# First World War
## and Army of Occupation
# War Diary
## France, Belgium and Germany

41 DIVISION
124 Infantry Brigade
Royal Fusiliers (City of London Regiment)
26th Battalion
4 May 1916 - 30 September 1919

WO95/2644/1

The Naval & Military Press Ltd
www.nmarchive.com
**Published in association with The National Archives**

Published by

The Naval & Military Press Ltd

Unit 10 Ridgewood Industrial Park,

Uckfield, East Sussex,

TN22 5QE England

Tel: +44 (0) 1825 749494

www.naval-military-press.com

www.nmarchive.com

*This diary has been reprinted in facsimile from the original. Any imperfections are inevitably reproduced and the quality may fall short of modern type and cartographic standards.*

# Contents

| Document type | Place/Title | Date From | Date To |
|---|---|---|---|
| Heading | WO95/2644/102 | | |
| Heading | 41st Division 124th Infy Bde 26th Bn Roy. Fus. May 1916 Oct 1917 Mar 1918-1919 Sep | | |
| Miscellaneous | D.A.G. 3rd Echelon. | 01/06/1916 | 01/06/1916 |
| War Diary | Aldershot | 04/05/1916 | 04/05/1916 |
| War Diary | Havre | 05/05/1916 | 06/05/1916 |
| War Diary | Greenbecque | 07/05/1916 | 07/05/1916 |
| War Diary | Shaple | 08/05/1916 | 09/05/1916 |
| War Diary | Oultersteene | 10/05/1916 | 25/05/1916 |
| War Diary | Albert Bapaame Rd. Ligny Church | | |
| War Diary | Poggeres | 01/06/1916 | 04/06/1916 |
| War Diary | In The Line | 05/06/1916 | 10/06/1916 |
| War Diary | Piggeries | 11/06/1916 | 16/06/1916 |
| War Diary | In The Line | 17/06/1916 | 17/07/1916 |
| War Diary | Creslow | 18/07/1916 | 22/07/1916 |
| War Diary | In The Line | 23/07/1916 | 30/07/1916 |
| War Diary | Riggeres | 24/07/1916 | 30/07/1916 |
| War Diary | In The Line | 31/07/1916 | 31/07/1916 |
| Operation(al) Order(s) | I.B. Order No. 28. Battalion Detail. | 10/07/1916 | 10/07/1916 |
| Operation(al) Order(s) | 124th Infantry Brigade Order No. 26 | 10/07/1916 | 10/07/1916 |
| Operation(al) Order(s) | 124th Infantry Brigade Order No. 35 | 19/07/1916 | 19/07/1916 |
| Operation(al) Order(s) | 124th Infantry Brigade Order No. 38 | 24/07/1916 | 24/07/1916 |
| Miscellaneous | To Headquarters, 124th Infantry Brigade. | 02/08/1916 | 02/08/1916 |
| War Diary | In The Line | 01/08/1916 | 02/08/1916 |
| War Diary | Rue De Sac to In the Line | 03/08/1916 | 09/08/1916 |
| War Diary | In The Line | 10/08/1916 | 17/08/1916 |
| War Diary | Rue De Sac to Meteren | 18/08/1916 | 23/08/1916 |
| War Diary | Meteren | 23/08/1916 | 23/08/1916 |
| War Diary | Vauchelles | 31/08/1916 | 31/08/1916 |
| War Diary | France (Vauchelles) | 01/09/1916 | 07/09/1916 |
| War Diary | Longpre | 07/09/1916 | 07/09/1916 |
| War Diary | Mericourt | 07/09/1916 | 07/09/1916 |
| War Diary | Dernancourt | 10/09/1916 | 10/09/1916 |
| War Diary | Fricourt | 13/09/1916 | 13/09/1916 |
| War Diary | France | 15/09/1916 | 30/09/1916 |
| War Diary | Wernancourt | 01/10/1916 | 07/10/1916 |
| War Diary | Girdtrench | 07/10/1916 | 09/10/1916 |
| War Diary | Becordel | 10/10/1916 | 10/10/1916 |
| War Diary | Buire-Sur Ancre | 13/10/1916 | 15/10/1916 |
| War Diary | Airaines | 16/10/1916 | 31/10/1916 |
| Operation(al) Order(s) | 124th Infantry Brigade Order No. 61 | 06/10/1916 | 06/10/1916 |
| Operation(al) Order(s) | Barrage Time Table. To accompany 124 Infy Bd de Order No. 61 of 5-10-16 | 06/10/1916 | 06/10/1916 |
| Miscellaneous | | 27/10/1916 | 27/10/1916 |
| Operation(al) Order(s) | 26th. Battalion Royal Fusiliers. Operation Order No. 14 | 27/10/1916 | 27/10/1916 |
| Operation(al) Order(s) | 26th. Battalion Royal Fusiliers. Operation Order No. 9 | | |
| Map | Map A | | |
| Map | 26 Rf | | |
| War Diary | Frontline Franch Diependaal Sector | 01/11/1916 | 03/11/1916 |
| War Diary | Ridgewood | 03/11/1916 | 03/11/1916 |

| | | | |
|---|---|---|---|
| War Diary | Frontline Diependaal Sector | 09/11/1916 | 09/11/1916 |
| War Diary | La Clytte | 15/11/1916 | 15/11/1916 |
| War Diary | Diependaal Sector | 21/11/1916 | 28/11/1916 |
| War Diary | Ridgewood | 28/11/1916 | 30/11/1916 |
| War Diary | 26th. Royal Fusiliers. Operation Order No. 21 | 30/11/1916 | 30/11/1916 |
| War Diary | | 01/12/1916 | 31/12/1916 |
| Operation(al) Order(s) | 26th. Bn. Royal Fusiliers. Operation Order No. 22 | 05/12/1916 | 05/12/1916 |
| Operation(al) Order(s) | 26th. Bn. Royal Fusiliers. Operation Order No. 23 | 12/12/1916 | 12/12/1916 |
| Operation(al) Order(s) | 26th Battalion Royal Fusiliers. Operation Order No. 24 | | |
| Operation(al) Order(s) | 26th. Battalion Royal Fusiliers. Operation Order No. 25 | | |
| Miscellaneous | Copy Of Letter To Company Commanders. | 15/12/1916 | 15/12/1916 |
| Miscellaneous | Copy Of Report by 2nd. Lt. P.A. Egan. | 15/12/1916 | 15/12/1916 |
| Miscellaneous | From Officer Commanding, 26th. Bn. Royal Fusiliers. | 15/12/1916 | 15/12/1916 |
| Miscellaneous | Copy Of Report By Lieut. M.B. Maude. O/C "C" Company. | | |
| Miscellaneous | Copy Of Wires Despatched. | | |
| War Diary | Diependaal Sector Front Line | 01/01/1917 | 01/01/1917 |
| War Diary | La Clytte | 03/01/1917 | 07/01/1917 |
| War Diary | Diependaal Sector Front Line | 08/01/1917 | 13/01/1917 |
| War Diary | Diependaal Sector | 14/01/1917 | 14/01/1917 |
| War Diary | Ridgewood | 14/01/1917 | 20/01/1917 |
| War Diary | Diependaal Sector | 20/01/1917 | 20/01/1917 |
| War Diary | Front Line | 21/01/1917 | 25/01/1917 |
| War Diary | La Clytte | 26/01/1917 | 28/02/1917 |
| Operation(al) Order(s) | 26th Bn Royal Fusiliers Operation Order No. 31 | | |
| Operation(al) Order(s) | 26th Bn Royal Fusiliers Operation Order No. 32 | 01/02/1917 | 01/02/1917 |
| Operation(al) Order(s) | Operation Order No. 33 | 04/02/1917 | 04/02/1917 |
| Operation(al) Order(s) | 26th. Bn. Royal Fusiliers. Operation Order No. 34 | 09/02/1917 | 09/02/1917 |
| Operation(al) Order(s) | 26th. Bn. Royal Fusiliers. Operation Order No. 35 | 16/02/1917 | 16/02/1917 |
| Operation(al) Order(s) | 26th. Bn. Royal Fusiliers. Operation Order No. 36 | 21/02/1917 | 21/02/1917 |
| Operation(al) Order(s) | 26th. Bn. Royal Fusiliers. Operation Order No. 37 | 27/02/1917 | 27/02/1917 |
| War Diary | Ridgewood | 01/03/1917 | 01/03/1917 |
| War Diary | Diependaal Sector | 06/03/1917 | 11/03/1917 |
| War Diary | La Clytte | 12/03/1917 | 12/03/1917 |
| War Diary | Piependaal Sector | 18/03/1917 | 18/03/1917 |
| War Diary | Ridgewood & Steenvoorde | 22/03/1917 | 22/03/1917 |
| War Diary | Steenvoorde | 23/03/1917 | 31/03/1917 |
| Operation(al) Order(s) | 26th. Bn. Royal Fusiliers. Operation Order No. 38 | 05/03/1917 | 05/03/1917 |
| Operation(al) Order(s) | 26th. Bn. Royal Fusiliers. Operation Order No. 39 | 11/03/1917 | 11/03/1917 |
| Operation(al) Order(s) | 26th. Bn. Royal Fusiliers. Operation Order No. 40 | 17/03/1917 | 17/03/1917 |
| Operation(al) Order(s) | 26th. Bn. Royal Fusiliers. Operation Order No. 41 | 19/03/1917 | 19/03/1917 |
| Operation(al) Order(s) | 26th. Bn. Royal Fusiliers. Operation Order No. 42 | 20/03/1917 | 20/03/1917 |
| Operation(al) Order(s) | 26th. Bn. Royal Fusiliers. Operation Order No. 43 | | |
| Map | 41st Divisional Front Left Sector | | |
| War Diary | Steenvoorde | 01/04/1917 | 06/04/1917 |
| War Diary | Reninghelst | 11/04/1917 | 11/04/1917 |
| War Diary | Trenches St Eloi Sheet 28 S.W. Square O.2 | 12/04/1917 | 12/04/1917 |
| War Diary | Trenches St Eloi | 15/04/1917 | 18/04/1917 |
| War Diary | Reninghelst | 18/04/1917 | 22/04/1917 |
| War Diary | Alberta Camp Renningheld | 23/04/1917 | 23/04/1917 |
| War Diary | Trenches St Eloi | 24/04/1917 | 30/04/1917 |
| War Diary | Royal Fusiliers. Operation Order No. 1 | | |
| Operation(al) Order(s) | Royal Fusiliers. Operation Order No. 2 | 11/04/1917 | 11/04/1917 |
| Operation(al) Order(s) | 26th Bn. Royal Fusiliers. Operation Order No. 2 | | |
| Miscellaneous | | 13/04/1917 | 13/04/1917 |
| Operation(al) Order(s) | Royal Fusiliers. Operation Order No. 3 | 17/04/1917 | 17/04/1917 |

| | | | |
|---|---|---|---|
| Operation(al) Order(s) | 'B' Bn. Royal Fusiliers. Operation Order No. 4 | | |
| Diagram etc | Dome House O.8.d. 9/3/3-6/3/4 | | |
| Map | | | |
| War Diary | Trenches St Eloi Sheet 28 S.W. Square 0.2 | 01/05/1917 | 01/05/1917 |
| War Diary | Trenches St Eloi | 02/05/1917 | 02/05/1917 |
| War Diary | Chippawa Camp A Sheet 28 S.W. | 03/05/1917 | 06/05/1917 |
| War Diary | Maulle Sheet 27 A.S.E. Square 11 | 06/05/1917 | 12/05/1917 |
| War Diary | Sheet 28 S.W. | 12/05/1917 | 12/05/1917 |
| War Diary | Mucmao Camp Sheet 28. S.W. | 13/05/1917 | 15/05/1917 |
| War Diary | Misoman Camp | 15/05/1917 | 17/05/1917 |
| War Diary | Sheet 28 N.W. | 17/05/1917 | 17/05/1917 |
| War Diary | Basseboom G. 21.a.27 | 17/05/1917 | 18/05/1917 |
| War Diary | Moulle Sheet 27 A.S.E. Square II | 19/05/1917 | 19/05/1917 |
| War Diary | Training Area Sheet 27 S.E. P29.30.36 Q. 31 | 20/05/1917 | 23/05/1917 |
| War Diary | Sheet 27 S.E. Square P 29.30 36 & Q31 | 23/05/1917 | 25/05/1917 |
| War Diary | Training Area Square P 29.30 36 Q31. Sheet 27 S.E. | 25/05/1917 | 25/05/1917 |
| War Diary | Moully | 26/05/1917 | 27/05/1917 |
| War Diary | Training Area | 28/05/1917 | 30/05/1917 |
| War Diary | Moully | 31/05/1917 | 31/05/1917 |
| Operation(al) Order(s) | 'B' Bn. Royal Fusiliers. Operation Order No. 3 | 04/05/1917 | 04/05/1917 |
| Operation(al) Order(s) | 'B' Bn Royal Fusiliers Operation Order No. 5 | 30/04/1917 | 30/04/1917 |
| Operation(al) Order(s) | 'B' Bn Royal Fusiliers Operation Order No. 7 | 05/05/1917 | 05/05/1917 |
| Operation(al) Order(s) | 26th Bn Royal Fus. Operation Order No. 8 | 11/05/1917 | 11/05/1917 |
| Miscellaneous | 26th Bn Royal Fusiliers. Battalion Order No. 1 | 16/05/1917 | 16/05/1917 |
| War Diary | Arrecke | 01/06/1917 | 01/06/1917 |
| War Diary | Micmac Camp North | 02/06/1917 | 05/06/1917 |
| War Diary | Micmac Camp (East) | 05/06/1917 | 05/06/1917 |
| War Diary | In The Line | 06/06/1917 | 08/06/1917 |
| War Diary | Elzenwalle | 09/06/1917 | 10/06/1917 |
| War Diary | In The Line | 11/06/1917 | 22/06/1917 |
| War Diary | Old Reserve Line | 23/06/1917 | 26/06/1917 |
| War Diary | Front Line Cyster | 27/06/1917 | 29/06/1917 |
| War Diary | Ontario Camp | 30/06/1917 | 30/06/1917 |
| Operation(al) Order(s) | 26th. Bn. The Royal Fusiliers. Operation Order No. 6 Appendix II | | |
| Operation(al) Order(s) | 26th. Bn. The Royal Fusiliers. Operation Order For Practice Attack Appendix III | 20/07/1917 | 20/07/1917 |
| Operation(al) Order(s) | 26th. Bn. The Royal Fusiliers. Operation Order No. 7 Appendix IV | 25/07/1917 | 25/07/1917 |
| Operation(al) Order(s) | 26th. Bn. The Royal Fusiliers. Operation Order No. 8 Appendix V | 25/07/1917 | 25/07/1917 |
| Operation(al) Order(s) | 26th. Bn. The Royal Fusiliers. Operation Order No. 7 Appendix VI | 20/07/1917 | 20/07/1917 |
| Miscellaneous | A Form Messages And Signals. | | |
| Operation(al) Order(s) | 26th. Bn. The Royal Fusiliers. Administration Orders | 23/07/1917 | 23/07/1917 |
| Miscellaneous | Appendix "A" Details To Be Left Behind | 23/07/1917 | 23/07/1917 |
| War Diary | Philcboom | 01/07/1917 | 18/07/1917 |
| War Diary | Westoutre | 19/07/1917 | 25/07/1917 |
| War Diary | La Clytte | 26/07/1917 | 29/07/1917 |
| War Diary | Ridgewood | 30/07/1917 | 30/07/1917 |
| War Diary | Bluff Tunnels | 31/07/1917 | 31/07/1917 |
| Miscellaneous | 26th. Bn. The Royal Fusiliers. Appendix I | | |
| Miscellaneous | Programme | | |
| War Diary | Moueumly Drec Camp La Clytte | 29/07/1917 | 29/07/1917 |
| War Diary | Ridgewood | 30/07/1917 | 30/07/1917 |
| War Diary | Spoil Camp Sumile | 31/07/1917 | 31/07/1917 |

| | | | |
|---|---|---|---|
| War Diary | Fusilier Wood | 01/08/1917 | 06/08/1917 |
| War Diary | Scottish Wood | 07/08/1917 | 08/08/1917 |
| War Diary | Wiltshire Farm | 09/08/1917 | 10/08/1917 |
| War Diary | Front Line | 11/08/1917 | 15/08/1917 |
| War Diary | Thieshouck | 16/08/1917 | 26/08/1917 |
| War Diary | Longuenesse | 27/08/1917 | 01/09/1917 |
| War Diary | Sheet 27A S.E. Map Infrence X 15 | 01/09/1917 | 01/09/1917 |
| War Diary | Longuenesse | 14/09/1917 | 14/09/1917 |
| War Diary | St Marie Cappelle | 15/09/1917 | 15/09/1917 |
| War Diary | Thieushouk | 16/09/1917 | 16/09/1917 |
| War Diary | La Clytte | 17/09/1917 | 17/09/1917 |
| War Diary | Ridgewood | 18/09/1917 | 18/09/1917 |
| War Diary | Voormezeele | 19/09/1917 | 20/09/1917 |
| War Diary | In The Line | 21/09/1917 | 22/09/1917 |
| War Diary | Wiltshire Camp | 23/09/1917 | 23/09/1917 |
| War Diary | Borre | 24/09/1917 | 28/09/1917 |
| War Diary | Ghyvelde | 29/09/1917 | 30/09/1917 |
| War Diary | America | 01/10/1918 | 01/10/1918 |
| War Diary | Kruiseecke Road | 07/10/1918 | 07/10/1918 |
| War Diary | Kairn Camp | 08/10/1918 | 15/10/1918 |
| War Diary | Moorseele | 16/10/1918 | 26/10/1918 |
| War Diary | Courtrai Area | 27/10/1918 | 31/10/1918 |
| War Diary | Ghyvelde | 01/10/1917 | 05/10/1917 |
| War Diary | Coxyde Bains | 06/10/1917 | 15/10/1917 |
| War Diary | Newpoirt Bains | 16/10/1917 | 23/10/1917 |
| War Diary | East Durkergu Bains | 24/10/1917 | 28/10/1917 |
| War Diary | Uxem | 29/10/1917 | 29/10/1917 |
| Operation(al) Order(s) | Dwindle Operation Order. No. 16 | 22/10/1917 | 22/10/1917 |
| Heading | 124th Inf. Bde. 41st Div. Battn. with Bde. returned to France from Italy 2/7.3.18 26th Battn. The Royal Fusiliers. March 1918 | | |
| War Diary | Villa Franca | 01/03/1918 | 02/03/1918 |
| War Diary | Mondicourt Pas | 07/03/1918 | 07/03/1918 |
| War Diary | Sus St. Leger | 08/03/1918 | 21/03/1918 |
| War Diary | Achite Le Chancd | 22/03/1918 | 31/03/1918 |
| Heading | Report On Operation between 22nd March 1918 and night 29th/30th March 1918 | | |
| Miscellaneous | Report on Operation Between 22nd March 1918 and night 29th/30th March 1918 | 06/04/1918 | 06/04/1918 |
| Heading | 41st Division. 124th Infantry Brigade 26th Battalion The Royal Fusiliers April 1918 | | |
| War Diary | Bucquoy | 30/03/1918 | 02/04/1918 |
| War Diary | Halloy | 03/04/1918 | 03/04/1918 |
| War Diary | Bonnieres | 04/04/1918 | 04/04/1918 |
| War Diary | Winnizeele | 05/04/1918 | 07/04/1918 |
| War Diary | St. Lawrence Camp. Brandhoek | 08/04/1918 | 08/04/1918 |
| War Diary | Cartekeep & Mills Keep | 12/04/1918 | 12/04/1918 |
| War Diary | Low Farm | 13/04/1918 | 13/04/1918 |
| War Diary | Ypres Menin Rd | 15/04/1918 | 25/04/1918 |
| War Diary | Ypres Ramparts | 25/04/1918 | 27/04/1918 |
| War Diary | Ypres Outpost Line | 28/04/1918 | 30/04/1918 |
| War Diary | Ypres Outposts Pilkem Line | 01/05/1918 | 02/05/1918 |
| War Diary | Dambre Camp | 03/05/1918 | 09/05/1918 |
| War Diary | Siege Camp | 09/05/1918 | 11/05/1918 |
| War Diary | Pilkem Line Ypres Reserve | 11/05/1918 | 19/05/1918 |
| War Diary | Ramparts Ypres Support | 19/05/1918 | 23/05/1918 |

| | | | |
|---|---|---|---|
| War Diary | Ecole Ypres | 23/05/1918 | 25/05/1918 |
| War Diary | Siege Camp | 26/05/1918 | 28/05/1918 |
| War Diary | Siege Camp 28 N.W. B20d. | 01/06/1918 | 03/06/1918 |
| War Diary | Wulverdinghe (Hazebrouck 5A) | 04/06/1918 | 08/06/1918 |
| War Diary | Audenfort (Calaie 13) | 08/06/1918 | 24/06/1918 |
| War Diary | Wulverdinghe (Hazebrouck 5A) | 25/06/1918 | 25/06/1918 |
| War Diary | Ouderzeele Area (Hazebrouck 5A) | 26/06/1918 | 29/06/1918 |
| War Diary | Abeele Area (Sheet 27) | 30/06/1918 | 30/06/1918 |
| War Diary | Scherpenberg Sheet 28. S.W. | 01/07/1918 | 01/07/1918 |
| War Diary | Westoutre Area Shts 27 N.E. & 28 S.W. | 05/07/1918 | 06/07/1918 |
| War Diary | Scherren Berg | 10/06/1918 | 15/06/1918 |
| War Diary | Westoutre Area | 20/06/1918 | 21/06/1918 |
| War Diary | Renninghelst Sht 28 N.W. | 22/07/1918 | 25/07/1918 |
| War Diary | Scherpenberg Sht 28. S.W. | 25/06/1918 | 31/06/1918 |
| War Diary | | 28/06/1918 | 28/06/1918 |
| War Diary | Scherpenberg Sht 28 SW | 01/08/1918 | 10/08/1918 |
| War Diary | Lappe Area (Sht 27) | 10/08/1918 | 11/08/1918 |
| War Diary | Scherpenberg | 18/08/1918 | 23/08/1918 |
| War Diary | Scherpenberg (Sht 28 S.W.) | 24/08/1918 | 31/08/1918 |
| War Diary | Sht 28 SW | 31/08/1918 | 01/09/1918 |
| War Diary | Sht 28 NW Dickebusch | 02/09/1918 | 04/09/1918 |
| War Diary | Sht 28 S.W. | 05/09/1918 | 08/09/1918 |
| War Diary | Sht 28 NW Dickebusch | 09/09/1918 | 11/09/1918 |
| War Diary | Dominion Camp (Sht 28 N.W.) | 12/09/1918 | 15/09/1918 |
| War Diary | Audenfort (Calais 13) | 15/09/1918 | 27/09/1918 |
| War Diary | Toronto Camp (Sht 28) | 27/09/1918 | 27/09/1918 |
| War Diary | Sht 28 | 28/09/1918 | 29/09/1918 |
| Miscellaneous | Report Of Operations. 4/9/18 to 8/9/18 | | |
| War Diary | Siege Camp | 28/09/1918 | 31/09/1918 |
| War Diary | Report on Operations. 28-9-18 to 30/10/18 | | |
| Miscellaneous | | 19/10/1918 | 19/10/1918 |
| Miscellaneous | Report On Operations. October 14th and 15th, 1918 | | |
| War Diary | Courtrai Area | 01/11/1918 | 01/11/1918 |
| War Diary | O.18.b.4.3 Sheet 29 | 02/11/1918 | 04/11/1918 |
| War Diary | Vichte | 04/11/1918 | 07/11/1918 |
| War Diary | Deerlyck | 08/11/1918 | 09/11/1918 |
| War Diary | Tieghem | 10/11/1918 | 10/11/1918 |
| War Diary | M21d (Sheet 30) | 11/11/1918 | 11/11/1918 |
| War Diary | Nederbrakel | 12/11/1918 | 12/11/1918 |
| War Diary | Hemelverdegem | 13/11/1918 | 13/11/1918 |
| War Diary | Idegem | 14/11/1918 | 18/11/1918 |
| War Diary | Denderwindeke | 19/11/1918 | 20/11/1918 |
| War Diary | Bievene | 21/11/1918 | 30/11/1918 |
| Miscellaneous | Report On Operations, 21st October to 26th October, 1918 | 03/11/1918 | 03/11/1918 |
| War Diary | Bievene | 01/12/1918 | 12/12/1918 |
| War Diary | Engien | 13/12/1918 | 13/12/1918 |
| War Diary | Hal | 14/12/1918 | 14/12/1918 |
| War Diary | Waterloo | 15/12/1918 | 16/12/1918 |
| War Diary | Ways De Genappe | 17/12/1918 | 17/12/1918 |
| War Diary | Nagwalee | 18/12/1918 | 18/12/1918 |
| War Diary | Temploux | 19/12/1918 | 19/12/1918 |
| War Diary | Bonnine | 20/12/1918 | 20/12/1918 |
| War Diary | Huy | 21/12/1918 | 31/12/1918 |
| Heading | London Division (Late 41st Division) 124th Infy Bde 26th Bn Roy. Fusiliers. Jan-Sep 1919 | | |

| | | | |
|---|---|---|---|
| War Diary | Huy | 01/01/1919 | 07/01/1919 |
| War Diary | Steinenbruck | 08/01/1919 | 08/01/1919 |
| War Diary | Ehreshoven | 09/01/1919 | 31/01/1919 |
| War Diary | Coln Kalk | 01/04/1919 | 30/04/1919 |
| War Diary | Coln Kalk | 01/04/1919 | 13/05/1919 |
| War Diary | Volberg | 14/05/1919 | 31/05/1919 |
| War Diary | Volberg | 01/05/1919 | 31/05/1919 |
| War Diary | Hoffnungstahl and Volberg. | 01/06/1919 | 17/06/1919 |
| War Diary | Unter Vilkerath | 18/06/1919 | 30/06/1919 |
| War Diary | | 01/06/1919 | 30/06/1919 |
| War Diary | Unter Vilkerath | 01/07/1919 | 01/07/1919 |
| War Diary | Overath | 02/07/1919 | 31/07/1919 |
| War Diary | Overath | 29/07/1919 | 25/08/1919 |
| War Diary | Marialinden | 26/08/1919 | 07/09/1919 |
| War Diary | Overath | 16/09/1919 | 16/09/1919 |
| War Diary | Marialinden | 30/09/1919 | 30/09/1919 |

41ST DIVISION
124TH INFY BDE

26TH BN ROY. FUS.

MAY 1916-~~DEC 1918~~ OCT 1917
MAR 1918 - 1919 SEP

~~HQ~~ ITALY 1917 NOV - 1918 FEB

D.A.G.
3rd Echelon.

Herewith War Diary compiled up to 3qst May,1916

W. J. North

Lieut.Col.Commanding
26th Battn:Royal Fusiliers

1st June,1916.

ORDERLY ROOM
1 JUN 1916
No. 1432
26th (S.) BATTN. ROYAL FUSILIERS (BANKERS)

26 R.F. Army Form C. 2118

XL1 Vol 1

# WAR DIARY
or
# ~~INTELLIGENCE SUMMARY~~
*(Erase heading not required.)*

Instructions regarding War Diaries and Intelligence Summaries are contained in F. S. Regs., Part II. and the Staff Manual respectively. Title Pages will be prepared in manuscript.

| Place | Date | Hour | Summary of Events and Information | Remarks and references to Appendices |
|---|---|---|---|---|
| Aldershot | 4/5/16 | 3 a.m. | Battalion entrained (three separate parties) from Farnborough for Southampton. Embarked on S.S. Mona Queen and arrived at Havre – 5/5/16. Transport came over on S.S. Bellerophon | |
| Havre | 5/5/16 | 7.30 am | Battalion marched to No 1 Rest Camp, Havre, and rested. | |
| Havre | 6/5/16 | 7.30 am | Battalion entrained in two parties at the Gare des Marchandises, Havre at points 1 & 3. | |
| Steenbecque | 7/5/16 | 9 a.m. | Battalion detrained at Steenbecque and marched to Staple and were billeted in the vicinity | |
| Staple | 8/5/16 | | Battalion rested at Staple | |
| Staple | 9/5/16 | 9.30 am | Battalion marched from Staple to new billets in the vicinity of Oultersteene. | |
| Oultersteene | 10/5/16 | 7 a.m. | 1st Party of Officers & men proceeded to trenches for instruction, and were attached to 5th Camerons. | |
| " | 23/5/16 | " | Party of Officers and 1 section of N.C.Os and men per platoon of A & B Coys proceeded to trenches for instruction and were attached to 5th Cameron Highlanders | |
| " | 25/5/16 | " | Party of Officers and 1 section of N.C.Os and men per platoon of C & D Coys proceeded to trenches for instruction and were attached to 5th Cameron Highlanders | |
| " | 30/5/16. | 5.30 pm | Battalion marched from Oultersteene to new billets at the Driggeries where they arrived on the morning of the 31st instant, after spending the night at La Creche | |

1/6/16

W. F. North
Lt. Colonel
Commanding
26th Battn. R. Fusiliers



1/5 (12 sheets)

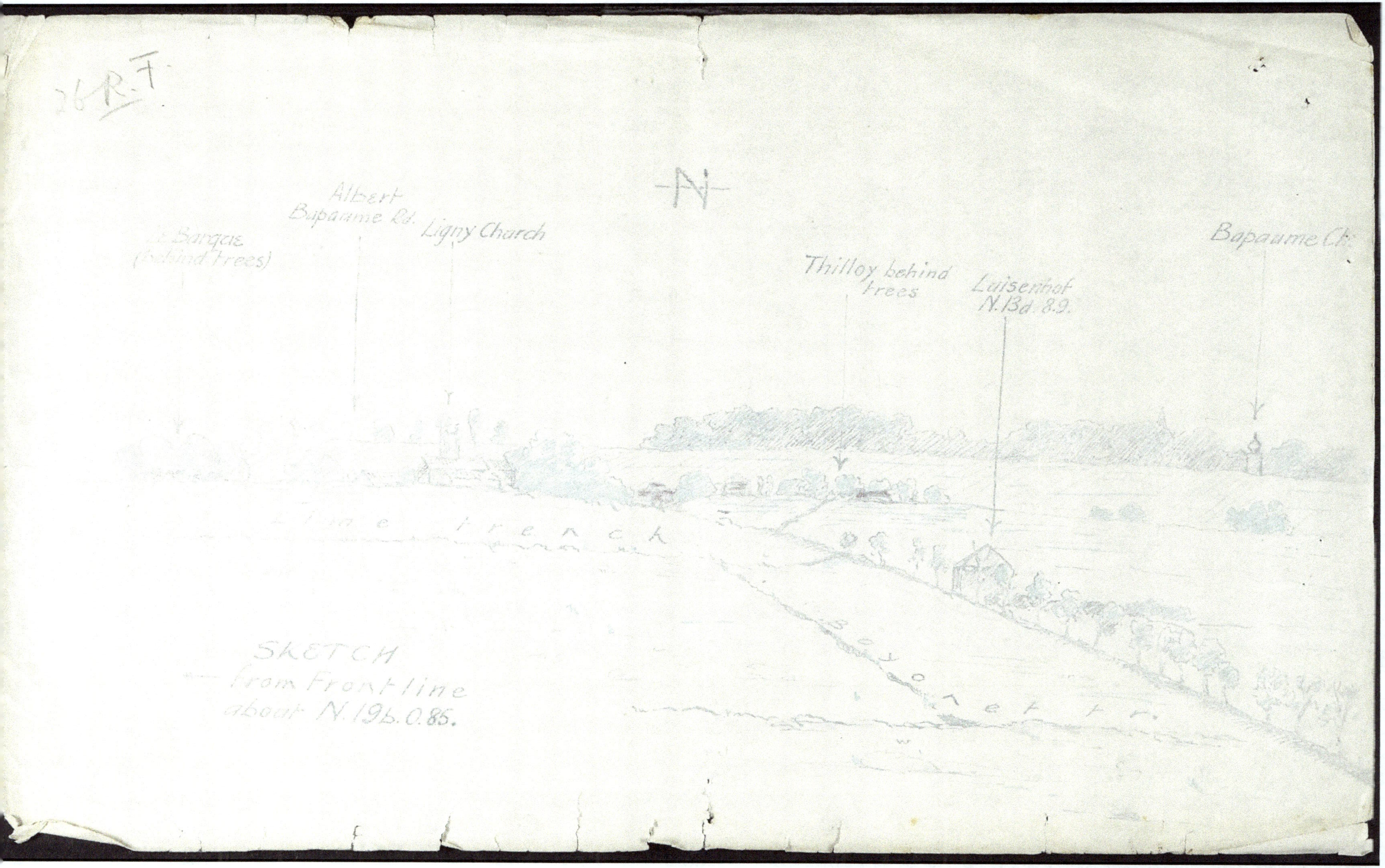
26 R.F.
N
Barque (behind trees)
Albert Bapaume Rd.
Ligny Church
Thilloy behind trees
Luisenhof N.13d.8.9.
Bapaume Ch.
Bayonet Tr.
SKETCH from Front line about N.19b.0.85.

41 JUNE

16th Royal Fusrs.

Instructions regarding War Diaries and Intelligence Summaries are contained in F. S. Regs., Part II. and the Staff Manual respectively. Title pages will be prepared in manuscript.

# WAR DIARY
*or*
# INTELLIGENCE SUMMARY.
*(Erase heading not required.)*

for June 1916.

Army Form C. 2118.

26 R. Fus

Map Ref. Sheet 28. S.W. STYLES. 10.

Vol 2

2.K (7 sheets)

| Place | Date | Hour | Summary of Events and Information | Remarks and references to Appendices |
|---|---|---|---|---|
| Piggeries | 1.6.16 | | In Brigade Reserve at The Piggeries ROEGSTEERT. The day was quiet & there is nothing to record. We suffered our first casualties on active service having 2 men killed & 10 wounded on working parties. | |
| do. | 2.6.16 – 4.6.16 | | Remained in reserve at the Piggeries. Things were generally quiet & there is nothing to report. One of the wounded men reported above died in hospital at BAILLEUL. | |
| In the line | 5.6.16 | 6am | The Battalion for the first time occupied the trenches, relieving the 18th K.R.R.C. in the line, & taking over Tp 124. 125. 126. 127. The day was very quiet. There was a little Artillery fire on Enemy's part & Enemy snipers were troublesome. There was a good deal of movement in rear. Enemy were seen putting up wires along MESSINES GAPAARD road. | |
| do. | 6.6.16 | | Our Patrols reported enemy had wiring parties out. Enemy was quiet during the day there being little artillery fire or sniping. There was some aircraft activity during the day on both sides. | |

Instructions regarding War Diaries and Intelligence Summaries are contained in F. S. Regs., Part II. and the Staff Manual respectively. Title pages will be prepared in manuscript.

# WAR DIARY
*or*
# INTELLIGENCE SUMMARY.
*(Erase heading not required.)*

Army Form C. 2118.

| Place | Date | Hour | Summary of Events and Information | Remarks and references to Appendices |
|---|---|---|---|---|
| In the line | 7.6.16 | | An officers patrol visited the ruins of MACHINE GUN HOUSE. at U.15. b. 3½.1. They found that one small room which was sandbagged & loopholed & was evidently used as a sniper post. Other patrols report enemy working party out. In reply to our shelling the enemy shelled our front line rather severely. Machine Gun & Rifle fire on both sides very active. During the day the enemy put up a large notice board which read "Kitchener has been taken by the devil" Aircraft on both sides active during the day. Casualties: killed 2 wounded | [illegible] |
| do | 8.6.16 | | Our patrols reported all quiet in front. Our snipers were busy & recorded a hit at BARRICADE AVE. U.15.a. 5.10. as well as hits on enemy periscopes & loopholes. Enemy sniper smashed one of our periscopes. The day was otherwise very quiet. The enemy wire has been strengthened. Continued aircraft activity. | [illegible] |
| do | 9.6.16 | | Our patrols visited enemy wire, found same strong & brought back specimens. Another of our patrols was surprised & bombed about | |

T2131. Wt. W708–776. 500000. 4/15. Sir J. C. & S.

Instructions regarding War Diaries and Intelligence Summaries are contained in F. S. Regs., Part II. and the Staff Manual respectively. Title pages will be prepared in manuscript.

# WAR DIARY
*or*
# INTELLIGENCE SUMMARY.
*(Erase heading not required.)*

Army Form C. 2118.

| Place | Date | Hour | Summary of Events and Information | Remarks and references to Appendices |
|---|---|---|---|---|
| In the line (Continued) | 9.6.16 | | 30 yards in front of our own wire. One of the patrol was killed & 2 wounded. An officer went out later & after a difficult search the man who was killed was found & brought in. Enemy's attitude was normal during the day but much more active than usual at night. Enemy shelled between PROVISE POINT & POOLES COTTAGE at O.13.d.5.6. The flash & position of enemy field gun was noted. There was much enemy machine gun fire at night. A good deal of movement in rear of enemy lines observed. We silenced an enemy sniper who was troublesome & in return enemy put a shot through our L.O.P. & slightly damaged a telescope. Continued aircraft activity on both sides. [illegible] | |
| do. | 10.6.16. | | Our patrols out as usual had nothing special to report. Enemy's attitude was normal during the day, but more aggressive at night with M.G. fire. There was no artillery fire. Some new works in enemy lines were noted. Again there was much aircraft activity. Casualties 1 killed 2 wounded. [illegible] | |

Instructions regarding War Diaries and Intelligence Summaries are contained in F. S. Regs., Part II. and the Staff Manual respectively. Title pages will be prepared in manuscript.

# WAR DIARY
*or*
# INTELLIGENCE SUMMARY.
*(Erase heading not required.)*

Army Form C. 2118.

| Place | Date | Hour | Summary of Events and Information | Remarks and references to Appendices |
|---|---|---|---|---|
| Piggeries | 11.6.16 to [illegible] | 6am | We were relieved at 6am by the 18th K.R.R.C & proceeded to Brigade Reserve at the Piggeries. We remained here until the morning of the 17th. There is nothing of importance to record during the week. We had 2 men wounded during these 6 days. | [signature] |
| In the line | 17.6.16 | 6am | At 6am we relieved the 18th K.R.R.C. in the trenches. Except for aerial activity the enemys attitude was quiet throughout the day & night. Our attitude was also quiet. Observers report that enemy has done considerable work during the past week & a good deal of work going on. Enemy aircraft were active & observation balloons up | [signature] |
| -do- | 18.6.16 | | Our patrols out on whole Battalion front & reported enemy repairing their wire at points on the front. These parties were dispersed by our M.G. fire & cries were heard. Enemys artillery was fairly active & retaliatory. Enemy M.G. & rifle fire active. A good deal of movement in rear of enemys lines was observed | |

Instructions regarding War Diaries and Intelligence Summaries are contained in F. S. Regs., Part II. and the Staff Manual respectively. Title pages will be prepared in manuscript.

# WAR DIARY
*or*
# INTELLIGENCE SUMMARY.
*(Erase heading not required.)*

Army Form C. 2118.

| Place | Date | Hour | Summary of Events and Information | Remarks and references to Appendices |
|---|---|---|---|---|
| In the line | 18.6.16 | | There was no enemy sniping & our snipers had a quiet time. Enemy aircraft busy during the day. [signature] | |
| do | 19.6.16 | | Patrols report enemy busy on their wire & parapet & also grass cutting. Enemy replied vigorously to our shelling & sent over a number of aerial torpedoes & rifle grenades during the afternoon & evening. Enemy machine guns were fairly active & a good deal of movement was observed in rear. Casualties 2 killed 3 wounded [signature] | |
| do | 20.6.16 | | Our patrols reported everything quiet on the front. Our snipers hit enemy sniper who was firing over the parapet, & also claimed a hit on firing at enemy working party at dawn. Enemys attitude quiet during day & night. A good deal of movement in rear of enemys trenches was observed & a good deal of fresh work noted. Enemy aeroplanes active & 5 enemy observation balloons up. Casualties 2 wounded [signature] | |

T2134. Wt. W708—776. 500000. 4/15. Sir J. C. & S.

Instructions regarding War Diaries and Intelligence Summaries are contained in F. S. Regs., Part II. and the Staff Manual respectively. Title pages will be prepared in manuscript.

# WAR DIARY
*or*
# INTELLIGENCE SUMMARY.
*(Erase heading not required.)*

Army Form C. 2118.

| Place | Date | Hour | Summary of Events and Information | Remarks and references to Appendices |
|---|---|---|---|---|
| In the line | 21.6.16 | | A Quiet day. There being no artillery fire or sniping by the enemy. M.G. & Rifle fire normal. A few rifle grenades were fired at our lines by enemy without causing much damage. Enemy aircraft again active & observation balloons up. Our patrols reported all quiet. Casualties 1 wounded. | [illegible] |
| | 22/6/16 | | Our patrols reported enemy working parties out. A Gas alarm was sounded at night. This resulted in our shelling enemy line & consequent retaliation. We received no gas. Enemy was very quiet during the day & there was no artillery fire or sniping. Work was continued in enemys lines & there was continued aircraft activity. Casualties 1 wounded | [illegible] |
| | 23/6/16 | | A Quiet day. Very little artillery fire, sniping & rifle fire. Our patrols report working parties on enemy wire. Work still continues in enemys lines. Our snipers were busy on enemy loopholes & periscopes. Casualties 1 wounded | [illegible] |

26th Royal Fusiliers

-41- July 26 R FUS

Army Form C. 2118

Instructions regarding War Diaries and Intelligence Summaries are contained in F. S. Regs., Part II. and the Staff Manual respectively. Title Pages will be prepared in manuscript.

# WAR DIARY
*or*
# INTELLIGENCE SUMMARY
*(Erase heading not required.)*

Map Reference. STYVES Part sheet 28 S.W Sheet 10

VOL 3

| Place | Date | Hour | Summary of Events and Information | Remarks and references to Appendices |
|---|---|---|---|---|
| In the line | 1/7/16 | 6 am | We relieved the 18th K.R.R.C & took over Tr. 124 125 126 127. After the heavy bombardment which they had suffered during the night the enemy was particularly quiet. The Enemy's trenches & wire had suffered very badly as the result of our shelling. Aircraft were very active during the day. We suffered no casualties. | |
| do | 2/7/16 | | Things continued quiet. Our patrols reported that enemy had no working parties out & their damaged wire remained unrepaired. They further reported that our wire had suffered little damage in consequence of Enemy Artillery Retaliation. There was no sniping on either side. 5 T.M's were fired into our lines by the enemy. No casualties reported. | |
| do | 3/7/16 | | During the night our artillery was very active shelling all roads behind enemy's lines which could be used for transport. A great deal of smoke was observed at LA BASSE VILLE – probably the result of our shelling. | |
| do | 4/7/16 | | During the early hours of the morning our right Coy. occupying T.124 were relieved by the 32nd R.F. & proceeded to rest billets at PAPOT. The remainder of the Battalion were relieved at 10.30 pm & also proceeded to PAPOT. The day was very quiet & there is nothing of importance to record | |
| do | 5/7/16 to 10/7/16 | | The Battalion remained in Billets at PAPOT. There is nothing of any Event to record. | 3.K. (15 sheets) |

Instructions regarding War Diaries and Intelligence Summaries are contained in F. S. Regs., Part II. and the Staff Manual respectively. Title Pages will be prepared in manuscript.

# WAR DIARY
*or*
# INTELLIGENCE SUMMARY
*(Erase heading not required.)*

Army Form C. 2118

| Place | Date | Hour | Summary of Events and Information | Remarks and references to Appendices |
|---|---|---|---|---|
| In the line | 11/7/16 | 5 am | We relieved the 3rd Royal Fusrs, taking over partly new & partly old trenches – viz:- TO 121. 122. 123. 124. This change brought our right Coy. practically in front of the BIRDCAGE. The night & early morning were reported as having been very quiet. No unusual occurrences reported during the day. Enemy snipers were fairly active & succeeded in hitting two of our periscopes. Shortly before midnight a patrol of the 3rd RF went out & endeavoured to find a Machine Gun which their raiding party had left out in NO MANS LAND, after having taken it from enemy's line. They were unsuccessful. Our patrols reported everything quiet. [illegible signature] | |
| do | 12/7/16 | | During the morning our Artillery was active shelling Enemy's lines. This activity continued throughout the day. Enemy's reply was very feeble & only a few Trench Mortars & grenades were fired back in return, together with a few 10 cm shells which fell well behind our lines. At night a raid on the enemy's line by the 18th KRRC on our left was attempted. Our early patrols reported everything quiet & no enemy working parties were out. The enemy appeared watchful & nervous & a large number of 'VERY' lights were fired. [illegible signature] | |

1875 Wt. W593/826 1,000,000 4/15 J.B.C. & A. A.D.S.S./Forms/C. 2118.

Army Form C. 2118

# WAR DIARY
*or*
# INTELLIGENCE SUMMARY
*(Erase heading not required.)*

Instructions regarding War Diaries and Intelligence Summaries are contained in F. S. Regs., Part II. and the Staff Manual respectively. Title Pages will be prepared in manuscript.

| Place | Date | Hour | Summary of Events and Information | Remarks and references to Appendices |
|---|---|---|---|---|
| In the line | 13/7/16 | | The day was exceedingly quiet there being practically no artillery fire. Our Patrol reported an enemy wiring party on our left. There is no evidence of any new wire having been put up. This working party was dispersed by our M.G. fire. Our snipers were more active & a number of shots were fired at enemy periscopes & loopholes, with good effect. During the night gas was discharged from the trenches on our left. This caused enemy Artillery retaliation which was very feeble. We had 4 men wounded. [signature] | Ref. 124 I.B. O. 26 of 10.7.16. |
| do | 14/7/16 | | The day opened with the enemy Artillery shelling ST YVES & ROTTEN ROW. Otherwise the morning was quiet: During the afternoon our Artillery continued to cut enemys wire. Observation was rather difficult owing to the thickness of the grass but it is thought that good results were obtained. Our T.M.Bs assisted Artillery in wire cutting. Enemys support lines were also shelled. Our Patrol reported that enemy attempted to repair his wire opposite T 121 but was prevented by M.G fire. They further reported a great deal of talking & walking about in Enemys line & it is thought that a relief was taking place. Enemys attitude in reply to our wire cutting was more active & they kept up an intermittent artillery bombardment during the afternoon of ST YVES. LONE HOUSE AVE. HULLS BURNT FARM & T.O 122. 123. [signature] | |

1875 Wt. W593/826 1,000,000 4/15 J.B.C. & A. A.D.S.S./Forms/C. 2118.

Instructions regarding War Diaries and Intelligence Summaries are contained in F. S. Regs., Part II. and the Staff Manual respectively. Title Pages will be prepared in manuscript.

# WAR DIARY
*or*
# INTELLIGENCE SUMMARY
*(Erase heading not required.)*

Army Form C. 2118

| Place | Date | Hour | Summary of Events and Information | Remarks and references to Appendices |
|---|---|---|---|---|
| In the line 14/7/16. | Continued. | | A good deal of new work was observed in enemys lines. Aircraft were active throughout the day. Casualties. 2 killed. 5 wounded. | [illegible] |
| [illegible] In the line | 15/7/16 | | During the day our Artillery shelled enemys support & communication trenches & at night a raid on the enemys trenches was attempted. The raiding party however found that the enemys short wire had not been cut by our Artillery fire & so could not proceed. They however put a charge of dynamite under the wire & exploded it. This party was brought back under heavy rifle & M.G. fire without a casualty. Their only casualties occured just as they started out. Our snipers were busy on enemy periscopes & loopholes. Enemys retaliation for our fire was fairly heavy & more active than usual. A deal of new work in enemy line was observed & reported. Casualties - 3 wounded | Ref 1 B.O. 31 10/7/16 |
| do. | 16/7/16 | | Co-operating with our raiding party our Artillery severely bombarded the enemys lines in the early hours of the morning. This brought about retaliation on enemys part with H.E. & Trench Mortars on LONE HOUSE AVE In YVES & DEAD HORSE CORNER. No appreciable damage was done | [illegible] |

1875 Wt. W593/826 1,000,000 4/15 J.B.C. & A. A.D.S.S./Forms/C. 2118.

Instructions regarding War Diaries and Intelligence Summaries are contained in F. S. Regs., Part II. and the Staff Manual respectively. Title Pages will be prepared in manuscript.

Army Form C. 2118

# WAR DIARY
*or*
# INTELLIGENCE SUMMARY
*(Erase heading not required.)*

| Place | Date | Hour | Summary of Events and Information | Remarks and references to Appendices |
|---|---|---|---|---|
| In the line Continued. | 16/7/16 | | During the morning, afternoon & evening an intermittent bombardment of the enemy's front & support line was kept up & between 9.30 & 11 pm the enemy's line were treated to intense fire. Our patrols reported enemy working parties near BROKEN TREE FARM, which were dispersed by our M.G. fire. The enemy made no attempt to repair his wire. No opportunity for sniping was given by the enemy. There was a little retaliation for our bombardment during the day. New work observed in several places in enemy's lines. | [illegible] |
| do | 17/7/16 | 6 am | We were relieved by the 3rd Royal Innis. F. & proceeded to Brigade Reserve at CRESLOW. The relief was completed in very quick time. The day was quiet & there is nothing of importance to record. Casualties 1 killed, 3 wounded. | [illegible] |
| CRESLOW | 18/7/16 | | Our billets were subject to shell fire from an unexpected direction. I am of opinion that enemy either had one of their heavy guns in vicinity of ARMENTIERS trained on us or else had brought up an armoured train. Casualties – 2 wounded. | [illegible] |
| do | 19/7/16 | | We were subject to same fire as yesterday. Casualties 2 killed 2 wounded. | [illegible] |

1875 Wt. W593/826 1,000,000 4/15 J.B.C. & A. A.D.S.S./Forms/C. 2118.

Instructions regarding War Diaries and Intelligence Summaries are contained in F. S. Regs., Part II. and the Staff Manual respectively. Title Pages will be prepared in manuscript.

# WAR DIARY
*or*
# INTELLIGENCE SUMMARY
*(Erase heading not required.)*

Army Form C. 2118

| Place | Date | Hour | Summary of Events and Information | Remarks and references to Appendices |
|---|---|---|---|---|
| CRESLOW | 20/7/16 | | Nothing of importance to record. Casualties 1 killed | |
| do | 21/7/16 | | — do — — do — 4 wounded | [illegible] |
| do | 22/7/16 | | — do — | |
| In the line | 23/7/16 | 6 a.m. | We relieved the 3rd R.F. Relief quickly completed. The day was remarkably quiet, probably the quietest day we had yet spent in the trenches. A little sniping was done. A good deal of work was going on in the enemy's lines. Enemy attempted to repair his wire but was dispersed by M.G. fire | [illegible] |
| do | 24/7/16 | | Our Artillery was active during the day cutting the enemy's wire opposite our trenches. Our M.G.s were also active preventing the enemy from working on his wire. Our heavy T.M.B's fired 2 of their heavy mortars into enemys lines which caused great damage just N of Factory Farm, & which occasioned much retaliation from enemy T.M.B's. Enemy's [illegible] fairly active. Their Artillery retaliated for our wire cutting with H.E. Their T.M.B's too were active & retaliated on LONE HOUSE AVE. [illegible] | |

1875 Wt. W593/826 1,000,000 4/15 J.B.C. & A. A.D.S.S./Forms/C. 2118.

Instructions regarding War Diaries and Intelligence Summaries are contained in F. S. Regs., Part II. and the Staff Manual respectively. Title Pages will be prepared in manuscript.

# WAR DIARY
*or*
# INTELLIGENCE SUMMARY
*(Erase heading not required.)*

Army Form C. 2118

| Place | Date | Hour | Summary of Events and Information | Remarks and references to Appendices |
|---|---|---|---|---|
| In the line Continued | 24/7/16 | | A good deal of work continues to be going on in the enemy's lines & a great deal of movement observed in vicinity of Fme de la CROIX. Casualties 2 killed | [illegible] |
| do | 25/7/16 | | Continued artillery activity on our part & the cutting of enemy's wire was proceeded with. Our patrols reported that enemy attempted to repair his wire but was prevented. Sniping on both sides quiet. Enemy was again retaliatory & shells were sent over into ST YVES locality. Our heavy T.M.'s again caused the enemy much annoyance. Machine Gun & Rifle fire normal. Enemy continues to work on his lines & there is much evidence of activity. A good deal of movement observed in rear of enemy's lines & much traffic heard on MESSINES GAPAARD road | [illegible] |
| do | 26/7/16 | | Wire cutting continued throughout the day. Our snipers did some good firing at enemy periscopes & loopholes. Enemy's attitude was again active & retaliatory. Far [?] more we received much back for our heavy T.M. Enemy ~~T.M.s~~ snipers fired a good deal without success. At night we cooperated with operations which took place | |

1875 Wt. W593/826 1,000,000 4/15 J.B.C. & A. A.D.S.S./Forms/C. 2118.

Instructions regarding War Diaries and Intelligence Summaries are contained in F. S. Regs., Part II. and the Staff Manual respectively. Title Pages will be prepared in manuscript.

# WAR DIARY
*or*
# INTELLIGENCE SUMMARY
*(Erase heading not required.)*

Army Form C. 2118

| Place | Date | Hour | Summary of Events and Information | Remarks and references to Appendices |
|---|---|---|---|---|
| In the line (continued) | 26/7/16 | | on our right & smoke bombs were discharged from our line. The enemy immediately sent up red rockets but there was little reply on our line. Enemy's line were being strengthened throughout the day & a great deal of movement in rear was observed. | Ref. I.B.O. no 35. of 19/7/16 + I.B.O. no 38 of 20/7/16 [signature] |
| do | 27/7/16 | | A quiet day. There was much activity for a short time during the early hours of the morning owing to a raid by the 10th. R.W.S. Regt. Our snipers were active on enemy loopholes & periscopes. Enemy snipers did a great deal of firing with no success. Evidence & sounds of work in enemy's line noted & reported. A good deal of movement was observed behind enemy's line. Our Patrols report no enemy wiring parties out but there is evidence of new wire having been put up round BROKEN TREE FARM. One of our patrols report that an enemy M.G. was firing from a sap head. Casualties 8 wounded. | [signature] |
| do | 28/7/16 | | During the early hours we were relieved in T's 121. 122. & 123 by the 32nd R.F. & we took over T's 125. 126. 127. from the 18th K.R.R.C. thus occupying the original trenches held by us. The day was particularly | |

1875 Wt. W593/826 1,000,000 4/15 J.B.C. & A. A.D.S.S./Forms/C. 2118.

Instructions regarding War Diaries and Intelligence Summaries are contained in F. S. Regs., Part II. and the Staff Manual respectively. Title Pages will be prepared in manuscript.

# WAR DIARY
*or*
# INTELLIGENCE SUMMARY
*(Erase heading not required.)*

Army Form C. 2118

| Place | Date | Hour | Summary of Events and Information | Remarks and references to Appendices |
|---|---|---|---|---|
| In the field (Continued). | 28/7/16 | | Quiet although in the early morning a good deal of hammering was heard in the enemy's lines. Aircraft were very active during the day & both ours & enemy's planes were reconnoitering. | [signature] |
| do | 29/7/16 | | General Quietness continued. Except for an occasional round there was no Artillery fire. Our snipers recorded a 'kill'. Enemy snipers quiet. A few rifle grenades fired by enemy did no damage. The flashes & smoke of an enemy field gun battery observed. In the evening one of our shells seemed to drop on enemy bomb store for a series of explosions resulted. | [signature] |
| do | 30/7/16 | | General conditions - Very quiet. Our Patrols reported enemy working parties in vicinity of BROKEN TREE FARM. These parties were dispersed. Our Artillery fired a few shots into Enemy front & support lines & shelled E.S.E. of MESSINES. Sniping on both sides was very quiet. There was a great deal of aircraft activity during the day. Machine Gun & Rifle fire normal. We had one officer wounded. | [signature] |

1875 Wt. W593/826 1,000,000 4/15 J.B.C. & A. A.D.S.S./Forms/C. 2118.

Instructions regarding War Diaries and Intelligence Summaries are contained in F. S. Regs., Part II. and the Staff Manual respectively. Title pages will be prepared in manuscript.

# WAR DIARY
*or*
# INTELLIGENCE SUMMARY.
*(Erase heading not required.)*

Army Form C. 2118.

| Place | Date | Hour | Summary of Events and Information | Remarks and references to Appendices |
|---|---|---|---|---|
| Riggers | 26/7/16 to 30/7/16 | | Remained in Brigade Reserve at the Riggers. Nothing of importance to record. Casualties 2 wounded | [illegible] |
| | | | W. J. North<br>Lieut. Col.<br>Commanding 26th Royal Fusiliers | |

T2134 W. ... 500000 4/15. Sir J. C. & S.

Instructions regarding War Diaries and Intelligence Summaries are contained in F. S. Regs., Part II. and the Staff Manual respectively. Title Pages will be prepared in manuscript.

# WAR DIARY
*or*
# INTELLIGENCE SUMMARY
*(Erase heading not required.)*

Army Form C. 2118

| Place | Date | Hour | Summary of Events and Information | Remarks and references to Appendices |
|---|---|---|---|---|
| In the line | 31/7/16 | | Another very quiet day. Our Artillery shelled MESSINES ridge. This occasioned no retaliation on our front. Our patrols reports enemy working parties on their wire. These were fired on & dispersed. Enemy was very quiet altho' sounds of working could be heard going on in their lines throughout the day. There was continuous aircraft activity on ours & the enemy's part. | |
| | | | W. J. North Lt Col<br>Officer Commanding 26th Royal Fus. | |

1875 Wt. W593/826 1,000,000 4/15 J.B.C. & A. A.D.S.S./Forms/C. 2118.

SECRET.

I. B. Order No. 28.
Battalion Detail.

---

Map reference of portion of enemy's trenches to be raided is from U 15 b 6.1 to U 15 d 8.8½. This portion will have its wire cut by R.A.

Two dud wirecutting will take place about U 15 b 4.4½ to U 15 b 0.5 and from U 15 d 9¾.3½ to U 15 d 8½.5.

Preparatory Measures.

On the nights of July 11th & 12th standing patrols, consisting of 2 Officers, 2 N.C.O's and 30 men from each company will cover the front of my trenchesfrom 12¼ to 124 inclusive and will endeavour to capture prisoners who may be attempting to work outside their trenches.

On the night of July 15/16th the raiding party will consist ofone party as above.

Barrage required from U 15 b 8¾.3 to U 16 c 2.8.

The raid will be made at Zero (exact time will be forwarded later). Signals for the raid will be thefirst shell fired in the barrage. Simultaneously with the raid Trench Mortars will bombard from U 21 b 9.7 to U 15 d 9½.0. The barrage will also be cut from U 15b4.4½ to U 15 b 0.5

Composition of raidingparty.

It is groups of 3 men armed with bombs and knob kerries. 2 Officers, one on theleft flank and the other in the centre. 2 N.C.O's, one on theright flank. Officers and N.C.O's will be armed with revolvers.

On reaching the enemys trench the flank groups of 3 men will bomb the approach trenches from either side. The Officers and N.C.O. on the right flank will carry whistles and give the signal for retiring. The trenches will be occupied for no longer than ten minutes, but each group on achieving its purpose will retire on our trenches with prisoners, or trophy or anything they can get. Flanking parties remain until the last man has left the trench, the senior Officerremaining also.

In case of retaliation being made men will lie in the grass on their wayback and returnto our trenches when possible before daylight.

If possible a party of R.E's consisting of 1 N.C.O. and 5 men will endeavour to destroy the enemy's wire by means of bangolore torpedoes connected with a wirefrom our trenches to the enemy's wire. In that case the Officer in the centre will guide his party bymeans of this wire. Very shortly before the raid takes place the raiding party will move up from their positions of standingpatrol to as near the enemy wire as possible.

A Vickers Machine gun should be placed on our parapet to the right and left of thepointto be attacked and should deliver Machine gun fire on the flank of point to be attacked. Care being taken that our own raiding party is not interfered with.

(Sgd.) [illegible]

10th July, 1916.

IMPORTANT. Copy No.7

SECRET. 124th Infantry Brigade Order No. 26.

1. Provided the wind is favourable, from W. to S.S.W. a surprise Gas Attack will be carried out by the personnel of "M" Company Special Brigade, R.E. at 2.a.m. on the 13th instant from Trench 124, T's 127, 128 and Southern half of T. 129.

2. Bays of the above mentioned trenches which contain cylinders and accessories will be temporarily cleared of Infantry during the discharge of gas.

3. Any sentry posts left in bays not containing accessories will wear gas helmets.

4. Smoke will also be discharged bythe personnel of "M" Company Special Brigade, R.E. from the following trenches at the same hour:-
N half of T.123, N. half of T. 124, T's 125, 126, South half of T. 130.

5. Troops in T. 123 will take Gas Alert precautions.

6. No artillery, machine gun or rifle fire will be employed in connection with the Gas Attack.

7. The gas discharge will cease at 2.20.a.m. at which hour the troops will reoccupy trenches temporarily vacated by them.

8. Please acknowledge.

(Sgd). E.B.North, Major.
Brigade Major.
124th Infantry Brigade.

10/7/16.

Issued at 11.a.m. 11/7/16.

SECRET. Copy No.4.

## 124th Infantry Brigade Order No. 35.

INFORMATION. 1. In order to inflict considerable losses on the enemy, prevent him withdrawing troops from our front capture prisoners, and do as much damag as posible, a combined raid by one company, 123rd Infantry Brigade, and one company, 124th Infantry Brigade, will be carried out on a date to be notified later, in accordance with the attached time table.

ARTILLERY. 2. The above combined raid will be prepared and supported by the Divisional Artillery, supplemented by a group of heavy artillery.

Arrangements will be madefor co-operation of Stokes Guns, and Machine Guns.

OBJECTIVES. 3. (a). One company 123rd Inf. Bde. will attack the hostile front and support line trenches in the RED HOUSE locality.

(b). One company, 10th Bn. "QUeens" R.W.S. Regt. will attack the hostile front line trenches from U 28 a 3½.8 to U 22 c 4.2 and the support trenches behind them.

Boththe companies will be accompanied by demolition Companies, provided by the R.E.

ZERO HOUR. 4. The time of Zero Hour will be notified to all concerned from Brigade Headquarters.

WATCHES. 5. Watches will be synchronised at 5 p.m. on the day of attack.

REPORTS. 6. Result of he raid will be reported by PRIORITY telegram to Brigade Headquarters by the unit concerned following by a detailed account in writing.

7. Please acknowledge.

(Sgd). E.B.North. Major
Brigade Major
124th Infantry Brigade.

19/7/16.

Issued at........

SECRET. Copy No.2.

## 124th InfantryBrigade Order No. 38.

With reference to 124th InfantryBrigade Order No.35 of the 19/7/16, the operations detailed therein will be carried out on the night of the 26/27th July.

On the night 26/27th July, smoke will be discharged from Trenches 120, 121-123 for three periods of two minutes each at intervals of 12 minutes.

The first discharge will commence at 1 hour before Zero
will cease at 58 minutes " "

The second discharge will commence at 46 mins. before Zero
will cease at 44 minutes " "

The third discharge will commence at32 mins. before Zero
will cease at 30 minutes " "

This operation is intended to conceal flashe of heavy trench mortars.

The time of Zero will be notified to all concerned by D.R.

Please acknowledge.

(Sgd). E.B.North, Major
Brigade Major
124th Inf. Brigade.

24/7/16.

Issued at 8.30.p.m.

SECRET.

To Headquarters.
124th Infantry Brigade.

---

Herewith are Battalion Intelligence Officer's copies of War Diary for July.

2nd August, 1916.

Lieut. & Adjutant.
26th Royal Fusiliers.

Vol 4

26th Royal Fusiliers

Instructions regarding War Diaries and Intelligence Summaries are contained in F. S. Regs., Part II. and the Staff Manual respectively. Title pages will be prepared in manuscript.

# WAR DIARY
*or*
# INTELLIGENCE SUMMARY.
*(Erase heading not required.)*

for August 1916

Army Form C. 2118.

Map Ref. St YVES Part of Sheet 28.

| Place | Date | Hour | Summary of Events and Information | Remarks and references to Appendices |
|---|---|---|---|---|
| In the line | 1/8/16 | | General conditions throughout the day were very quiet. Our snipers were active on enemy periscopes & loopholes but no other targets were presented. The enemy were very quiet during the day. There was no hostile artillery fire on our front during the day. Enemy snipers fired a good many shots during the day without effect. Enemy seems to be doing a good deal of work in his lines for sounds of hammering were heard throughout the day. There was continued aircraft activity on both sides. Our patrols out at night reported enemy working parties out. | |
| do | 2/8/16 | | There was slightly more activity on our part during the day & we shelled ground in rear of enemy lines, without occasioning retaliation. Our snipers claimed hits on enemy periscopes. There was no sniping on the enemys part. In the early morning a ruse attempted on us failed. Some of the enemy kept calling out "Hullo Tommy" & on our observers looking over the parapet they were treated to bursts of rapid fire from various directions. Our patrols reported | A–K (9 sheets) |

T2131. Wt. W708–776. 500000. 4/15. Sir J. C. & S.

Instructions regarding War Diaries and Intelligence Summaries are contained in F. S. Regs., Part II. and the Staff Manual respectively. Title pages will be prepared in manuscript.

# WAR DIARY
*or*
# INTELLIGENCE SUMMARY.
*(Erase heading not required.)*

Army Form C. 2118.

| Place | Date | Hour | Summary of Events and Information | Remarks and references to Appendices |
|---|---|---|---|---|
| | | | no Enemy wiring parties out, but continued work in enemy lines. At night the enemy was continually bombing his own wire. | |
| Rue de Sac to | 3/8/16 to 9/8/16 | | At 6 hours we were relieved by the 18th K.R.R.C. and proceeded to Divisional Reserve at RUE de SAC where we remained until the 9th inst. Nothing of interest happened during the stay in Reserve but on the 8th of August Brigadier General Clemson presented two of our NCOs with the ribbons of the Military Medal gained for gallant conduct in bringing in wounded men under fire. These are the Regiment's first decorations. | |
| In the line | 9/8/16 | 6 am | At 6.am we again relieved the 18th K.R.R.C. in the line. The day was exceedingly quiet. There being practically no sniping, & artillery fire. During the past week the 18th K.R.R.C. had jumped new saps built out of our line & the work on these was proceeded with. This enterprise is the means of straightening up the | |

Instructions regarding War Diaries and Intelligence Summaries are contained in F. S. Regs., Part II. and the Staff Manual respectively. Title pages will be prepared in manuscript.

# WAR DIARY
*or*
# INTELLIGENCE SUMMARY.
*(Erase heading not required.)*

Army Form C. 2118.

| Place | Date | Hour | Summary of Events and Information | Remarks and references to Appendices |
|---|---|---|---|---|
| | | | front line. The enemy has apparently during the past week strengthened his parapet. Aircraft were very active during the day & there was much anti aircraft fire. | Awm |
| [illegible] in the line | 10/8/16 | | General artillery much more active on our front. Our artillery shelled enemy's lines intermittently throughout the day, even as far back as the Messines Ridge. This activity was the cause of retaliation on the enemy's part, and the following points were heavily shelled - ST YVES, LONE HOUSE AVE & PROWSE POINT. Our Patrols were out during the early hours of the morning but reported all quiet in NO MANS LAND. The enemy were bombing their own wire. Sniping was quiet on both sides. During the early morning the roads behind the enemy lines were much used & sounds of a great deal of transport were heard. A bugle & drum band was heard & it is believed that a relief has taken place | Awm |

T2134. Wt W708—776. 500000. 4/15. Sir J. C. & S.

Instructions regarding War Diaries and Intelligence Summaries are contained in F. S. Regs., Part II. and the Staff Manual respectively. Title pages will be prepared in manuscript.

# WAR DIARY
*or*
# INTELLIGENCE SUMMARY.
*(Erase heading not required.)*

Army Form C. 2118.

| Place | Date | Hour | Summary of Events and Information | Remarks and references to Appendices |
|---|---|---|---|---|
| In the line | 11/8/16 | | General conditions were much quieter than on previous day. Our patrols reported enemy working parties out. These were fired on by our M.Gs. About 6 am this morning on the mist clearing away an enemy party was seen in front of the parapet. They were immediately fired on by a M.G. with good results.<br>Enemy artillery was fairly active during the day. Our Artillery replied on enemy front & support lines.<br>Our snipers had a busy day. A remarkable number of periscopes were up in Enemy's lines, probably owing to new troops being in & a number were smashed by our snipers. There was little enemy sniping.<br>There was practically no machine gun fire at night as we had large working parties out. | |

Aw

Army Form C. 2118.

# WAR DIARY
*or*
# INTELLIGENCE SUMMARY.
*(Erase heading not required.)*

Instructions regarding War Diaries and Intelligence Summaries are contained in F. S. Regs., Part II. and the Staff Manual respectively. Title pages will be prepared in manuscript.

| Place | Date | Hour | Summary of Events and Information | Remarks and references to Appendices |
| --- | --- | --- | --- | --- |
| In the Line | 12/8/16 | | General Conditions were again quiet. There was practically no Artillery fire on either side. Our patrols reported large enemy working parties out. These were fired at & dispersed. Our working parties got through a good deal of work during the night & a large quantity of wire was put out. There was practically no sniping during the day but increased rifle fire at night. Much aircraft activity on our part during the day. Casualties :- 1 O.R. Wounded. [initials] | |
| do | 13/8/16 | | The Conditions continued quiet. Little Artillery fire on both sides. We had strong fighting patrols out all night. The enemys wire was examined & found very thick & strong. Enemy had no working parties out. Practically no machine gun or rifle fire. [initials] | |

Instructions regarding War Diaries and Intelligence Summaries are contained in F. S. Regs., Part II. and the Staff Manual respectively. Title pages will be prepared in manuscript.

# WAR DIARY
*or*
# INTELLIGENCE SUMMARY.
*(Erase heading not required.)*

Army Form C. 2118.

| Place | Date | Hour | Summary of Events and Information | Remarks and references to Appendices |
|---|---|---|---|---|
| In the line | 14/8/16 | | Both ours & Enemys attitude fairly Quiet. Our Artillery was active on Enemys lines. Enemy replied on PROWSE POINT & PLOEGSTEERT WOOD. A small patrol consisting of an officer & 3 other ranks, were examining our wire when they were surprised by a strong enemy patrol & bombed. The officer was wounded by rifle fire. The Enemy patrol immediately ran off to their own lines. There was little sniping during the day. Machine Guns were inactive. Our aircraft were busy during the early morning & Evening. Casualties :- 1 officer & 1 OR wounded | |
| do | 15/8/16 | | Our Artillery were active during the day & the Enemys lines were heavily shelled. This occasioned a good deal of retaliation on T.W. & LONE HOUSE AVE. We had strong patrols out but no Enemy patrol was encountered & no Enemy working parties were out. | |

T2134. Wt W708–776. 500000. 4/15. Sir J. C. & S.

Instructions regarding War Diaries and Intelligence Summaries are contained in F. S. Regs., Part II. and the Staff Manual respectively. Title pages will be prepared in manuscript.

# WAR DIARY
*or*
# INTELLIGENCE SUMMARY.
*(Erase heading not required.)*

Army Form C. 2118.

| Place | Date | Hour | Summary of Events and Information | Remarks and references to Appendices |
|---|---|---|---|---|
| | | | Machine Gun fire & sniping, Quiet on both sides. Enemy appears to have been at work on his parapet. Signalling was observed behind Enemy lines at LA POTTERIE FARM<br>Casualties :- 1 OR wounded | |
| In the Line | 16/7/16 | | Our artillery continued their activity & shelling of Enemy lines the ground behind the Enemy line was well searched & buildings were treated to HE shells. There was no retaliation on our front<br>Our patrols reported no movement in Enemy's line & No Mans land<br>Machine Gun fire & sniping - Quiet. Our Air Craft were active during the day<br>Casualties :- 1 Officer & 1 O.R. killed. 1 O.R. wounded | |

T2134. Wt. W708-776. 500000. 4/15. Sir J. C. & S.

Instructions regarding War Diaries and Intelligence Summaries are contained in F. S. Regs., Part II. and the Staff Manual respectively. Title pages will be prepared in manuscript.

# WAR DIARY
*or*
# INTELLIGENCE SUMMARY.
*(Erase heading not required.)*

Army Form C. 2118.

| Place | Date | Hour | Summary of Events and Information | Remarks and references to Appendices |
|---|---|---|---|---|
| In the line | 17/7/16 | 5 am | We were relieved at this hour by the 8th Batt. K.O. Yorkshire L.I. & we proceeded to RUE du SAC. The new battalion were agreeably surprised at the amount of valuable information given them as to the enemy's lines & our system of observation was much admired. | |
| | | | We remained at Rue du Sac during the day. Nothing of importance to note. | [initials] |
| Rue du Sac to | 18/7/16 | 9 am | We left our billets at RUE du SAC – they having been taken over by the 11th West Yorks Regt & the whole Battalion marched to the Meteren district where they remained until | |
| | 23/8/16 | | the 23rd August. | |
| | | | The week at Meteren was spent in training & there is nothing of importance to record. | [initials] |
| Meteren | 23/8/16 | 9 am | At this hour the Battalion entrained at BAILLEUL for PONT REMYS (on the Somme). We arrived at PONT REMYS | |

T2134. Wt. W708—776. 500000. 4/15. Sir J. C. & S.

Instructions regarding War Diaries and Intelligence Summaries are contained in F. S. Regs., Part II. and the Staff Manual respectively. Title pages will be prepared in manuscript.

# WAR DIARY
*or*
# INTELLIGENCE SUMMARY.
*(Erase heading not required.)*

Army Form C. 2118.

| Place | Date | Hour | Summary of Events and Information | Remarks and references to Appendices |
|---|---|---|---|---|
| | | | at 7 pm. the journey taking 10 hrs. From PONT REMYS we marched to our billets at VAUCHELLES de QUESNOY. Training was continued & schemes for the attack were practised. | |
| VAUCHELLES | 31/8/16 | | We remained at VAUCHELLES during the remainder of the month | |
| | | | Awn | |
| | | | W. F. North Lt. Col. Commanding 26 Ser Bn Royal Fus. | |

T2134. Wt W708—776. 500000. 4/15. Sir J. C. & S.

26th (S) Batn Royal Fusiliers.

124/41

Instructions regarding War Diaries and Intelligence Summaries are contained in F. S. Regs., Part II. and the Staff Manual respectively. Title pages will be prepared in manuscript.

# WAR DIARY
*or*
# INTELLIGENCE SUMMARY.
*(Erase heading not required.)*

September 1916.

Army Form C. 2118.

Vol. 5

| Place | Date | Hour | Summary of Events and Information | Remarks and references to Appendices |
|---|---|---|---|---|
| | 1916. | | | |
| France (Vanchelles) | 1st Sept. to 7th Sept | | During this time the Battalion remained in training at Vanchelles & Quesnoy, near Abbeville. There is nothing of importance to record | [initials] |
| LONGPRE | 7th Sept | 10 pm | At about 10 pm the Battalion left Vanchelles & marched to LONGPRE where they entrained about 6 am. for MERICOURT. We arrived at | |
| MERICOURT | | | MERICOURT at about 10 am. The Battalion was fed at the B.E.F. Canteen & after a rest proceeded to camp at E.9.a (Map ref. | |
| DERNANCOURT | | | France Sheet 62 D) We remained at this camp until | [initials] |
| | 10th Sept | | When we moved to camp at BECORDEL - E.12. (map ref France Sheet 62 D) Here we remained until | [initials] |
| FRICOURT | 13th Sept | | When we moved nearer the line & encamped at E.14.b (Same map reference. During the time spent in the above camp the training was proceeded with. After their long rest from trench work & the large amount of training got in, the men are in splendid condition & eagerly looking forward to the fight. | [initials] |



5K (11 sheets)

Instructions regarding War Diaries and Intelligence Summaries are contained in F. S. Regs., Part II. and the Staff Manual respectively. Title pages will be prepared in manuscript.

# WAR DIARY
*or*
# INTELLIGENCE SUMMARY.
*(Erase heading not required.)*

Army Form C. 2118.

| Place | Date | Hour | Summary of Events and Information | Remarks and references to Appendices |
|---|---|---|---|---|
| France | 15th Sept | 5.15 pm | At this hour the Battalion left the last named camp and marched up into the line. The journey was very long owing to continual stoppages on the road on account of heavy traffic. At about 9 pm we arrived at the Brigade Dump, East of MONTAUBAN where after having received stores ammunition &c we proceeded via FLARE LANE up to our point of assembly in front of DELVILLE WOOD, the Companies taking up their positions for the attack which was timed to commence at 6.20. The Battalion arrived & took up their position about 10 mins only before the attack commenced. They had been on the march from 5.15 the previous evening & went into attack on the morning of the 15th without a rest or sleep. | |
| | 15th Sept | 6.20 am | The order of Battle of our Brigade (the 124th Infantry Bde) was as follows Front line 21st K.R.R.C & 10th Queens R.W.S Regt. The 26th Battalion Royal Fusiliers were in support | |

T2134. Wt. W708—776. 500000. 4/15. Sir J. C. & S.

Instructions regarding War Diaries and Intelligence Summaries are contained in F. S. Regs., Part II. and the Staff Manual respectively. Title pages will be prepared in manuscript.

# WAR DIARY
*or*
# INTELLIGENCE SUMMARY.
*(Erase heading not required.)*

Army Form C. 2118.

| Place | Date | Hour | Summary of Events and Information | Remarks and references to Appendices |
|---|---|---|---|---|
| | | | of the 21st K.R.R.C. & the 32nd Royal Fusiliers in support of the 10th Queens. | |
| | | | Map Reference. Trench map. FRANCE. Sheet 57c S.W. Edition 3A. | |
| 15th Sept. | | 6.20 am. | The 21st K.R.R.C. were in position for attack on SWITCH trench supported by 26th R.F. (two Companies in Edge Trench & two Companies in Green Trench). Attack commenced at 6.20 am. | |
| | | 6.30 am | 26th R.F. were within 80 yds of 1st objective (SWITCH trench) & found that 1st five waves were advancing through our own artillery barrage in a half right direction the left flank being about 300 yds East of FLERS village. The position of our left flank should have been on FLERS road. A halt was ordered & mistake was as far as possible rectified | |
| | | 6.50 am | The left sector of 1st objective was taken with very little opposition. Our barrage advanced & infantry followed & took up position in front of 2nd objective – FLERS trench | |

T2131. Wt. W708—776. 500000. 4/15. Sir J. C. & S.

Instructions regarding War Diaries and Intelligence Summaries are contained in F. S. Regs., Part II. and the Staff Manual respectively. Title pages will be prepared in manuscript.

# WAR DIARY
*or*
# INTELLIGENCE SUMMARY.
*(Erase heading not required.)*

Army Form C. 2118.

| Place | Date | Hour | Summary of Events and Information | Remarks and references to Appendices |
|---|---|---|---|---|
| | | | At this point men from various Battalions straggled back through our barrage on the right - 2nd LIEUT GAUTHERN (26th RF) did excellent work in bringing men out of the barrage at great personal risk. | |
| | 7.45 a.m. | | Our barrage lifted from 2nd objective & the infantry moved forward & took the trench. Casualties were suffered here from hostile rifle & M.G. fire. A number of prisoners were taken. Our D Company took something like 150 prisoners. The 2nd Objective FLERS TRENCH had been severely damaged by our Artillery fire. | |
| | | | The infantry remained in this trench until the 122 I B. on our left commenced to clear the village of FLERS | |
| | | | In the attack on the first two objectives the infantry was assisted by TANKS of the Heavy Machine Gun Coy but by the time the 2nd Objective was taken there was only 1 Tank in our sector which had not been put out of action | |

T2134. Wt. W708—776. 500000. 4/15. Sir J. C. & S.

Instructions regarding War Diaries and Intelligence Summaries are contained in F. S. Regs., Part II. and the Staff Manual respectively. Title pages will be prepared in manuscript.

# WAR DIARY
*or*
# INTELLIGENCE SUMMARY.
*(Erase heading not required.)*

Army Form C. 2118.

| Place | Date | Hour | Summary of Events and Information | Remarks and references to Appendices |
|---|---|---|---|---|
| | | | This tank was sent forward along the right of [illegible] village to assist the 122nd Brigade & to cover their right flank. A small party under 2/Lt Atwood followed the tank to keep in touch with the troops clearing the village. The Battalion was re-organised, & as our barrage moved forward, & advanced in two waves. | |
| | 15 | 11.15 | The Tank moved forward in front of our waves to the 2nd object-ive - HOGS HEAD - & FLEA TRENCH. Our first wave was advancing, but when about 200 yards from the HOGSHEAD Lt. Col. Oakley, of the 10th "Queen's" ordered a withdrawal to FLERS TRENCH, the reason being that the troops that had been in the village of FLERS had lost all their Officers & had retired. We proceeded to consolidate FLERS TRENCH | |
| | | 3 pm | An advance was ordered & under heavy machine gun & rifle fire they occupied the line of the 3rd objective. Shortly afterwards the line again moved forward on the signal of Lieut. Colonel the Earl of Feversham, commanding 21st K.R.R.C. | |

T2134. Wt. W708—776. 500000. 4/15. Sir J. C. & S.

Instructions regarding War Diaries and Intelligence Summaries are contained in F. S. Regs., Part II. and the Staff Manual respectively. Title pages will be prepared in manuscript.

# WAR DIARY
*or*
# INTELLIGENCE SUMMARY.
*(Erase heading not required.)*

Army Form C. 2118.

| Place | Date | Hour | Summary of Events and Information | Remarks and references to Appendices |
|---|---|---|---|---|
| | | | We advanced towards GIRD TRENCH under heavy & increasing fire, but at a point about 150 yards away from our objective, when our left flank was held up by a part of the enemy, who had advanced in front of their trench & lay concealed in a corn field. | |
| | | 5pm | An order was passed down to retire. We could not find out where this order originated & movement backwards was as far as possible prevented: but men on our right flank commenced to double back & the right flank was quickly broken. The enemy immediately opened heavy artillery fire along the whole front & we were forced to withdraw to an old trench, situated about N.32 a 1.5. which we found occupied by 20 to 30 men & 2 "Vickers" Guns. We could not find anybody on either flank with whom to get into touch & therefore the men were ordered to "stand to" until dusk. At dusk we retired to a new line which was being consolidated | |

T2134. Wt. W708—776. 500000. 4/15. Sir J. C. & S.

Instructions regarding War Diaries and Intelligence Summaries are contained in F. S. Regs., Part II. and the Staff Manual respectively. Title pages will be prepared in manuscript.

# WAR DIARY
*or*
# INTELLIGENCE SUMMARY.
*(Erase heading not required.)*

Army Form C. 2118.

| Place | Date | Hour | Summary of Events and Information | Remarks and references to Appendices |
|---|---|---|---|---|
| | | | between the 2nd. & 3rd. objectives. We remained here & proceeded with consolidation. | |
| | | 11pm | The Brigade was relieved by the 123rd. Brigade & proceeded into the support line with the exception of a Company under Capt. Etchells which was in front of the line & was unable to reach the remainder of the Battalion. | [initials] |
| | 16th. | | The Battalion remained in the support lines & was subject to heavy artillery fire throughout the whole day. We were not called upon during the day by the Brigade in front. Capt. Etchells & his Company were relieved on Saturday evening & in view of the heavy fighting they had done they were ordered to remain at the Brigade camp during Saturday night & on Sunday morning they were ordered to proceed back to the Transport lines. | [initials] |
| | 17th. | | The rest of the Battalion, remained ~~was~~ in support during Sunday & although subjected to heavy artillery fire suffered | |

Instructions regarding War Diaries and Intelligence Summaries are contained in F. S. Regs., Part II. and the Staff Manual respectively. Title pages will be prepared in manuscript.

# WAR DIARY
*or*
# INTELLIGENCE SUMMARY.
*(Erase heading not required.)*

Army Form C. 2118.

| Place | Date | Hour | Summary of Events and Information | Remarks and references to Appendices |
|---|---|---|---|---|
| | | | no casualties. | |
| | 18th. | | During the early hours of the morning we were relieved by the North Lancashire Regt. & the Battalion proceeded back to the Transport lines, & after a meal & a rest returned to camp at E.Q. | |
| | | | Our casualties during the action were as follows:- Officers, Lts. M. J. Shaw, A. J. Bright (killed). Lts. G. W. Havelock, G. L. Ashwood (died of wounds). 2/Lts. Sir W. A. Blount, Bart. & H. K. Patterson, R. J. H. Lane & C. F. Neale (wounded). Other ranks 33 (killed) 58 (missing ~~[illegible]~~) & 140 (wounded). | |
| | | | Prisoners taken by the Battalion - 2 Officers, 158 other ranks. | |
| | 19th to 30th. | | The Battalion remained in camp at E.Q. where training was proceeded with. On the 27th Lieut. Colonel ~~The Hon.~~ W. F. North relinquished command | |

T2134. Wt. W708—776. 500000. 4/15. Sir J. C. & S.

Instructions regarding War Diaries and Intelligence Summaries are contained in F. S. Regs., Part II. and the Staff Manual respectively. Title pages will be prepared in manuscript.

# WAR DIARY
*or*
# INTELLIGENCE SUMMARY.
*(Erase heading not required.)*

Army Form C. 2118.

| Place | Date | Hour | Summary of Events and Information | Remarks and references to Appendices |
|---|---|---|---|---|
| | | | of the Battalion & Lieut. Colonel Gwyn Thomas took over from him. Otherwise there is nothing of importance to report between these dates. | |
| | | | Gwyn Thomas<br>Lieut. Col. Commanding<br>11th Royal Fusiliers. | |

T2134. Wt. W708—776. 500000. 4/15. Sir J. C. & S.

26th Bn. Royal Fusiliers; — October 1916. Army Form C. 2118.

Vol 6

# WAR DIARY
*or*
# INTELLIGENCE SUMMARY.
*(Erase heading not required.)*

Instructions regarding War Diaries and Intelligence Summaries are contained in F. S. Regs., Part II. and the Staff Manual respectively. Title pages will be prepared in manuscript.

| Place | Date | Hour | Summary of Events and Information | Remarks and references to Appendices |
|---|---|---|---|---|
| Henencourt | 1 Oct | | The Battalion remained at Camp at E.14. + training was continued with. | Map Ref France Sheet 62.D |
| | 2nd | 2pm | The Battalion moved by road to POMMIERS REDOUBT (S.26c7.) near MONTAUBAN, where we arrived at 6 o'clock. The march was a very trying one, being conducted throughout in heavy rain along very muddy roads. The men bivouaced here for the night under very unfavourable conditions. | Map Ref France 57 C. N.W |
| | 3rd. | | On the morning of the 3rd, Company Commanders were sent | |
| | | 2pm | up to reconnoitre the trenches. At 2 p.m. the Battalion marched out of camp and arrived at THISTLE DUMP (S.16a3.9) at 5 p.m. Tea was served + we then proceeded into support lines in relief of 3rd Bn. New Zealand Infantry Brigade. | |
| | | 3am | Relief was completed at 3 a.m. Disposition of companies:- "A" + "B" Coys — FLERS [redacted] TRENCH: "C" + "D" Coys - FLERS [redacted] SUPPORT. | |
| | 4th + 5th. | | The Battalion remained here during the 4th + 5th. During this time it was subject to fairly heavy shelling. Large | |

T2134. Wt. W708—776. 500000. 4/15. Sir J. C. & S.

Instructions regarding War Diaries and Intelligence Summaries are contained in F. S. Regs., Part II. and the Staff Manual respectively. Title pages will be prepared in manuscript.

# WAR DIARY
*or*
# INTELLIGENCE SUMMARY.
*(Erase heading not required.)*

Army Form C. 2118.

| Place | Date | Hour | Summary of Events and Information | Remarks and references to Appendices |
|---|---|---|---|---|
| | | | fatigue parties were found, for digging purposes in the front line. The front held by the Battalion was close on 3000$^{x}$ yards. | CRW |
| | 5th to 7th. | 6 pm. | The Battalion moved up into GIRD TRENCH, GIRD SUPPORT & NEW LINE. Disposition – 2 Coys. in NEW LINE (front line trench) & 2 Coys in GIRD SUPPORT & GIRD TRENCH, where they remained until the forenoon of the 7th. During the stay in these trenches, both "C" & "D" Coys did good work in digging a new trench forward of GIRD SUPPORT. We were subject to intermittent shelling by the enemy, but our casualties were very slight. | CRW |
| GIRD TRENCH | 7th | 1.45 pm. | At 1.45 pm. (ZERO HOUR) the Battalion was in the assembly trenches prepared to attack, & moved forward (X) at that hour. Disposition was as follows:– "A" & "B" Coys. in front line; "C" & "D" Coys in support. The disposition of the 124th. Infantry Brigade was – 26th. Royal Fusiliers on the left: 32nd. Royal Fusiliers on the right: 21st King's Royal Rifle | 124th Inf Bde Order No 5? dated 6/10/ (attached) |

(X) In 4 waves of ½ Companies at 50$^{x}$ distance

9

Instructions regarding War Diaries and Intelligence Summaries are contained in F. S. Regs., Part II. and the Staff Manual respectively. Title pages will be prepared in manuscript.

# WAR DIARY
*or*
# INTELLIGENCE SUMMARY.
*(Erase heading not required.)*

Army Form C. 2118.

| Place | Date | Hour | Summary of Events and Information | Remarks and references to Appendices |
|---|---|---|---|---|
| | | | Corps supporting Left Battalion: 10th "Queens" R.W.K. Regt. supporting Right Battalion. On the left of our Brigade was the 122nd. Infantry Brigade, & on the right of our Brigade the 12th. Division. The right of our A Coy. directed the attack. | |
| | | | The objectives allotted to the Battalion were as follows:- | |
| | | | (a) line running from M 18 d 6.5 to N 14 c 3.2. | |
| | | | (b) line running from M 18 b 3.3 to N 14 a 3.0. | |
| | | | The Battalion went forward into the attack in good formation. The men were in good spirits. Our artillery barrage was very heavy: but the result of this fire, owing to a steep bank immediately to our front, was unobserved. On reaching the above-mentioned bank our lines were subject to extremely brisk & heavy enemy machine gun fire. The enemy had evidently managed to push several of his machine guns forward of our barrage, & our Infantry, | |

T2134. Wt. W708—776. 500000. 4/15. Sir J. C. & S.

4/

Instructions regarding War Diaries and Intelligence Summaries are contained in F. S. Regs., Part II. and the Staff Manual respectively. Title pages will be prepared in manuscript.

# WAR DIARY
*or*
# INTELLIGENCE SUMMARY.
*(Erase heading not required.)*

Army Form C. 2118.

| Place | Date | Hour | Summary of Events and Information | Remarks and references to Appendices |
|---|---|---|---|---|
| | | | advancing over the crest formed a very easy target for accurate shooting. We, unfortunately, suffered heavy casualties, but nevertheless the men continued to press forward, under the very fine leadership of our officers. Our first wave managed to reach a point estimated at about 50 yards from the first objective: but the enemy fire proved too much of an obstacle, & the men were forced to stay & dig in as best they could, at a point about 350 yards from our starting point. On the approach of dusk, the line reached by the Battalion, which up to the present could only be marked by a chain of shell holes, was dug, & by continued hard digging for several hours, a good line of resistance was made & communication with both flanks was obtained. This new line was held. During the attack, troops of various units became rather mixed | |

5

Instructions regarding War Diaries and Intelligence Summaries are contained in F. S. Regs., Part II. and the Staff Manual respectively. Title pages will be prepared in manuscript.

# WAR DIARY
*or*
# INTELLIGENCE SUMMARY.
*(Erase heading not required.)*

Army Form C. 2118.

| Place | Date | Hour | Summary of Events and Information | Remarks and references to Appendices |
|---|---|---|---|---|
| | | | but they nevertheless all worked together with one object – that of remaining in the line & holding the ground which they had fought so well for. All our Company officers were casualties, & it reflects great credit upon our N.C.O's. that the above object was attained. By 2 am. on | C.R.W. |
| | 8th. | 2 am | the morning of the 8th, a Communication trench was dug through our newly gained territory, & safe means of communication was established between our original & new front lines. This work was splendidly carried out by the 19th (Pioneer) Battalion Middlesex Regiment. During the whole of the evening & night our men were troubled by enemy snipers, but there was no sign of an enemy counter attack, although we were well prepared for such an event. The Battalion remained in its new position during the whole of the next day & the work of consolidation was | |

6/

Instructions regarding War Diaries and Intelligence Summaries are contained in F. S. Regs., Part II. and the Staff Manual respectively. Title pages will be prepared in manuscript.

# WAR DIARY
*or*
# INTELLIGENCE SUMMARY.
*(Erase heading not required.)*

Army Form C. 2118.

| Place | Date | Hour | Summary of Events and Information | Remarks and references to Appendices |
|---|---|---|---|---|
| | | | proceeded with. | |
| | | | We were relieved on the evening of the 8th. by a batt. 10th Queens ~~of the 123rd Infantry Brigade~~, & the Battalion moved a | |
| | 8th. | 6 pm | few hundred yards back from the front line. & occupied FACTORY ~~[illegible]~~ TRENCH (N 19 c 8.2). Here we were subject to even more shelling than in the front line, but our casualties were slight. We remained in this support during the whole of Sunday night (8th) & the following day | CRW |
| | 9th | 9 pm | & were relieved by the 17th Battalion Manchester Regt. | CRW |
| | | | We proceeded to bivouacs at CATTERPILLAR WOOD. | |
| | | | Our casualties during the above period in the line were:- Officers, killed - 3. | |
| | | | missing - 2 | |
| | | | wounded - 7. | |
| | | | Other Ranks, Killed - 35. | |
| | | | died of wounds. - 3. | |

Instructions regarding War Diaries and Intelligence Summaries are contained in F. S. Regs., Part II. and the Staff Manual respectively. Title pages will be prepared in manuscript.

# WAR DIARY
*or*
# INTELLIGENCE SUMMARY.
*(Erase heading not required.)*

Army Form C. 2118.

| Place | Date | Hour | Summary of Events and Information | Remarks and references to Appendices |
|---|---|---|---|---|
| | | | Missing - 15 | |
| | | | Wounded · 164. | |
| BECORDEL | 10th | 8am | The following day we entrained for bivouacs at BECORDEL (F.S.C: ). Here we received drafts of reinforcements, & the work of training & reorganisation was proceeded with. (Draft of 150 from Royal Fusiliers & Essex Bns) | CRW |
| BUIRE-sur-ANCRE | 13th | 1.15 pm | The Battalion left BECORDEL & proceeded to BUIRE-sur-ANCRE. | CRW |
| | 15th | 11am | On the 15th. the Battn. marched to EDGEHILL RAILHEAD where it entrained at 11.25 am for AIRAINES. Detrainment was effected | CRW |
| AIRAINES. | 16th | 12 noon | by 12 noon on the 16th. & the men marched to billets, situate in & near this town. | CRW |
| | | | At each of the above places, drafts of reinforcements were received & the reorganisation & training of the Battalion was continued. | CRW |

T2134. Wt. W708—776. 500000. 4/15. Sir J. C. & S.

(6)

Instructions regarding War Diaries and Intelligence Summaries are contained in F. S. Regs., Part II. and the Staff Manual respectively. Title pages will be prepared in manuscript.

# WAR DIARY
*or*
# INTELLIGENCE SUMMARY.
*(Erase heading not required.)*

Army Form C. 2118.

| Place | Date | Hour | Summary of Events and Information | Remarks and references to Appendices |
|---|---|---|---|---|
| | 18th | 5pm | The Battalion left AIRAINES & by road proceeded to LONGPRE. | |
| | | 10.11 | After some refreshment, we entrained at 10.11 pm. for | |
| | | pm. | CASTRE, where we arrived on the 19th. about 9 am. | CRW |
| | 19th. | | The men then marched to billets in the METEREN area. | |
| | 21st. | | The Battalion proceeded by road to CONNAUGHT. | CRW |
| | 22nd. | | CAMP (L 34 b 4.4) & from thence on the 22nd to billets at LA CLYTTE. | CRW |
| | | | On this day the 124th. Infantry Brigade relieved the 12th. Australian Infantry Brigade in the line. | |
| | | | During our stay at LA CLYTTE the Battalion | |
| | 27th. | | training was proceeded with: & on the 27th. it was inspected | CRW |
| | | | by Gen. Sir Herbert C. Plumer, G.C.M.G. K.C.B. Commander of 2nd Army, who expressed his satisfaction at the good turn-out of the Battalion. He also congratulated the men on the work they had done in the SOMME fighting. | CRW |

T2134. Wt. W708–776. 500000. 4/15. Sir J. C. & S.

9/

Instructions regarding War Diaries and Intelligence Summaries are contained in F. S. Regs., Part II. and the Staff Manual respectively. Title pages will be prepared in manuscript.

# WAR DIARY
*or*
# INTELLIGENCE SUMMARY.
*(Erase heading not required.)*

Army Form C. 2118.

| Place | Date | Hour | Summary of Events and Information | Remarks and references to Appendices |
|---|---|---|---|---|
| | 28th. | | The Battalion relieved the 21st. Bn. K.R.R.C. in the left sub-sector of the line. | O7b.6.10 to O.7.c.0.9 Sheet 28 cRuf |
| | 29th to 31st | | The work of improving the trenches for the winter months was carried on. Patrols reconnoitred each night to ascertain the strength with which the Germans hold their front line. Our wire was inspected and found to need much repair which work was started. Casualties wounded 2 O.R. | see operation order 14 cRuf. |

Gwyn Thomas
Lieut. Col. Comm^d^g.
26th Royal Fusiliers

3/12
EB

SECRET.                                                    Copy No. 11

124th.Infantry Brigade Order No.61.

Reference maps GUEUDECOURT to BAPAUME, 1/10,000.
LIGNY THILLOY 1/20,000.

---

1. This order is supplementary to 124th.Infantry Brigade Warning Order No.4 and 124th.Infantry Brigade Order No.60.

2. INFORMATION.
The 38th.Infantry Brigade, 12th.Division, will be on the right and the 140th.Infantry Brigade, 47th.Division, on the left of the 41st.Division.

3. ASSEMBLY AREAS.
3 Vickers Guns of 124th.Machine Gun Coy(instead of 2 as previously detailed)will be attached to each 32nd.Bn.Royal Fusiliers and 26th.Bn.Royal Fusiliers, 2 guns for indirect fire at N 19 a 6.3. The remaining Vickors Guns will be held in reserve in FAT TRENCH near its junction with FISH ALLEY.
Attached half sections Field Co. R.E. will join their respective Battalions (at 5am) on the ~~afternoon of the~~ 7th.Octr.
Arrival of units in ~~possess~~ positions of assembly will be reported thus, "DERBY". Time....."

4. Preliminary Work.
On night 6/7th. October 32nd.Bn.R.Fusiliers and 26th.Bn. R.Fusiliers will complete the new trenches in front of GIRD SUPPORT in their respective sectors.
During the night 6/7th.October constant fire from rifles, Lewis and Vickers Guns must be maintained on LINE TRENCH, BAYONET TRENCH and the new German trench.

5. OBJECTIVES.
The attack will be preceded by a bombardment commencing at 3.15 pm. 6th,October till ZERO Hour. There will be no intense fire before ZERO Hour.
The attack will be carried out in two stages as follows:-
First objective. Green line on attached Map "A".
Second objective. Brown line on attached Map "A".
Details and Time Table of the Creeping and Stationery Barrages will be issued later.
Heavy artillery is dealing with hostile defences, approaches, villages, etc.
At 2 minutes before ZERO the sub-section of the 124th.L.T.M.Batty. in rear of GIRD SUPPORT will bombard the portion of the GIRD LINE still held by the enemy.

6. DIRECTION.
The right of the 26th.Bn.R.Fusiliers will direct, maintaining direction by the dividing ~~LINE~~ ROAD.
LINE

7. DIVIDING LINES.
The Dividing Lines (a) between the 36th.Infantry Brigade and 124th.Infantry Brigade (b) between 124th.Infantry Brigade and 122nd.Infantry Brigade (c) between 32nd.Bn.R.Fusiliers and 26th.Bn.R.Fusiliers are marked by dotted red line on the attached Map "A".
The dividing road between Battalions is inclusive to 32nd.Bn.R.Fusiliers.

RUNNER

14. VISUAL SIGNALLING AND RELAY POSTS.

Visual Stations have been notified. The Brigade Signalling Officer will maintain runner Posts and telephone wire between Brigade Headquarters and advance report centre at H 30 b 5.3 where the trench crosses the Sunken Road from FACTORY CORNER. Forward from this point Battns. must maintain their own runner posts.

15. PIGEONS.

32nd.Bn.R.Fusiliers and 26th.Bn.R.Fusiliers will be provided with four pigeons for use if other means of communication fail.

16. LIAISON.

O.C. 32nd.Bn.R.Fusiliers will detail an Officer as Liaison Officer with Headquarters, 36th.Infantry Brigadd. This Officer will report at 124th.Infantry Brigade Headquarters for instructions at 7 am. on the 7th.October.

17. MEDICAL.

Advanced Dressing Stations will be established at THISTLE and GREEN DUMPS and a Divisional Collecting Station at FLAT IRON COPSE.

18. WATCHES.

Watches will be synchronised by the Brigade Signalling Officer at 9.15 am. and 1.15 pm. on the 7th.October.

19. BRIGADE HEADQUARTERS.

124th.Infantry Brigade will move to S 6 a 8.7 (FERRET TRENCH) as soon as it is vacated by 122nd.Infantry Brigade Time will be notified later.

20. HOUR OF ZERO.

The ZERO Hour will be notified later.

21. REPORTS.

Units will send Situation Reports to Brigade Headquarters at the end of every hour after ZERO. Important events, e.g. capture of objective, will be reported at once. If the situation is unknown it will be so stated.

22. WORK.NIGHT 7/8th.

Strong Officers Patrols must be sent out on the night 7/8th.October.

The following work will be carried out on the night 7/8th.October:-

(a) Troops occupying our new trenches in front of GIRD SUPPORT will dig two Communication trenches, one to connect with the new GERMAN TRENCH in N 13 c, the other to connect with western point of BAYONET TRENCH.
If O.C. 21st.Bn.K.R.R.Corps is still in our original front line he may call upon O.C. 10th.Bn."Queens" R.W.S. for 200 men to assist.

(b) Troops occupying 1st. objectivewill join BAYONET TRENCH and NEW TRENCH if not already done, and ~~defend~~ deepen and improve this line.

(c) Troops occupying 2nd.objective will clear diagonal trench leading from BAYONET TRENCH to LIME TRENCH so as to make a good Communication Trench.

Every effort will be made to continue the above work during daylight on the 8th.Oct. in order to facilitate an early relief.

8. CLEARING PARTIES.
Officers Commanding 32nd.Bn.R.Fusiliers and 26th.Bn. Royal Fusiliers will detail special mopping parties to clear the hostile trenches and dugouts passed over in the attack. The attached map "B" shews these trenches so far as they are known to exist.
Special attention must be paid to the diagonal trench running N.W. of BAYONET TRENCH. Wire cutters must be carried as LIME TRENCH is wired.

9. CONSOLIDATION.
Special parties will be detailed by 32nd.Bn.R.Fusiliers to construct Strong Point about N 13 b 3.1 and by 26th.Bn. R.Fusiliers about N 13 c 5.7. Each of these will be provided with a Vickers Gun. The sub-section 124th. L.T.M.B. attached to 32nd Royal Fusiliers or one gun of it, will be detailed to the strong point about N.13.b.3.1.
The remainder of the 32nd. Royal Fusiliers and 26th Royal Fusiliers less the above strong point parties and clearing parties will dig in along the line of the 2nd objective, advanced posts with Lewis Guns being pushed out in front.
1 Company, 21st K.R.R.C. [illegible] with 2 Lewis Gunswill advance immediately in rear of the 26th. Royal Fusiliers, and consolidate new German Trench between N.13 c 9.5 and N.13.c.1½.5.
1 Coy. 21st K.R.R.C. less 2 platoons, with 1 Lewis Gun will advance immediately in rear of 32nd. Royal Fusiliers, andconsolidate portion of BAYONET TRENCH in our sector.
If BAYONET TRENCH and the New Trench to the west of it have been joined up by the enemy the whole line will be consolidated.

10. SUPPORTING BATTALIONS.
As the leading battalions advance the 21st.Bn.K.R.R.C. less parties detailed for consolidation of 1st. objective, [illegible]
will move up into the trenches vacated by the leading Battns. The former will not advance beyond our front line trenches unless required to reinforce either of the leading Battalions, on their own consolidating parties.
If 21st Bn.K.R.R.C. reinforce ~~the leading Battalions~~ O.C. 10th.Bn."Queens" will move his Battalion forward into the trenches vacated by the 21st.Bn.K.R.R.C.
Both supporting Battalions will be ready to reinforce at a moments notice.

11. BOMBS.
Every Officer, N.C.O. and man will carry two Mills bombs in his pockets. "P" bombs will also be provided for clearing dugouts.

12. S.O.S.ROCKETS.
S.O.S.Rockets will be taken forward by each Battalion.

13. COMMUNICATION WITH AEROPLANES.
Every Officer and N.C.O. and 50 men per Company, will carry two yellow flares. These are to be lighted in front line only on reaching each objective and at 4 pm. and 5 pm. 7th.October and at 7 am. 8th.October. Panels, lamps, and ground sheets will also be used to communicate with the contact aeroplanes.

23. Strong Points will be constructed by adjoining Brigade as follows:-

(a) By 36th.Infantry Brigade on right:-

GREEN LINE - N 20 a 8.2.
N 20 a 2.9.

BROWN LINE - N 14 b 7.0
N 14 a 8.2
N 13 b 2.2.

(b) By 122nd.Infantry Brigade on right:-
N 18 d 6.9.
N 18 c 45.70.

24. Acknowledge.

P Lloyd-Pearce
Major,
Brigade Major,
124th.Infantry Brigade.

6/10/16.

Issued at 3.15 p.m.

Copy No.1 File
2 War Diary
3 41st.Division.
4 C.R.E. 41st.Division.
5 A.D.M.S.41st.Division.
6 122nd.Inf.Bde.
7 123rd.Inf.Bde.
8 36th. Inf.Bde.
9 No. Section, 237th.Fd.Co.R.E.
10 10th.Bn."Queens" R.W.S.Regt.
11 26th.Bn.R.Fusiliers.
12 32nd.Bn.R.Fusiliers.
13 21st.Bn.K.R.R.Corps.
14 124th.M.G.Coy.
15 124th.T.M.Btty.
16 Staff Captain
17 Brigade Intelligence Officer.
18 Brigade Transport Officer.
19 Signal Officer.

SECRET. COPY NO. 7

ADDENDUM
TO
124th.INFANTRY BRIGADE ORDER NO.61.

1. 21st.Bn.K.R.R.Corps will construct Strong Points at N 13 c 35.50 and N 13 d 0.5. Each of these will be provided with a Lewis Gun.

2. The 122nd.Infantry Brigade will construct additional Strong Points at M 18 d 5.4 and M 18 c 6.2.

3. Time Table for barrages attached.

4. 124th.I.B .Report Centre will close at CARLTON TRENCH at 4 am. on 7th.October and re-open in FERRET TRENCH, S 6 a 8.7 at the same hour. It will close at FERRET TRENCH at 5 am. on 8th.October and reopen at CARLTON TRENCH at the same hour.

4. Acknowledge.

P Hoy-Treane
Major,
Brigade Major,
124th.Infantry Brigade.

6/10/16.

Issued at 7.45 p.m

Copy No.1 File
2 War Diary
3 41st.Division.
4 122nd.Inf.Bde.
5 123rd.Inf.Bde.
6 36th.Inf.Bde.
7 No.3 section, 237th.Fd.Co.R.E.
8 10th."Queens" R.W.S.
9 26th.Bn.R.Fuslrs.
10 32nd.Bn.R.Fuslrs.
11 21st.Bn.K.R.R.C.
12 124th.M.G.Coy.
13 124th.L.T.M.B.
14 Brigade Intelligence Officer.
15 Brigade Signal Officer.

No 3 Sect 237 F Co

SECRET. BARRAGE TIME TABLE.

To accompany ~~41st Division Order No. 49~~ 124 Infy Bde Order No 61. of 5-10-16.

---

| TIME. | |
|---|---|
| 00.00 (ZERO) | Barrage will open on a line about 150 yards in front of our line. Leading Infantry will advance and get close up under the Barrage. |
| 00.02 - (ZERO plus 2 mins.) | The Barrage will creep forward at the rate of 50 yards per minute until it reaches a line 200 yards beyond the first objective (GREEN LINE). The Barrage will remain on this line till 00.X (ZERO plus X mins.) The GREEN LINE will be altered in front of the 41st Division Sector so as to include the new Trench running E. and W. through N 13 c 4½.5. and conform with the advance of the 47th Division, and will run as follows :- N 13 d 5.5. - N 13 c 45.50 - M 18 d 5.6. - M 18 d 6.3. - M 18 c 0.3. - thence to III Corps Area about M 17 d Central. 122nd Infantry Brigade will, however, arrange to follow up the Creeping Barrage along the GIRD Trench and GIRD SUPPORT and establish blocks as close as possible to the Barrage which will be on German trenches 200 yards beyond the GREEN LINE. (I.E. as marked on map "A" attached to 124 I.B. Order 61) |
| 00.Y (ZERO plus Y mins) | The Infantry will again advance from the GREEN LINE and place itself close under the Barrage. |
| 00.Z (ZERO plus Z mins) | The Barrage will creep forward at the rate of 50 yards per minute until it reaches a line 200 yards in advance of the BROWN LINE and will remain on this line until the position of our Infantry on the BROWN LINE has been consolidated. |

From ZERO Hour Stationary Barrages have been arranged on certain objectives but will lift off them in front of the Creeping Barrages, the movements of which only concern the attacking Infantry.

6-10-16. X,Y and Z minutes will be communicated later.

| Unit. | Company. | In relief of. | Trenches taken over. | Remarks. |
|---|---|---|---|---|
| 26th. R.F. | B | B Coy. xx 21st. K.R.R.C. | Strong Points EASTERN, WESTERN and SOUTHERN REDOUBTS; and Strong Point No. 7. 1 Platoon in each Strong Point. | Guides, 1 per Platoon, meet at LE BRASSERIE 8.30 a.m. |
| 26th. R.F. | D | D Coy. 21st. K.R.R.C. | Left of Front Line. 2 platoons in front line and 2 platoons in support. | Guides at Le BRASSERIE 9.15 a.m. Proceed by P. & O. TRENCH to front line. |
| 26th. R.F. | C | C Coy. 21st. K.R.R.C. | Right of Front Line 2 platoons in front line and 2 platoons in support. | Guides at LE BRASSERIE at 10.15 a.m. Proceed to front line via CHICRORY LANE |
| 26th. R.F. | A | Reserve Platoons of C and D Coys. 21st. K.R.R.C. | Reserve Line. | Guides at LE BRASSERIE at 11 a.m. Proceed via CHICHORY LANE. |

HEADQUARTERS will proceed to LE BRASSERIE arriving there at 11.15 a.m. and will be located at LE BRASSERIE.

27.10.16.

SECRET. COPY NO ..2..

# 26TH. BATTALION ROYAL FUSILIERS.

## OPERATION ORDER NO. 14.

1. The Battalion will relieve the 21st. Bn. K.R.R.C. in the left sub-sector of the line to-morrow, the 28th. instant, in accordance with the attached movement, relief and time table.

2. East of the DICKEBUSCH - LA CLYTTE Road all movements will be made by sections at 200 yards interval.

3. Officers' trench bundles, mess boxes and Orderly Room box will be ready stacked outside this Orderly Room at 8.30 a.m. and will be taken by Transport as far as RIDGE WOOD.

One G.S. wagon for Headquarters and one limber per Company will be available for the conveyance of the above and of cooking utensils.

4. Company Commanders will forward to Bn.H.Q. within two hours of relief a complete list (in duplicate) of all trench stores taken over and the receipt given by the relieved Company.

5. The bootmaker and master tailor will accompany Headquarters and be located at LE BRASSERIE. Details not proceeding to the trenches will be located at the Transport Lines.

6. Details proceeding to the Transport will parade at 9.0 a.m. on the Battalion parade ground, and will be marched to the Transport Lines under 2/Lieut. Brown.

A party of 10 men per Company and 5 from Headquarters will be detailed from men proceeding to the Transport Lines to see that the Camp and huts are left in an entirely clean state

7. The Commanding Officer directs that all shall be done to leave the camp in such a state as will bring credit to the Battalion and conduce to the comfort of the incoming unit.

8. Attention is again drawn to Bn.R.O. No. 302 of 23rd. instant. Company Commanders are warned that in addressing messages over the telephone they must use the code words.

9. Company Commanders will report completion of relief to Bn.H.Q. by wire, as follows:-

"O.O. NO. 14 O.K. at (time) ."

----------

(sgd) A.M.MACKAY,
2/Lieut. & Actg. Adjutant,
26th. Bn. Royal Fusiliers.

27.10.16

Copy No. 1 ..File.
2 ..Adj.
3 .. 124 I.B.
4 ..A Coy.
5 ..B "
6 ..C "
7 ..D "
8 ..Qmr.
Copy No. 9 ..T.O.
10 ..Bombing Officer.
11 ..O.C.Hqrs.

331

SECRET. COPY NO ......

## 26TH. BATTALION ROYAL FUSILIERS.

### OPERATION ORDER NO. [illegible]

1. The Battalion will move from FRICOURT CAMP this evening.

Order of march:- Headquarters, "A", "B", "C", "D" Coys.
The Head of the column to pass S.P. Road Junction F.8 a 4.0 at 4.15 p.m. Route:- via. horse track just North of MEAULTE-FRICOURT-MONTAUBAN Road, via. Brigade Dump at S.25 d 1.5 to place of assembly at EDGE TRENCH and GREEN TRENCH.
A and B Coys. will occupy part of GREEN TRENCH, and
C and D Coys do. EDGE TRENCH,
the other portion of these trenches being held by the 32nd. Royal Fusiliers.
Places of assembly and avenues of approach will be taped or otherwise marked by the 10th. Bn. "Queen's" R.W.Surrey Regt.
Avenue of approach for the Battalion FLARE LANE.

2. Distribution:-

| | | |
|---|---|---|
| The First Line - | 10th. Bn. "Queen's" | Right. |
| | 21st. Bn.K.R.R.C. | Left. |
| Support " | 32nd. Bn. Royal Fusiliers. | Right. |
| | 26th. Bn. Royal Fusiliers. | Left. |

Section 4, Machine Gun Company will be attached to this Battalion, together with Half Section of 237th. Field Company, R.E.

3. LEWIS GUNS, will be conveyed on limbers as far as POMMIERS and thence by handcarts as far as QUARRY DUMP, where carts will be handed over to the Brigade Bombing Officer

4. METHOD OF ATTACK. The attack will be made in waves, the first wave in extended order, following as closely as possible to the barrage. Succeeding waves in small shallow columns, not more than 50 yards distance.
Supporting Battalions will follow in rear of First line Battns.
When the barrage rests on an objective and the advance is held up, advantage must be taken of all available cover.

5. CARRYING PARTIES. Lieut. Berry and 30 other ranks [illegible] each from A and B Coys. and 8 each from C and D Coys. to report to Brigade Bombing Officer at 124th. Infantry Brigade Dump (QUARRY DUMP) S 25 c 1.6 at 11 p.m. to-night to act as carrying parties. Companies will detail the following ammunition carriers:-
(a) 4 men per Lewis Gun.
(b) 12 men per Vickers Gun attached.

6. BOMBS. Every man will carry two Mills Bombs in his pockets. These are to be looked upon as reserve for the use of the Bombing Squads, and are to be dumped and collected in each line gained. They will not be thrown by the men carrying them.

7. COMMUNICATION WITH AEROPLANES. Every Officer and N.C.O. and [illegible] men per Company will carry [illegible] red flares. [illegible] lighted in the front line only, at intervals of 20 [illegible] gaining the line of each objective, as soon as the contact aeroplane appears (or calls for flares [illegible]) and again at 2 p.m. and 5 p.m. on the 15th. [illegible], and at 7 a.m. on the day following. [illegible]
[illegible]

8. MEDICAL. Advanced dressing and collecting stations will be established as follows:-

Advanced dressing station .. THE QUARRY S 23 c 1.5.
Divisional Collecting Station .. E 6 a 2.0. MAMETZ-
MONTABAN Road.

9. DOCUMENTS. No maps or documents giving information of British trenches must be taken over the parapet.

10. STRONG POINTS will be constructed as follows with the assistance of R.E:-

S 6 d 72.67 will be constructed by "D" Coy.
S 1 a 2.5. do. "C" "
N 31 b 19.80 do. "B" "
N 26 a 8.8. do. "A" "

These Strong Points will be garrisioned by one platoon, strength not less than 25 men. One Vickers Gun from No. 4 Section 124th. Machine Gun Company will be detailed to each of these strong points. If Vickers Guns are not available, Lewis Guns will be detailed.

11. REPORTS. O.C. Companies will keep Battalion Headquarters posted, as requested in list of returns and reports already issued.

(sgd) A.W.MACKAY,
2/Lieut. & Acting Adjutant,
26th. Bn.Royal Fusiliers.

No. 1 .. Filed.
" 2 .. 124 I.B.
" 3 .. "A" Coy.
" 4 .. "B" "
" 5 .. "C" "
" 6 .. "D" "
" 7 .. Qmr, & T.O.
" 8 .. Bombing Off. and L.G.Officer.
" 9 .. Sig. Officer and Med. Officer.
" 10.. Adjutant.

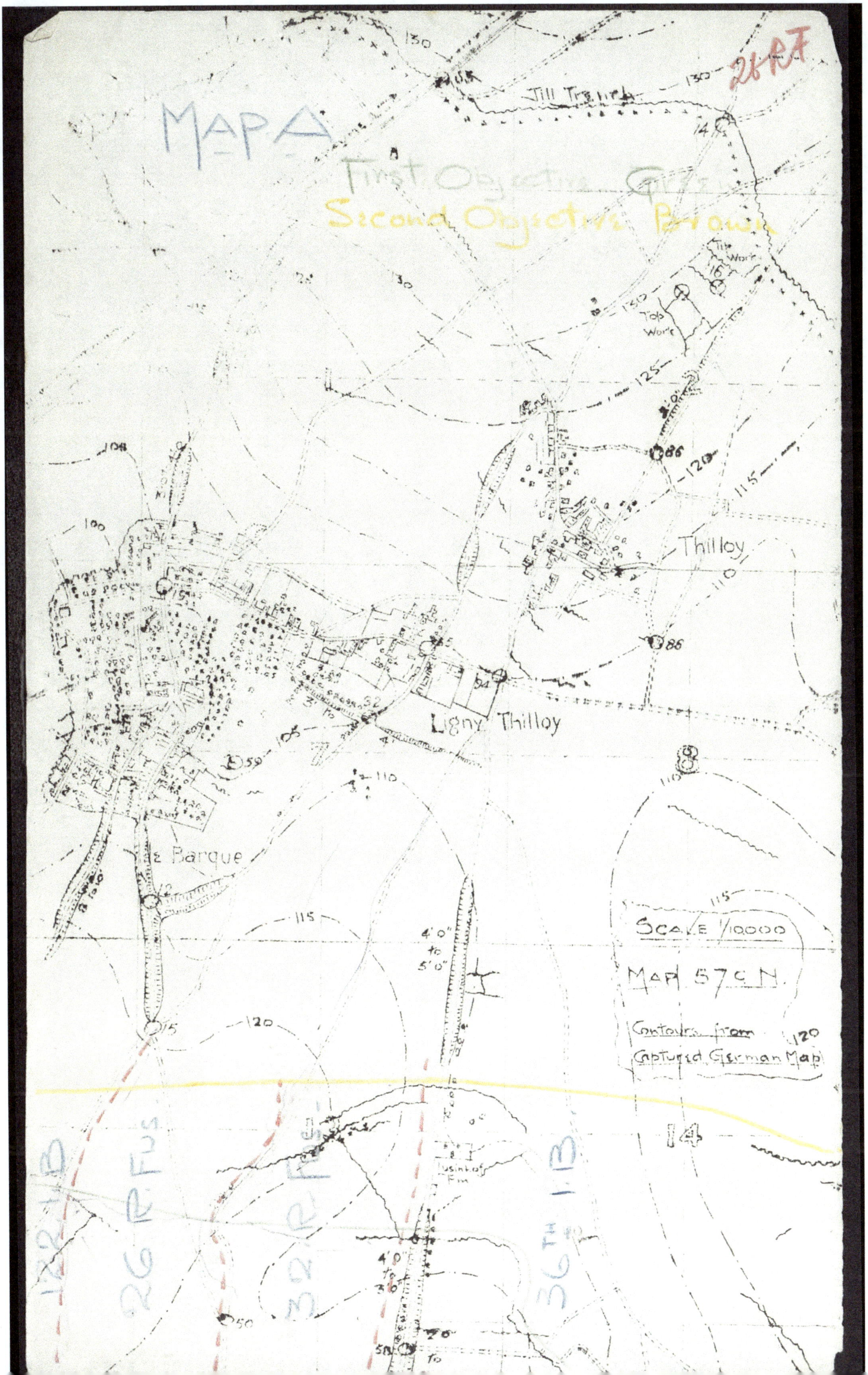
26RF
MAP A
Jill Trench
First Objective Green
Second Objective Brown
Tip Work
Top Work
Thilloy
Ligny Thilloy
Le Barque
4'0" to 5'0"
SCALE 1/10,000
MAP 57c N.
Contours from Captured German Map
Dusinhof Fm
122 I.B
26 R. FUS
32 R. FUS
36TH I.B
14

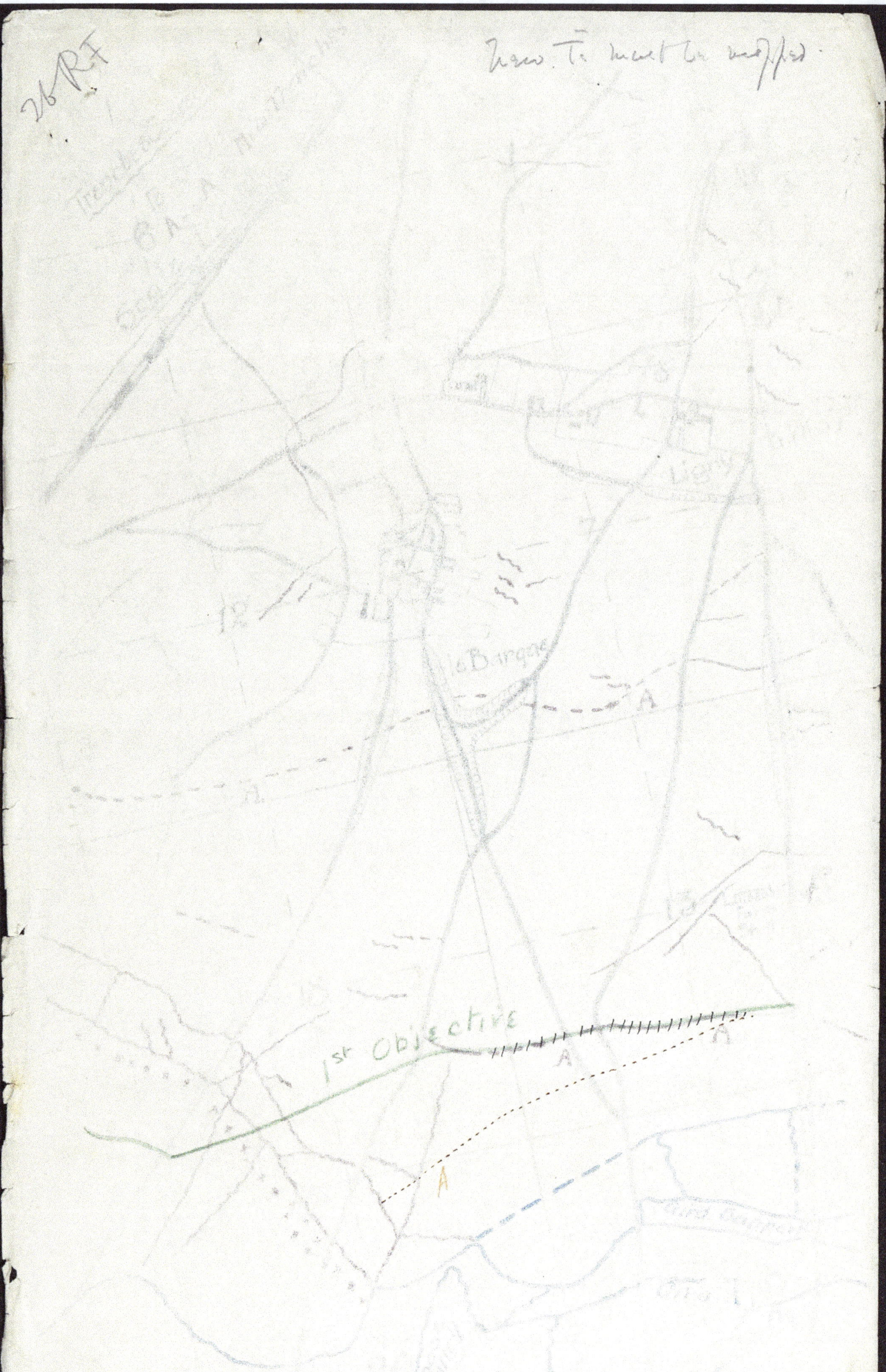
26 RF
1st Objective
le Barque
Ligny
A
A
A
A
A

(18) 26th Royal Fusiliers

Instructions regarding War Diaries and Intelligence Summaries are contained in F. S. Regs., Part II. and the Staff Manual respectively. Title pages will be prepared in manuscript.

# WAR DIARY
*or*
# INTELLIGENCE SUMMARY.
*(Erase heading not required.)*

November ~~October~~ 1916

Vol 7

Army Form C. 2118.

| Place | Date | Hour | Summary of Events and Information | Remarks and references to Appendices |
|---|---|---|---|---|
| Front line Trenches DIEPENDAAL SECTOR. | Nov 1st – Nov 3. | } | The daily trench routine & work on trenches was continued | CRuf |
| | Nov. 3rd | | The Battn. was relieved at 11.45 pm by the 21st K.R.R. and went into Support in Ridge Wood. While there, large working parties were supplied day & night for work on the front line & the new reserve line. As far as possible, the training of specialists was continued with. The erection of a drying room in Ridge Wood was commenced. | reference Operation order No. 15. CRuf. |
| RIDGEWOOD | | | | |
| FRONT LINE DIEPENDAAL SECTOR. | Nov 9th | | The Battn. relieved the 21st KRR's in the line, and continued the work of constructing strong points in the front line (at eleven selected points.) The weather was good, and exceptionally good work was done by the men, who were keenly interested in the strong points. Patrols were sent out every night, & much information was obtained with regard to the Enemy front line. During these six days our own divisional artillery relieved the Australians behind our sector of line | CRuf |
| LA CLYTTE | Nov 15th | | The Battn was relieved by the 21st KRR's at 4.30 pm & went into Brigade Reserve at La Clytte. Large working parties were supplied, day and night for work in the trenches & for R.E. fatigues. The training of Lewis Gunners, Signallers, and Snipers was continued. Many of the men | Reference Operation order No 18. |



75 (2 sheets)

(11)

Instructions regarding War Diaries and Intelligence Summaries are contained in F. S. Regs., Part II. and the Staff Manual respectively. Title pages will be prepared in manuscript.

# WAR DIARY
*or*
# INTELLIGENCE SUMMARY.
*(Erase heading not required.)*

Army Form C. 2118.

| Place | Date | Hour | Summary of Events and Information | Remarks and references to Appendices |
|---|---|---|---|---|
| | | | had baths, but all did not receive clean underclothing. | CRW |
| DIEPENDAAL SECTOR. | 21st to 28th | | The Battn. relieved the 21st KRRs. in the line at 1·30 pm. Work was continued on the front line and the new Reserve trench. The Strong Points were also worked on, and much progress was made. Patrols were ~~used~~ sent out every night | Reference Operation Order No 19. CRW |
| RIDGEWOOD | 28th to 30th. | | The Battn was relieved by the 21st KRRs. & went into Support in Ridge Wood Large parties were provided every day for work & carrying parties in the trenches. These parties were so large that great difficulty was experienced in finding them. Work of reconstruction of dugouts, & the building of the new drying room was carried on. On the 30th the drying room was ready for use. | CRW CRW |
| | | | Casualties during this month — Date / Killed / Wounded: 2nd — 2 — 1; 3rd — 1 — 0; 12th — 0 — 1; 13th — 1 — 0; 23rd — 0 — 1; 24th — 0 — 1. 4 Killed – 4 wounded. | CRW |

[illegible]

T2134. Wt. W708–776. 500000. 4/15. Sir J. C. & S.

SECRET.

397

COPY NO.1....

## 26th.BN. ROYAL FUSILIERS.

### Operation Order No.21

1. The Battalion will releive the 21st. Bn. K.R.R.Corps in the tomorrow 1st. December 1916, relief to commence at 4 p.m.

2. Companies will be disposed as follows :-

"A" Redoubts.
"B" Right Front.
"C" Left Front.
"D" Sleepy Hollow.

3. Order of relief, times at which relieving Sections and Companies will be at LA BRASSERIE, and routes to be taken will be as follows:-

| | | | |
|---|---|---|---|
| Machine Gunners, Signallers, Snipers and C.S.M's | | | 12 noon |
| "A" | 4 p.m. | CHICORY LANE | |
| "B" | 4-30p.m. | " " | |
| "C" | 5 p.m. | P & O TRENCH | |
| "D" | 5-30p.m. | CHICORY LANE | |

4. O.C. Campanies are responsible that the Trench Store return reaches Battalion Orderly Room within two hours of taking over.

5. The Camp,dugouts etc. in RIDGEWOOD must be left scrupulously clean and O.C. Companies must see that this order is carried out, also that all latrine buckets are emptied.

6. Each man will take one blanket with him tothe trenches. The remainder will be rolled in bundles of 10 and stacked outside R.S.M's dugout by 2 p.m. Officers valises, boxes etc. that are being returned to the TransportLines must be stacked at the same place and time.

7. Rations will brought up at the xxxx usual time by the Transport and O.C. Campanies must arrange for their rations parties to take same to the trenches.

8. Completion of taking over will be wired to Battalion Orderly Room as follows :-

"PIP" (time).

(sgd) B.W.E.Dunsford,
2/Lieut. for Adjutant,
26th. Royal Fusiliers.

30/11/16.

Copy No. 1 Filed.
2 124th. I.B.
3.Adjutant.
4 21st. K.R.R.C.
5 "A" Coy.
6 "B"
7 "C"
8 "D"
9 Lewis GunOfficer
10 Bombing Officer
11 Signalling & Intelligence Officer
12 Transport Officer & Quartermaster.

1/1 303 1-1-17. –

Instructions regarding War Diaries and Intelligence Summaries are contained in F. S. Regs., Part II. and the Staff Manual respectively. Title pages will be prepared in manuscript.

# WAR DIARY or ~~INTELLIGENCE~~ SUMMARY.

December 1916. Vol 8

(Erase heading not required.)

Army Form C. 2118.

| Place | Date | Hour | Summary of Events and Information of 26th Btn. Royal Fusiliers | Remarks and references to Appendices |
|---|---|---|---|---|
| | 1st | | On this day we relieved the 21st K.R.R's in the line. | Ref. O.O. No 21. |
| | 1st to 6th. | | The ordinary trench routine was carried on, and good progress made with the work of strengthening the front line, wiring and the dugouts behind S.P.7. During this tour we had our first case of trench feet. It occurred in the Coy. holding the left subsector of our line. | CRuf |
| | 6th | | The 21st K.R.R.S relieved this battalion, and we went into Brigade Reserve at LA CIYTTE. | Ref. O.O. No 22. CRuf |
| | 6th to 13th | | The battalion provided large working parties daily for the Reserve and the front line. The weather was alternately wet and cold. | CRuf |
| | 13th | | We relieved the 21st K.R.R's. in the trenches. On the night of 13th/14th the enemy shelled our right Coy with heavy trench mortars making two breaches in the parapet and damaging CHICORY LANE about 200yds from the front line | Ref. O.O. No 23. CRuf |
| | 14th | | By the morning of the 14th the damage to the parapet was sufficiently repaired to enable work to be continued by day. and the pioneers had cleared the communication trench. | CRuf |

8.K. (18 sheets)

T2134. Wt. W708—776. 500000. 4/15. Sir J. C. & S.

9/

Instructions regarding War Diaries and Intelligence Summaries are contained in F. S. Regs., Part II. and the Staff Manual respectively. Title pages will be prepared in manuscript.

# WAR DIARY
*or*
~~INTELLIGENCE~~ SUMMARY.

December 1916.

Army Form C. 2118.

(*Erase heading not required.*)

| Place | Date | Hour | Summary of Events and Information of 26th Btn. Royal Fusiliers | Remarks and references to Appendices |
|---|---|---|---|---|
| | 14/15th | | On the night of the 14th/15th an officer and one Lance Corporal entered the enemy trench at (0.76.4.4) between 7 and 8 pm. and shot a sentry. About 8-45 pm. the enemy attempted a raid on our right Coy. front at (0.7a.3.1). Ref. report attached | report attached. CRuf. |
| | 15th | | The right Coy. of the front line 'C' Coy., having sustained the shock of the raid, was relieved at 5.30 am by 'A' Coy. from SLEEPY HOLLOW. So much work was done during the early morning that by stand to the trench between the right and left Coys. was clear for traffic. The day passed quietly and much progress was made in repairing the trenches. The pioneers had cleared CHICORY LANE during the night. | CRuf. |
| | 16th | | The day passed quietly: work was continued. There was much aeroplane activity. On the night of the 16th/17th the 21st K.R.R's supplied a working party for wiring BOIS CARRÉ. | CRuf |
| | 17th | | The day was very foggy and advantage was taken of this to work on the wire of the front line, which was much broken on the night of the 14th/15th, and on the wire round BOIS CARRÉ. | CRuf |

T2134. Wt. W708—776. 500000. 4/15. Sir J. C. & S.

3/

Instructions regarding War Diaries and Intelligence Summaries are contained in F. S. Regs., Part II. and the Staff Manual respectively. Title Pages will be prepared in manuscript.

# WAR DIARY
or
# ~~INTELLIGENCE SUMMARY~~
(Erase heading not required.)

December 1916

Army Form C. 2118

| Place | Date | Hour | Summary of Events and Information of 26th Btn. Royal Fusiliers | Remarks and references to Appendices |
|---|---|---|---|---|
| | 17th | | On the night of the 17th/18th the 21st K.R.R's again wired in BOIS CARRÉ. A new drain down to the DIEPENDAALBEEK from the left Coy. front line was finished and the trench is much dryer in consequence. Finding the German front line very strongly held, on the night, the C.O. asked the battery and 124th Brigade for fire on the hostile trenches. This was given by the 18 pdrs. and heavies at intervals from 3.40 am to 5.30 am. | CRuf. |
| | 18th and 19th | | These days passed quietly and work was continued. | CRuf. |
| | 20th | | On the 20th the battn. was relieved by the 21st KRR's & went into Support in Ridgewood. Our Casualties during this tour in the line were<br>Killed — 2. (Died of wounds — 3)<br>Wounded — 21. Missing — 1<br>Total Casualties — 24 | Ref O.O. 24 |
| | | | | CRuf. |

1875 Wt. W593/826 1,000,000 4/15 J.B.C. & A. A.D.S.S./Forms/C. 2118.

A/

Instructions regarding War Diaries and Intelligence Summaries are contained in F. S. Regs., Part II. and the Staff Manual respectively. Title pages will be prepared in manuscript.

# WAR DIARY
*or*
# INTELLIGENCE SUMMARY.
*(Erase heading not required.)*

Army Form C. 2118.

| Place | Date | Hour | Summary of Events and Information | Remarks and references to Appendices |
|---|---|---|---|---|
| | 20th to 27th | | The Battalion remained in Support at RIDGE WOOD excepting on the 25th – Xmas DAY – working parties were found by the Battalion daily & every night a wiring party was found for work on wire in front of NEW RESERVE LINE. Xmas day was observed as a holiday by the men & a most enjoyable day was spent. Special attention was paid to the mens Xmas dinner and through the kindness of Lieut Col. The Hon W. F. North, & the 'Daily Telegraph' Pudding Fund, a good supply of Xmas Fare was available. There is nothing of importance to record during this week. There was no unusual activity on the part of the enemy during the period. | [illegible] |
| | 27th | | On the morning of the 27th we relieved the 21st K.R.R.C. in the line | Ref O.O. 25. [illegible] |

(5)

Instructions regarding War Diaries and Intelligence Summaries are contained in F. S. Regs., Part II. and the Staff Manual respectively. Title pages will be prepared in manuscript.

# WAR DIARY
*or*
# INTELLIGENCE SUMMARY.
*(Erase heading not required.)*

Army Form C. 2118.

| Place | Date | Hour | Summary of Events and Information | Remarks and references to Appendices |
|---|---|---|---|---|
| | 27th | | Owing to a 'Trench Mortar' Shoot in the afternoon the time of relief was altered & relief took place at 9.30 am. A good deal of retaliation on part of Enemy observed for our T.M. activity; our line was blown in in several places but our casualties were very light. Another T.M. shoot took place at 8.30 pm. | CRuf |
| | 28th 29th 30th 31st | | The Battalion remained in the line during this time. Ordinary Trench Routine was carried out and the work of improving & strengthening the line was proceeded with. The wire in front of the line was strengthened. The enemy showed increased Artillery activity & has undoubtedly increased the numbers of his guns in this sector. Enemy T.M's. caused our front line some damage but there was no increased activity in this respect. | CRuf |

SECRET.                                                                                    COPY NO....../

(354)

# 26th. BN. ROYAL FUSILIERS.

## OPERATION ORDER NO.22

1. The Battalion will be relieved tomorrow by the 21st. Bn.K.R.R.C. Relief to commence at 2 p.m. and will proceed to Brigade Reserve at LA CLYTTE.
2. Order and times at which companies will be relieved is as under -

| | | | |
|---|---|---|---|
| Machine Gunners, Snipers, Signallers and C.S.M's | | | 9 a.m. |
| "A" | Redoubts | 2p.m. CHICORY LANE | |
| "D" | Sleepy Hollow | 2.30p.m. " " | |
| "C" | Left Coy. | 3p.m. P. & O.TRENCH. | |
| "B" | Right Coy. | 3.30p.m.CHICORY LANE. | |

Headquarters as convenient to incoming Battalion.

All movements East of LA CLYTTE - DICKEBUSCH Road will be by sections at 200 yards interval.

3. Officers trench bundles, mess boxes, cooking ~~mai~~ utensils etc. will be brought down to RIDGEWOOD by 1 p.m.
The Transport Officer will arrange 1 G.S.Wagon for Headquarters and one limber per company to be at the ration dump at 1 p.m.to transport the above to LA CLYTTE.
4. Rations will be taken to LA CLYTTE tomorrow.
5. Officers valises, blankets for the men, and other boxes will be taken to LA CLYTTE by transport.
6. Company and Headquarter Cooks and Acting C.Q.M.S. will leave with the limbers at 1 p.m.
7. Disposition of Companies and specialists at LA CLYTTE will be the same as when the Battalion was last there.
8. Company Commanders, L.G.Officer's and Medical Officer's horses will be at the ration dump at 2 p.m. Commanding Officer's, Adjutant's and 2nd. in Command at 4 p.m.
9. Trenches and dugouts will be scrupulously clean and all latrine buckets emptied.
10. O.C.Companies will render to Battalion Orderly Room within two hours of arriving at LA CLYTTE duplicate lists of trench stores handed over by them and receipt obtained.
11. Intelligence Oggicer will arrange to hand over a summary of his reports for the week, and will furnish the incoming Intelligence Officer with all possible information.
O.C.Companies will h and over a summary of work done during the past week, and will furnish any information which will be useful to the incoming unit.
12. Completion of relief will be notified by O.C.Companies to B.H.Q. by wire as follows :-
O.O. No.22 complied with (time).

(sgd) B.W.E.Dunsford,
2nd. Lieut. for Adjutant,
26th. Royal Fusiliers.

5/12/16.

Copy No. 1 Filed.
2 124th. Infantry Brigade.
3. Adjutant.
4. 21st. K.R.R.C.
5. "A" Coy.
6 "B" "
7. "C" "
8. "D" "
9. Lewis Gun Officer.
10. Bombing Officer.
11. Signalling & Intelligenee Officer.
12. Transport Officer & Quartermaster.

SECRET. (677)

Copy No..1...

26th. BN. ROYAL FUSILIERS.

OPERATION ORDER NO.23.

1. The Battalion will relieve the 21stm BN.K.R.R.C. in the left sub sector tomorrow the 13th. December 1916, relief to commence at 1.30 p.m.

2. All moves East of DICKEBUSCH - LA CLYTTE Road will be by sections at 200 yards interval.

3. Companies will be disposed as gollows :-

| | |
|---|---|
| "D" Coy. | left front Coy. |
| "C" " | right front Coy. |
| "B" " | Strong Points. |
| "A" " | Sleepy Hollow. |

4. Times at which Companies are to be at LA BRASSERIE and the route are as follows :-

| | | |
|---|---|---|
| Snipers, Machine Gunners and C.S.M's | 11.0 a.m. | |
| "B" Coy | 1.30 p.m. | Chicory Lane |
| "C" " | 2.0 p.m. | - do - |
| "D" " | 2.30 p.m. | P.t.o. |
| "A" " | 3.0 p.m. | |
| Headquarters | 3.0 p.m. | |

5. Each man will take one blanket to the trenches on his pack. The remaining blankets will be rolled into bundles of ten and stacked outside Battalion Orderly Room by 1 p.m.

6. Officers trench bundles, cooking utensils, Orderly Room and Mess boxes will be stacked outside Battalion Orderly Room by 1 p.m. for collection by Transport.
Officers valises and boxes that are being returned to the Transport lines should be stacked outside Battalion Orderly Room by 1 p.m. separately

7. Rations will be taken to the ration dump, RIDGEWOOD, by Transport tomorrow afternoon and O.C.Companies will arrange ration parties to be there at 3 p.m.

8. One G.S.Wagon for Headquarters and one limber per company will be at Battalion Headquarters at 1 p.m. to convey Officers bundles etc. to the trenches.
Officers horses to be at Battalion Headquarters 2 hours before time mentioned in para. 4.

9. O.C.Companies must see that the camp and huts are left in a scrupulously clean condition and all latrine buckets emptied.

10. O.C.Companies willrender to Battalion Orderly Room two hours after taking over, list of trench stores in duplicate.

11. Completion of taking over will be wired by O.C.Companies bo Battn. Headquarters as follows :-
SNOW (time).

(sgd) A.W.Mackay,
Lieut. & A/Adjutamt.
26th. Royal Fusiliersm

12/12/16.

Copy No. 1 Filed.
2 124th. Infantry Brigade.
3. Adjutant.
4 21st. K.R.R.C.
5 "A" Coy.
6 "B" "
7 "C" "
8 "D" "
9 Signalling & I ntelligence Officer.
10 Quartermaster & Transport Officer.
11 Bombing Officer.
12 Lewis Gun Officer.

SECRET. Copy No.....1....

(831)

26th B ATTALION ROYAL FUSILIERS.

OPERATION ORDER No. 24.

---

1. The Battalion will be relieved tommorrow 20th December, 1916 by the 21st. Bn. K.R.R.Corps, relief to commence at 4.p.m. and will proceed into Support at RIDGEWOOD.

2. Order of relief, times at which relieving sections and Companies will be at LA BRASSERIE, and route to be taken will be as follows:-

| | | |
|---|---|---|
| Lewis Gunners, Snipers and C.S.M!s | 11. a.m. | |
| Redoubt Company | 4. p.m. | CHICORY LANE. |
| Right Company Front Lin e | 4.30.p.m. | do. |
| Left Company do. | 5 p.m. | P. & O. TRENCH |
| Sleepy Hollow Company . | 5.30p.m. | CHICORY LANE |
| Headquarters. | 4.30p.m. | |

No one will move out of the Redubts until the whole of the Right Company Front Lin e has moved out.

3. Companies will occupy exactly the same billets as when the Battalion was last in RIDGEWOOD.

4. O.C. Companies will have complete lists of Trench Stores ready for the incoming unit.

The signed portion will be sent to Battalion Orderly Room within two hours of arrival in RIDGEWOOD.

5. O.C. Companies are responsible that the trenches, dugouts and latrines are left scrupulously clean.

6. Tables of "work done" and "work in hand and proposed" should be made out and handed over for the information of the incoming unit.

7. The Intelligence Officer will arrange to provide the Intelligence Officer of the in coming Unit with a copy of his reports for the past week and give him all possible information.

Before handing over their posts, Snipers and Observers will give all possible information to the incoming Snipers and Observers.

8. O.C.Companies will make their own arrangements for getting cooking utensils, trench bundles etc.to RIDGEWOOD.

9. The Transport Officer will arrange to have Officers kits and all blankets for the men brought up to RIDGEWOOD tomorrow afternoon at the same time as rations.

Rations will be brought to the ration dump as usual and a guard from Headquarters placed over them until they drawn by Companies after relief.

10. Completion of relief will be wired to Battalion Orderly Room as follows :-

COLD (time).

(sgd) A.W.Mackay,
Lieut. & A/Adjutant,
26th.Royal Fusiliers.

Copy No. 1 Filed.
2 124th.Infantry Brigade.
3 Adjutant.
4 21st.K.R.R.C.
5 O.C."A"Coy.
6 O.C."B" "
7 O.C."C" "
8 O.C."D" "
9 O.C. Headqurters Details.
10 Intelligence & Sniping Officer
11 Transport Officer & Quartermaster.
12 Bombing Officer & Lewis Gun Officer.

SECRET. Copy No. 1

26th Battalion Royal Fusiliers.

OPERATION ORDER No. 25.

(94)

---

1. The Battalion will relieve the 21st Battalion King's Royal Rifle Corps in the line on 27th December, 1916, relief to commence at 9.a.m.

2. The Companies will be disposed as follows:-

"A" Sleepy Hollow.
"B" Redoubts.
"C" Right Front.
"D" Left Front.

3. Order of relief, times at which relieving sections and Companies will be at LA BRASSERIE, and routes to be taken will be as follows:-

| | |
|---|---|
| Machine Gunners, Snipers, and C.S.M's | 7.a.m. |
| "B" Company. | 9.a.m. Chicory Lane |
| "C" Company. | 9.30.a.m. do. |
| "D" Company. | 10.a.m. P & O |
| "A" Company. | 10.30.a.m. Chicory Lane |
| Headquarters. | 10.a.m. |

4. O/C Companies are responsible that the Trench Store return reaches Battalion Orderly Room within two hours of taking over.

5. The camp, dug-outs, etc., in RIDGEWOOD must be left scrupulously clean, and O/C Companies must see that this order is carried out, also that all latrine buckets are emptied.

6. Each man will take one blanket with him to the trenches. The remainder will be rolled into bundles of 10 and labelled; they will be stacked at the ration dump by 9.30. a.m. Officers valises, boxes, etc,. that are being returned to the Transport Lines must be stacked at the same place and time.

7. O/C Companies will make their own arrangements for getting trench bundles, cooking utensils, etc., up to the line.
Rations will be brought up by the Transport at the usual time, and O/C Companies will make usual arrangements.

8. Completion of taking over will be wired to the Battalion Orderly Room as follows: -

"DROP" (time).

(Sgd). A. W. Mackay.
Lieut. & Adjutant.
26th Royal Fusiliers

Copy No. 1. Filed.
2. 124th Infantry Brigade.
3. Adjutant.
4. 21st K.R.R.C.
5. O.C. "A" Coy.
6. O.C. "B" "
7. O.C. "C" "
8. O.C. "D" "
9. O.C. Headquarters Details.
10. Intelligence & Sniping Officer.
11. Transport Officer & Quartermaster.
12. Bombing Officer & Lewis Gun Officer.

COPY OF LETTER TO COMPANY COMMANDERS.

From Officer Commanding,

26 th Royal Fusiliers.

To O/C Company.

---

Will you kindly submit by 12 noon today a narrative report of your experiences during the night giving such times as you can remember, and bringing to notice the names of any men who, in your opinion, did well.

I particularly want to know how the Germans were first spo tted, and what action was taken by the wiring party.

1. Was there much bombing: -

(a). Before the Germans got into the trench.

(b). After the Germans got into the trench.

2. Did the Germans retire through our barrage, and, if so, is it possible that they suffered loss by so doing.

3. Estimated numbers of Germans who left their own parapet, and the numbers who penetrated our line.

4. What action was taken by the sentrygroup on the extreme right of "C" Company.

5. Did our men make good use of their rifles.?

6. Was our Artillery fire satisfactory.?

Please also ask your Company Officers to write me a narrative on the above lines.

(Sgd). Gwyn Thomas.
Lieut.-Col. Commanding
26th Bn. Royal Fusrs.

15th December, 1916.

## COPY OF REGRT BY 2nd. Lt. P.A. EGAN.

I put out covering party, three men. All thelarge stakes had been put in, and nearly all small stakes preparatory to putting up apron fencing. At about 8.45 p.m. the stakes having been driven in the men were standing by them, when the Germans opened up a barrage of high explosive, whiz-bangs, rifle grenades, rum jars, between the old support line and the fire trench, on CHICORY C.T., and also on the wire in front of mynworking party. I immediately gave the order for all men to lie down which they did, and were well extended. While lying there three men were badly wounded, one man having his leg blown off. The barrage on our fire trench and a heavy fire kept upon our wire the whole time, and also a heavy machine gun fire.

I heard a voice which I recognised as Lt. Maude's calling my name, and asking me to bring my party in his direction. I collected thr men into a ditch, and then altogether we made for the direction whence Mr. Maude's voice came, and got into the firing trench at N.5.Bay 7. We then came up against a barricade erected by Mr. Maude and Mr. Murdoch at S.P."D", and were challenged by the Lewis Gunners who were behind the barriacde.

Corporal Dawes rendered most excellent work the whole time and tended the wounded, and insisted upon staying behind with them until stretcher bearers could be brought to their aid.

It was about half an hour befor e our guns opened fire in in retalliation, which seemed most effective on the enemy front line.

Mr. Maude then organised my working party into a bombing party which he lead himself. I was ordered to erect another barricade outside Company Headquarters, and collect men and bombs.

(sgd) P.A. Egan, 2nd. Lieut.
"C" Company.
26th. Bn. Royal Fusiliers.

## REPORT BY LEWIS GUNNER, No. 19610 HENRY JONES. "B" Company attached "C" Company.

I was holding my position at S.P."C" when the Germans put up their barrage. I was firing at their front line parapet. After some time I noticed a party climbing over our parapet two bays to my right. I immediately moved my gun off the parapet on to a sheet of corrugated iron so as to enfilade the parapet on my right. I estimate the raiding party to be anything from 16 to 20. I opened fire on them but had a slight stoppage with my gun, which I handed down to my men who quickly repaired it. Meanwhile I took out my revolver and with the rest of my team opened fire on the Germans coming down the trench. I then got my gun into action again and opened fir e on to the raiding party as they were climbing over the parapet upon which they commenced to retreat back to their line. I had bombs ready but had no occasion to use them. The Germans did not throw any bombs either.

I fired four or five magazines traversing the front across which they had betreated.

Two Germans looked into our bay, upon which several of us fired and we heard an exclamation of pain which showed us that he had either been killed of badly wounded. We afterwards discovered that he was killed.

(sgd) Henry Jones, No. 19610
"B" Coy. attached "C" Coy. Lewis Gun Team.
(sgd) A.V. Todd, No. 2302
"C" Coy. Lewis Gun tea

P.T.O.

It was undoubtedly due to Private Jones, No.19610 and his team that the German Raid turned out an absolute failure, owing to his vigilance and prompt action taken.

(sgd) M.B.Maude, Lieut.
O/C "C" Company,
26th Royal Fusiliers.

-------------

REPORT ON ENEMY RAID. 14-12-16.

At about 8.45 p.m activity of the enemy artillery was noticed.

At about 9.10 p.m. my Adjutant returned from the line saying assistance was needed on the right. I had directed the Artillery primarily on my left Company front. as my right Company had reported O.K.

At about 9.20 p.m. the last message was received from the Right Companysaying "I wish the enemy straffed opposite Right Company front". This telephone then went dis, and remained so throughout the night.

Within about ten minutes of this (9.30 p.m.) my observers at Battalion Headquarters reported two red rockets. These I took to be the S.O.S. signal of my Right Company ( Trenches O.7.1. - O.7.4) I accordingly requested the Artillery Forward Observation Officer to give S.O.S. fire on my Right Sub-sector, which he did.

At approximately 9.40 p.m. I received a telephone message from Brigade Headquarters reporting that the enemy had entered my Right Company front line trench, and I was ordered to turn them out.

At 9.10 p.m. I had received intimation that my Reserve Comapny was standing to. I ordered my Second in Command (Major H.M.Tuite) to proceed to SLEEPY HOLLOW and there to await my orders. Prior to his arrival the situation had developed sufficiently to cause me to order my reserve company to the front line to assist in expelling the enemy raiders.

This was efficiently carried out by Captain A. Maxwell with my "A" Company; and I prsonally proceeded at about 9.45 p.m. to my Battle Headquarters at SLEEPY HOLLOW with all available men from the BRASSERIE, roughly about 50, who brought up bombs from the reserve.

Patrols were sent out from this Headquarter detachment to gain touch with my Right Front Company, and also to my Right and Left to intercept any enemy raiding party which might seek to pnetrate our rear lines.

Throughout the night my telephone wires to my Left Front Company, my Company in the Redoubts, and my Battalion Headquaters at LA BRASSERIE were intact.

At 10.35 p.m. I received intimation by telephone frommy Left Company Commander in the Front Line that no enemy now remained in my Right Sub-sector; this fact I reported to Brigade Headquarters pending confirmation. Written confirmation to this effect was received by me from Captain A. Maxwell (who had assumed command of my Right Sub-sector) at 10.45 p.m.

On receipt of this information I requested that the Artillery might slacken fire.

All was quiet by 11.15 p.m.at which time reports began to come in from the Front Line to the effect that my Officers and men were engaged in NO MAN'S LAND bringing in the wounded and that I might expect about

about ten casualities in the RightCompany. Further that my Front Line had been condiderably breached and that CHICORY LANE had been knocked in in about 20 places.

At 11.30 p.m. 2nd. Lieut. Jenkins who had gone forward to appreciate the position for me returned with the news that CHICORY LANE was not very seriously damaged; and that this damage was only between BOIS CARRE and the Front Line; but that the Front Line was considerably knocked about. He further reported that my men were considerably exhausted, and this was confirmed by requests from the Front Line for assistance in repairing the parapet. My Headquarter section was already en route for the Right Company Front Line to help in this work; but I considered it advisable to ask the O/C 10th. "Queens" R.W.S. Regt. for assistance which he most kindly gave me.

(sgd)

Lieut.-Col., Commanding
26th. Royal Fusiliers.

15th. December 1916.
1.30 a.m.

C O N F I D E N T I A L

From Officer Commanding,
26th. Bn.Royal Fusiliers.

To Headquarters,
124th. Infantry Brogade.

---------

In continuation of my reort No.104 of todays day, I have since obtained the folloing facts;-

1. The raiding party which left enemy front line is estimated at somewhere near 100, but of these not more than 10/20 crossed No Man's Land, and only about 6 entered my front line trench.

Although I had a wiring party in No.Man's Land, the the conformation of the ground prevented them noticing the enemy's advance. This advance appears to have been along the road from BOIS QUARANTE to O.7.a.3.1.

2. There does not appear to have been any bombing before the enemy entered the trench.

Although bombing parties were organsed in my Right Company, I cannot ascertain that bombs were used even after the enemy entered the trench.

3. There appears to have been little difficulty in expelling the enemy after he got in, thanks to the excellent action of Lewis Gunners, No.19610 Pivate Henry Jones, and No.2302 Private A. V. Todd, who showed skill and determination in their handling of the gun. Detailed reprt by O/C this Company will be found in Appendix "B", together with a report by Lewis Gunner Jones, endorsed by Lieut. Maude.

4. All agree that our Artillery fire was extraordinarily good. The delay in applying it may be explained by the fact that, although the bombardment was noticed by me at 8.47 p.m., O/C my Right Comany only asked "that the enemy front line mightnbe straffed", and I saw no reason to do this with S.O.S. fire.

I attach duplicates of messages sent by me regarding retalliation and S.O.S., which will be corroborated by the diary of F.O.O., "A" 190th. Brigade R.F.A. who was at my Battalion Headquarters on that night.

Lieut. Preston, the F.O.O. in question, assisted me throughout most ably, and I do not consider the blame attaches to the Artillery as regards delay in opening fire mentioned in report be Officer Commanding "C" Company.

5. There is little doubt that the German raiders must have crossed their parapet at about the same time as I called for S.O.S. i.e. about 9.30 p.m. This will account for the reported as having been seen crossing their own parapet, and the few who entered my front line. All agree that no more than half a dozen or so penetrated our line.

6. The enemy raiders were first spotted by No.19610 Private Henry Jones, "B" Company attached to "C"Company. As shown in his statement, which is corroborated by Lieut. Maude, the reason of the German raid being unsuccessful was in the main due to the good work of the Lewis Gunners of this Battalion.

7. From the duration and intensity of our barrage the Germans would certainly have had to retire through it, and there is a consensus of opinion amongst my Officers and Men that the enemy did so and suffered heavy casualities. All ranks, both Officers and Men, express their admiration of the Artillery barrage, which was most effective and w

8. As a result of the enemy bombardment my frontn line was seriously daaged.

To repair this damage I was most kindly assisted by O/C 10th. Bn. Royal West Surrey Regt."Queens", who placed a working party of 150 men with Officers at my disposal for the remainder of the night. I personally saw this work in progress from 3.30 a.m. onwards, and the spirit shown by all ranks in repairing the damage was very cmmendable. By dawn the damage had been sufficiently repaired to admit of through traffic from Right to Left of my line. For this I am greatly indebted to the excellent work done by the men placed at my disposal by O/C 10th."Queens". They worked splendidly

9. My casualties so far ~~xx~~ known are ascfollows :-

| | |
|---|---|
| Killed | 2 |
| Died of wounds | 1 |
| Wounded | 17 |
| do (at duty) | 1 |
| Missing | 1 |

The amn reported to be missing was on sentry on No.3 post in the trench which the enemy entered. I regret I have no clue as to what became of him.

10. Throughout the operation my Officers and Men showed a fine soldierly spirit, and I wish to bring certain names to your notice ; these will be submitted very shortly.

Major H.M.Tuite, my second in Command, was throughtout of the greatest assistance to me. His report is attached.

(sgd)

Lieut. Col. Commanding
26th. RoyalFusiliers.

15/12/16.

COPY OF REPORT BY LIEUT. M. B. MAUDE.

O/C "C" Company.

-------

Having taken the wiring party out I returned to the trench at C.2 (the same place that I wentnout.) I then went along to the right to see that the sentries were all on the alert, and returned to my Company Headquarters and got Sergeant Warner to collect 4 "A" Company men with rolls of wire to proceed out in frontto the wiring party. The barrage then commenced timed about 8.45 p.m. I immediately went along to the signallers, ordering the men about my Company Dugout to go down the sap until I was ready for them. I went into the Signals Station and got on to the Battery immediately and asked for a heavy barrage on the German front line as I thought they were raiding. I then went out and ordered the middle group of Lewis Gunners who were just on the right of Company Headquarters, to proceed farther to the right. I then, with the aid of my servant, tried to get a red rocket off, but it only fell flaming to the ground. 2nd. Lieut. Murdoch then got one off correctly outside my Company Headquarters, I then ran along to the sap shaft and got 4 men with rifles out on to the parapet in S.P."D" giving them orders to fire high. I then went down to the left and brought up a machine gun team who also had orders to fire high. I then returned to the sap shaft and got the rest of the men out on to the parapet. I then got the report from 2nd. Lieut. Murdoch that there were Germans coming along the trench. I immediately got the Machine Gun and the men off the parapet, and erected a barricade across the trench, and manned it with machine gun and rifles. I left Mr. Murdoch in charge and went down to the left to get bombs, at the same time sending a runn er down to "D" Company asking for reinforcements and bombs. I then sent two more runners down for bombs to "D" Company and along the trench ( four men in all).

I went out to try and get Mr. Egan's working party in order to work round the German raiding party. I heard his voice, but could not get him in my direction. I then endeavoured to return to the trench, but lost both my gum boots and socks.. Meanwhile, Mr. Murdoch had got up more bombs. I was organising a bombing party when Captain Maxwell came along. He informed me that his Company were coming up to support men I then met Mr. Munday and we went ahead with the bombing party, leaving Lt. Murdoch and Lt. Egan to erect a new barricade just outside Company Headquarters. We arrived at O.7.a.4.2. and found Privates Jones and Todd with their gun firing over the parapet. Mr.Munday and I with the bombing party then went along to the right and found that the raiding party had left the trench. Major Tuite, Mr. Egan, myself and L/Cpl. Whitehead then wentnout, and got in the two wounded men of the wiring party.

(sgd) M. B. Maude.
Lieut. O/C "C" Company.

COPY OF WIRES DESPATCHED.

9.3 p.m. To E.N.13.

Require SOUP opposite my lefy.

From E.W.7.

---------

9.7. p.m. To F.F.1.

Require SOUP my left front on CAT FRONT PATCH.

From E.W.7.

--------

9.14 p.m. To F.F.1.

CATS CARGO and BEASTS busy on my left PATCHES.

HAVE ASKED BEASTS for Soup on CATS FRONT PATCH.

Please ask for Soup from HRAVY BEASTS.

From E.W.7.

--------

9.30 p.m. To F.B.1.

We have asked for S.O.S. on our Right Company front.

From E.W.7.

---------

1. 230/1-1-17

Instructions regarding War Diaries and Intelligence Summaries are contained in F. S. Regs., Part II. and the Staff Manual respectively. Title pages will be prepared in manuscript.

Army Form C. 2118.

# WAR DIARY of 26th Battn. Royal Fusiliers or ~~INTELLIGENCE SUMMARY.~~

(Erase heading not required.)

January 1917.

Vol 9

| Place | Date | Hour | Summary of Events and Information | Remarks and references to Appendices |
|---|---|---|---|---|
| DIEPENDAAL Sector Front line | Jan. 1st | | On this day there was great artillery activity at 11 p.m. reaching from North of YPRES to KEMMEL | CRuf |
| | 2nd | | On this day the Battalion was relieved by the 21st KRRC and proceeded to LA CLYTTE. | Ref.O.O. No 26 CRuf. |
| LA CLYTTE | 3rd | | No working parties were required from the battalion on this day, which was given up to cleaning and training. | CRuf |
| | 4th | | A lecture was given to all officers by the Brigadier on open warfare. Large working parties were found by the battalion. | CRuf. |
| | 5th | | 'C' Coy. spent the day in Open Warfare training. The other companies were all out on fatigue. | CRuf |
| | 6th | | 'D' Company was out all day on Field Manoeuvres, the other Companies finding the working parties. 50 men of 'C' Company went up to the New Reserve Line to complete the wiring between P. and O. and BOIS CARRÉ. | CRuf |

9.K. (6 sheets)

T2134. Wt. W708—776. 500000. 4/15. Sir J. C. & S.

2/

Instructions regarding War Diaries and Intelligence Summaries are contained in F. S. Regs., Part II. and the Staff Manual respectively. Title pages will be prepared in manuscript.

WAR DIARY of 26th Batn. Royal Fusiliers
~~or~~
~~INTELLIGENCE SUMMARY.~~ January 1917
(Erase heading not required.)

Army Form C. 2118.

| Place | Date | Hour | Summary of Events and Information | Remarks and references to Appendices |
|---|---|---|---|---|
| Do | Jan. 7th | | On this day 'A' Company trained in open warfare; working parties being supplied by the rest of the Battalion. The remainder of 'C' Company joined the wiring party in the Reserve Line in order to get the work completed. | CRuf |
| DIEPENDAAL Sector front line | 8th | | On this day the battalion relieved the 21st K.R.R.C in the line; the disposition being:- Front line - left 'A' Company. - Right 'D' Company. Redoubts - 'C' Company Sleepy Hollow 'B' Company. The snipers were posted behind Strong Point 7 in order to increase the number available in the New Reserve Line, the band occupying their old billet in B.H.Q. | Ref. O.O. 27 CRuf |
| Do. | 9th. | | The enemy trench mortars were specially active against our right Sub-sector and caused several casualties. Dummy figures were put out in front of O.7.8. O.7.9 for use on the 10th. | CRuf |

T2134. Wt. W708-776. 500000. 4/15. Sir J. C. & S.

3/

Instructions regarding War Diaries and Intelligence Summaries are contained in F. S. Regs., Part II. and the Staff Manual respectively. Title pages will be prepared in manuscript.

# WAR DIARY of 26th Battn. Royal Fusiliers or ~~INTELLIGENCE SUMMARY~~. January 1917.

(Erase heading not required.)

Army Form C. 2118.

| Place | Date | Hour | Summary of Events and Information | Remarks and references to Appendices |
|---|---|---|---|---|
| Do | Jan 10th | | Again enemy trench mortars annoyed our right front company. At 7 p.m our artillery started an hours bombardment of the enemy front system of trenches along the divisional front. Two minutes before zero the dummy figures were pulled up and fire was opened with rifle and Lewis guns. The figures were pulled up and down in the hope of getting the enemy to man his parapet. He does not seem to have noticed the figures, but his trenches were very considerably damaged. The dummies were brought in and examined afterwards. Only two figures were damaged. | CRuf |
| Do | 11th | | This day passed much more quietly: the enemy evidently being engaged on repairs. | CRuf |
| Do | 11th / 12th | | At 1 a.m. the Germans suddenly cheered opposite our front for no apparent reason. | CRuf |
| Do | 12th | | Nothing unusual happened on this day | CRuf |

T2134. Wt. W708—776. 500000. 4/15. Sir J. C. & S.

4/

# WAR DIARY of 26th Battn. Royal Fusiliers

A.F.C. 2118

January 1917

| Place | Date | Summary of Events an Information | Remarks and reference to appendices |
|---|---|---|---|
| Do | 13th Jan. | The day passed quietly | C.R.f |
| DIEPENDAAL Secto | 14th Jan. | On this day the 21st K.R.R.C. relieved the battalion in the line and the battalion went into support in RIDGE WOOD. The weather became suddenly colder. | Ref. O.O. No 23 C.R.f |
| RIDGE WOOD | 14th – 20th Jan. | The battalion supplied large working parties. There was a fall of snow and the weather continued to be very cold. | C.R.f |
| DIEPENDAAL SECTOR FRONT LINE | 20th Jan. | On this day the battalion relieved the 21st K.R.R.C. in the line. | Ref. O.O. 29 C.R.f |
| | 21st Jan. | Owing to the crackly condition of the hard frozen snow patrolling was rendered very difficult indeed. Nevertheless good work was done in making sure that the salient opposite CHICORY LANE was unoccupied | |

5/

# WAR DIARY of 26th Battn. Royal Fusiliers

A.F.C. 2118

January 1917.

| Place | Date | Summary of Events and Information | Remarks and references to appendices. |
| --- | --- | --- | --- |
| | 22nd Jan. | On this day the German artillery bombarded our left front company very heavily all day. No action followed. | CRof |
| | 23rd - 25th Jan. | These days passed quietly. The cold weather still continuing with very severe frost after snow. | CRof |
| LA CLYTTE | 26th Jan. | On this day the 21st K.R.R.C. relieved the battalion in the line and the battalion went in Brigade Reserve at LA CLYTTE. | Ref. O.O. No 30<br>CRof |
| | 27th Jan. | This day was a rest day and there was a route march. The baths were allotted to the battalion, but as the water pipe was frozen very few men were able to bath. | CRof |
| | 28th Jan. | Working parties were provided on this day. | |
| | 29th Jan. | On this day 'D' Company spent a day in open warfare training | CRof |

6/

A.F.C. 2118

# WAR DIARY of 26th Battn Royal Fusiliers

January 1917.

| Place | Date | Summary of Events and Information | Remarks and references to Appendices |
|---|---|---|---|
| Do | 30th Jan | On this day 'B', 'C' and 'D' companies went for a route march and 'A' Company went out for Field Training. Fatigue parties were also found. | CRef |
| Do. | 31st Jan | 'A', 'B' and 'D' Companies went for a route march and 'C' Company did Field Training. Fatigue parties were found as usual. G.O.C. lectured in Evening | CRef |

G. George-Thomas Lt Col

Cmdg 26th Royal Fusiliers

Instructions regarding War Diaries and Intelligence Summaries are contained in F. S. Regs., Part II. and the Staff Manual respectively. Title Pages will be prepared in manuscript.

# WAR DIARY of 26th Battn. Roy. Fus.
~~or~~
~~INTELLIGENCE SUMMARY~~
(Erase heading not required.)

February 1917.

Army Form C. 2118

Vol 10

| Place | Date | Hour | Summary of Events and Information | Remarks and references to Appendices |
|---|---|---|---|---|
| | 1/2/17 | | The battalion relieved the 21st K.R.R.C. on this day in the line. | Ref. O.O. 31. [initials] |
| | 2/2/17 | | The frost being still severe patrolling was difficult. The disposition of companies was carried out after 'Standdown' | Ref. O.O. 32 [initials] |
| | 3/2/17 + 4 | | These days passed quietly the frost still continuing | [initials] |
| | 5/2/17 | | On this day the battalion was relieved in the line by the 21st K.R.R.C. and went into support in RIDGEWOOD. On the 5th, 1 slightly wounded (he remained at duty). | Ref. O.O. 33 [initials] |
| | 6 to 9/2/17 | | The battalion supplied large working parties. Clean changes of underclothing were only obtainable at the baths. Weather still freezing. On the 6th there were 5 killed | [initials] |

10 K (12 sheets)

1875 Wt. W593/826 1.000.000 4/15 J.B.C. & A. A.D.S.S./Forms/C. 2118.

2

Instructions regarding War Diaries and Intelligence Summaries are contained in F. S. Regs., Part II. and the Staff Manual respectively. Title Pages will be prepared in manuscript.

# WAR DIARY of 26th Battn. Roy. Fus.
~~or~~
~~INTELLIGENCE SUMMARY~~ February 1917.

(Erase heading not required.)

Army Form C. 2118

| Place | Date | Hour | Summary of Events and Information | Remarks and references to Appendices |
|---|---|---|---|---|
| | 10/2/17 | | On this day the battalion relieved the 21st K.R.R.C. in the line. | ref. 00. 34. [initials] |
| | 11/2/17 | | Our heavy artillery bombarded the German rear defences and in the afternoon our Medium trench mortars carried out a wire cutting shoot on NAGS NOSE. Otherwise all quiet. | [initials] |
| | 12/2/17 | | The T.M.B's again carried out a shoot on HOLLANDSCHESCHUUR SALIENT. Retaliation was slight. Two were wounded on this day. | [initials] |
| | 13/2/17 | | There was slight increased artillery activity on the part of the enemy on this day | [initials] |
| | 14/2/17 | | The frost began to give way on this day. The Germans were caught relieving in the early morning and shelled by our artillery. | [initials] |

1875 Wt. W593/826 1,000,000 4/15 J.B.C. & A. A.D.S.S./Forms/C. 2118.

3/

Instructions regarding War Diaries and Intelligence Summaries are contained in F. S. Regs., Part II. and the Staff Manual respectively. Title Pages will be prepared in manuscript.

# WAR DIARY of 26th Battn. Roy. Fus.
~~or~~
~~INTELLIGENCE SUMMARY~~ February 1917
(Erase heading not required.)

Army Form C. 2118

| Place | Date | Hour | Summary of Events and Information | Remarks and references to Appendices |
|---|---|---|---|---|
| | 15/2/17 | | The artillery of both sides was slightly more active than usual. Our T.M.B's. still continue to cut wire in HOLLANDSCHESCHOUR SALIENT | [illegible] |
| | 16/2/17 | | On this day the battalion was relieved in the line by the 21st K.R.R.C. and proceeded into Brigade Reserve at LA CLYTTE | Ref. 00.35 [illegible] |
| | 17/2/17 | | This day was a rest day and training was done. | [illegible] |
| | 18/2/17 | | Working parties were provided on this day. Lewis gunners of 'A' & 'B' Companies. Baths were obtained | [illegible] |
| | 19/2/17 | | The day passed quietly. | [illegible] |
| | 20/2/17 | | This day also passed quietly. | |

4

Instructions regarding War Diaries and Intelligence Summaries are contained in F. S. Regs., Part II. and the Staff Manual respectively. Title Pages will be prepared in manuscript.

# WAR DIARY of 26th Battn. Roy. Fus.
or
~~INTELLIGENCE SUMMARY~~ February 1917
(Erase heading not required.)

Army Form C. 2118

| Place | Date | Hour | Summary of Events and Information | Remarks and references to Appendices |
|---|---|---|---|---|
| | 22/2/17 | | On this day the battalion relieved the 21st K.R.R.C in the line | Ref. O.O. 86. [initials] |
| | 23/2/17 | | The day was misty. The morning passed quietly and in the afternoon our heavies, field guns and T.M's bombarded the enemy's defences and cut his wire. The German retaliation was heavy. | [initials] |
| | 24/2/17 | | There was a heavy bombardment by us this morning and 10th Battn. Queens R.W.S. raided the German line at 5.0 pm. on our right. There was considerable shelling of our battn. front. There were 2 killed on this day and 7 wounded. | [initials] |
| | 25/2/17 | | The day passed quietly. 1 officer + 1 O.R. killed, 2 died of wounds and 14 wounded. | [initials] |
| | 26/2/17 | | Except for a little artillery activity on the part of the enemy, the day passed quietly. On this day 1 was killed and one wounded | |

1875 Wt. W593/826 1,000,000 4/15 J.B.C. & A. A.D.S.S./Forms/C. 2118.

5

Instructions regarding War Diaries and Intelligence Summaries are contained in F. S. Regs., Part II. and the Staff Manual respectively. Title Pages will be prepared in manuscript.

# WAR DIARY of 26th Battn. Roy. Fus.
or
# ~~INTELLIGENCE SUMMARY~~ February 1917.
(Erase heading not required.)

Army Form C. 2118

| Place | Date | Hour | Summary of Events and Information | Remarks and references to Appendices |
|---|---|---|---|---|
| | 27/2/17 | | The day passed quietly. Weather was misty | [illegible] |
| | 28/2/17 | | The battalion was relieved by the 21st K.R.R.C. in the line and went into support in RIDGEWOOD. | Ref 0987 |

In the Field
5-3-17

H.W. [illegible] Major
Comdg 26th Roy Fus.

1875 Wt. W593/826 1,000,000 4/15 J.B.C. & A. A.D.S.S./Forms/C. 2118.

Secret.                                                                 Copy No. ______

# 26th Bn Royal Fusiliers

## Operation Order No 31

1. The Battalion will relieve the 21st Bn K.R.R.C. in the line tomorrow, 1st February, 1917, relief to commence at 4 pm.

2. Companies will be disposed as follows:-

| | |
|---|---|
| "A" Coy | Left Front |
| "B" Coy | Right Front |
| "C" Coy | Redoubts |
| "D" Coy | Sleepy Hollow. |

3. Order of relief, times at which relieving sections and Companies will be at LA BRASSERIE and route to be taken is as follows:-

| | | |
|---|---|---|
| "C" Coy | 1-30 pm. | Chicory Lane. |
| "B" Coy | 2 pm. | do. |
| "A" Coy | 2-30 pm | P.& O. Lane |
| "D" Coy | 3 pm | Chicory Lane. |
| Headquarters | 2-30 pm | — |
| Snipers, Lewis Gunners & C.M's. | 11 am. | |

4. O/c Companies must ensure that the return of trench stores taken over reaches Battalion Orderly Room not later than two hours after taking over

5. The camp, ~~billets~~ etc, must be left scrupulously clean. O/c Companies must see that this order is carried out and that all latrine buckets are emptied

6. Each man will take one blanket to the trenches on his pack.
The remaining blankets will be rolled into bundles of 10 tallied and stacked outside the Bn O.R. by 12 noon for collection by transport.
Officers valises and other boxes that are being returned to the Transport Lines will be stacked outside Bn O.R. by 12 noon in a separate heap.
The Transport Officer will arrange the necessary waggons for Transport.

7. Rations will be at Ration Dump as usual when Battalion is in the line

8. Completion of relief will be wired to Bn O.R. as follows:-
... (time)

(Sgd) A.W. Mackay,
Lieut & Adjutant
26th Bn Royal Fusiliers

SECRET. Copy No.

26th. BN. ROYAL FUSILIERS.

Operation Order No. 32.

---

1. After 'Stand down' on the 2nd. February 1917 the following will be he distribution of Companies.

(a) Front Line Trench O 7 1 to O 7 9
"B" Coy. with 6 Lewis Guns by day & 7 by night.

(b) Durham Strong Point and New Reserve Line.
Trenches R.N.12.7 to R.O.1.2. (i.e. between Chicory Lane & P & O)
"C" Coy. with 1 Lewi s Gun at Durham S.P. & 1 Lewis Gun at junction of Chicory Lane and New Reserve Line.

(c) Redoubts & S.P. 7.
"A" Coy. with 1 Lewis Gun at Southern Redoubt & 1 at Eastern Redoubt.

(d) SleepyHollow.
"D" Coy. The remaining Lewis Gun will be staioned at LA BRASSERIE and will be used as an Anti-aircraft gun by day.

2. Headqarters of Company in the Line will be at trench O 7 2.

3. At least one Officer of the Front Line Company will live in Trench O 7 9 and 1 Officer in Trench O 7 6.

4. O.C. Front Line Company will arrang always to have at least 1 Officer on watch by day and 2 on watch by night.
Duringhis watch the Officer must remain patrolling the Trench and must not enter his dugout.

5. 3 S.O.S. Rockets will be at the Headqurters of the front line Company. 2 S.O.S. Rockets will be kept at the old Headquarters on left of front line.
1 S.O.S. Rocket kept at Headquarters of Company in New Reserve Lin
1 S.O.S. Rocket kept by O.C. Redoubts & 1 at Headquarters.
Officers on watch in the front line are reminded that they must carry 'Very' lights of the same colour as the S.O.S. Rockets.

6. The front line Company will find all patrols unless otherwise ordered.

7. The front line Company will work from 9 -1 daily on repairing the front line.
The Company at Sleepy Hollow will furnish a ration party for the front line Company daily. O.C. front line Company will arrange with O.C. Company at Slepy Hollow the most convenient method of bringing up rations.

8. The Company occupying the New Reserve Line will be responsible for the wiring of the front line and will furnish nightly a party of 50 men under an Officer for this work. (This party of 50 men will be told off in 4 squads of 12).
O.C. this Company will submit indents for all material for the work at the usual hour.
Any other working parties required will be furnished by this Company and the Company occupying Sleepy Hollow.

9. The Company occupying Redoubts and S.P.7 will not usually be asked to provide any working parties outside the Redoubts and will beeployd dayad night improving redoubts and in wiring.

10. Os.C. "B" & "C" Companies will arrange as to what trench stores will remain in the front line and what taken back.
New trench store return will be rendered by "C" Coy. by Monday next at 10 am.

11. Os.C. "B" & "C" Companies will report by wire when the order in pra 1. of this Operation Order is completed usig the following code :-

"FRIDAY" (time).

12. Acknowledge.

(sgd) A.W.Mackay,
Lieut. & Adjutant,
26th Royal Fusiliers

1/2/17.

Operation Order No. 33.

1. The Battalion will be relieved by the 21st. K.R.R.C. tomorrow 5th. February, 1917, relief to commence at 4 pm. and will proceed to RIDGEWOOD.

2. Order of relief, times at which relieving section s and Coys will be at LA BRASSERIE & rote to be takenwill be as follows :-

| | | | |
|---|---|---|---|
| Lewis Gunners, Snipers and C.S.Ms | | | 1 pm. |
| Redoubts - Chicory Lane | | | 3.30 pm. |
| Front Line - | 2 Platoons | Chicory Lane | 4.0 pm. |
| | 2 " | P & O Trench | 4.0 pm. |
| Reserve Line | 2 " | " " " " | 4.15 pm. |
| | 2 " | Chicory Lane | 4.15 pm. |
| SleepyHollow | | ChicoryLane | 5.0 pm. |

Redoubts to file out as soon as last Company proceeding to New Reserve Line has passed up Chicory Lane.

3. Companies will occupy exactly the same billets as when the Battalion was last in RIDGEWOOD.

4. O.C. Companies will have complete lists of trenchstores prepared ready for the incoming unit.
The signed portion will be sent to Bn. O.R. immadiately on on arrival at RIDGEWOOD. A copy of this list will be rendered to Bn. O.R. by 10 am. on 5/2/17.

5. O.C. Companies ar e responsible that the trencks dugouts and latrines are left scrupulously clean.

6. Tables of 'work done' and 'work in hand and proposed' should be made out and handed over for the informaion of the incoming unit.

7. The Intelligece Officer will arrange to provide the Intelligence Officer of the incoming unit with a copy of his reports for the past week and give him all possible information.

8. O.C.Companies will make their own arrangements for getting cooking utensils, trench b undles, etc. to RIDGEWOOD.

9. The Transport Officer will arrange to have Officers valises and blankets for the men brought up to RIDGEWOOD at the same time as rations.

10. Completion of relief will be wired to Bn.O.R. as follows :-
"BEER" (time).

(sgd) A.W.Mackay,
Lieut & Adjutant,
26th. Royal Fusiliers.

4/2/17.

SECRET. Copy No...1.

# 26th. Bn. ROYAL FUSILIERS.

## Operation Order No. 34.

1. The Battalion will relieve the 21st. Bn. K.R.R.C. in the line tomorrow 10th. January, 1917, relief to commence at 4 p.m.
2. Companies will be disposed as follows :-
   "A" Coy. SLEEPY HOLLOW
   "B" " REDOUBTS.
   "C" " FRONT LINE.
   "D" " RESERVE LINE.
3. Order of relief, times at which relieving sections and Companies will be at LA BRASSERIE, and routes to be taken will be as follows:-
   Snipers, Lewis Gunners and C.S.Ms. 1.30 p.m.
   "B" Coy. 3.30p.m. CHICORY LANE
   "C" " 4 p.m. 2 Platoons CHICORY LANE, 2 Platoons P&O.TRENCH
   "D" " 4.30p.m. 2 " " " 2 " " "
   "A" " 5 p.m. CHICORY LANE
   Headquarters 5 p.m.
   Snipers, Lewis Gunners and C.S.Ms. will have dinner at 12 noon before leaving for the trenches.
4. O.C.Companies must ensure that the return of Trench Stores taken over reaches Battalion Orderly Room not later than two hours after taking over.
5. The camp, dugouts, etc. in RIDGEWOOD must be left scrupulously clean, and O.C.Companies must see that this order is carried out; also that all latrine buckets are emptied.
6. Each man will take with him one blanket to the trenches. The remainder will be rolled into bundles of 10, labelled and stacked at the Dressing Station by [illegible] p.m. ready for the Transport. Officers valises and other boxes that are being returned to the Transport Lines will be stacked at the same place and by the same hour.
7. O.C.Companies will make their own arrangements for taking Trench bundles, Mess boxes, cooking utensils etc. into the Trenches.
8. Rations will be brought up as usual by the Transport and O.C. Companies must arrange for their Ration parties to take same to the Trenches.
9. Completion of relief will be wired to Battalion Orderly Room as follows :-

"STOUT" (time).

(sgd) A.W.MACKAY,
Lieut. & Adjutant,
26th. Royal Fusiliers.

9/1/17.

Copy No. 1 Filed.
2 124th. Infantry Brigade.
3 Adjutant.
4 21st. Bn. K.R.R.C.
5 O.C. "A" Coy.
6 O.C. "B" "
7 O.C. "C" "
8 O.C. "D" "
9 O.C. Headquarters.
10 Transport Officer & Quartermaster.
11 Sniping & Intelligence Officer
12 Bombing Officer & Lewis Gun Officer.

SECRET. Copy No. 1..

580

26th Bn. ROYAL FUSILIERS.

Operation Order No. [illegible].

1. The Battalion will be relieved by the 21st. Bn. K.R.R.C. in the line tomorrow 16th. February, 1917, relief to commence at [illegible] p.m. and will proceed to LA CLYTTE.

2. Order of relief, times at which relieving sections and Companies will be at LA BRASSERIE and route to be taken will be as follows :-

Snipers, Lewis Gunners and C.S.Ms [illegible] a.m.
Redoubts Coy. 1.30 p.m. CHICORY LANE.
Front Line Coy. [illegible] p.m. [illegible] Platoons CHICORY LANE, [illegible] TRENCH
Reserve Line [illegible] p.m. [illegible] " " " "
Sleepy Hollow [illegible].45 p.m. CHICORY LANE.
Headquarters. [illegible].30 p.m.

3. Companies will occupy the same billets as when the Battalion was last at LA CLYTTE.

4. O.C.Companies will have complete lists of Trench Stores ready for the incoming unit and the signed portion will be rendered to Bn. Orderly Room immediately on arrival at LA CLYTTE.
A list of the Stores to be handed over will be rendered to Bn. Orderly Room by 10 a.m. tomorrow morning.

5. O.C.Companies are responsible that the dugouts, and latrines are left scrupulously clean.

6. Tables of "work done" and "work in hand and proposed" should be made out and handed over for the information of the incoming unit.

7. The Intelligence Officer will arrange to provide the Intelligence Officer of the incoming unit with a copy of his reports for the past week and give him all possible information.

8. All trench bundles, cooking utensils etc., will be taken to the Dressing Station by [illegible] p.m. ready for the Transport.

9. The Transport Officer will arrange to have all Officers kits, blankets etc., taken to [illegible] CAMP.
Officers horses to be at the Dressing Station [illegible] hour later than times mentioned in para. 2.
The Transport Officer will also have 1 limber at the Dressing Station at 1 p.m. for the use of the Lewis Gunners.

10. Completion of relief will be wired to Bn. Orderly Room as follows :-

"RATS" (time).

(sgd) A. [illegible],
Lieut. & Adjutant,
26th. Royal Fusiliers.

15/2/17.

Copy No. 1 Filed.
2. 124th. Infantry Brigade.
3 Adjutant.
4 21st. K.R.R.C.
5 O.C. "A" Coy.
6 O.C."B" "
7 O.C."C" "
8 O.C."D" "
9 O.C.Headquarters.
10 Transport Officer & Quartermaster.
11 Sniping & Intelligence Officer
12 Lewis Gun Officer & Bombing Officer.

SECRET. Copy No. 2..

# 26th. BN. ROYAL FUSILIERS.

## Operation Order No. 36.

1. The Battalion will relieve the 21st. Bn. K.R.R.C. in the line tomorrow 22nd. February 1917 relief to commence at 2 p. m.
2. Companies will be disposed as follows :-

"A" Coy. Reserve Line.
"B" " Sleepy Hollow.
"C" " Redoubts.
"D" " Front Line.

3. Order of relief, times at which relieving sections and Companies will be at LA BRASSERIE and route to be taken will be as follows :-

Lewis Gunners, Snipers and C.S.Ms 11 a.m.
"C" Coy. 1.30 p.m. CHICORY LANE
"D" " 2.0 p.m. 2 Platoons CHICORY, 2 Platoons P.& O TRENCH
"A" " 2.30 p.m. " " " " "
"B" " 3.0 p.m. CHICORY LANE.
Headquarters 2.30 p.m.

4. Each man will take one blanket to the trenches on his pack, the remaining blankets will rolled into bundles of 10, tallied, and stacked outside the Bn.O.R. by 11 a.m.

Officers trench bundles, cooking utensils and boxes will be stacked outside Bn.O.R. by 12 noon for collection by Transport.

Officers valises and other boxes that are being returned to the Transport Lines will be stacked outside the Bn.O.R. by 12 noon in a separate heap.

The Transport Officer will arrange the necessary waggons for Transport.

5. Rations will be at LA BRASSERIE as usual when the Battalion is in the line.
6. O.C.Companies will be responsible that the Camp and Huts are left scrupulously clean and latrine buckets emptied.
7. O.C.Companies will render to Bn.O.R. within two hours of taking over signed list of trench stores.
8. Completion of relief will be wired to Bn.O.R. as follows :-

"POST" (time).

(sgd) A.W.Mackay,
Lieut. & Adjutant,
26th. Royal Fusiliers.

21/2/17.

Copy No. 1 Filed.
2 124th. Infantry Brigade.
3 Adjutant.
4 21st. Bn.K.R.R.C.
5 O.C."A" Coy.
6 O.C."B" "
7 O.C."C" "
8 O.C."D" "
9 O.C.Headquarters, & Signalling Officer.
10 Transport Officer & Quartermaster.
11 Lewis Gun Officer & Bombing Officer.
12 Sniping & Intelligence Officer.

<u>Secret.</u> Copy No..1...

(897)

## <u>26th. BN. ROYAL FUSILIERS.</u>

### <u>Operation Order No. 37.</u>

1. The Battalion will be relieved tomorrow 28/2/17 by the 21st Bn.K.R.R.C. relief to commence at 10.3 p.m. and will proceed into Support at RIDGEWOOD.
2. Order of relief, times at which relieving sections and Companies will be at LA BRASSERIE and route to be taken will be as follows :-

| | | |
|---|---|---|
| Snipers, Lewis Gunners and C.S.Ms | ~~5~~ 10 a.m. | |
| Redoubt Coy. | ~~[illegible]~~ 11.30 am | Chicory Lane |
| Front Line Coy. | 12.~~[illegible]~~ pm. | 2 Platoons Chicory Lane, & 2 via P & O. |
| Reserve Line Coy. | 12.30 pm. | 3 " " " & 4 " " |
| Sleepy Hollow Coy. | 1.~~[illegible]~~ pm. | Chicory Lane. |
| Headquarters | 12.30 pm. | |

3. Immediately after having handed over the C.S.Ms will proceed to RIDGEWOOD to take over from the 18th. Bn. K.R.R.C.
4. Companies will occupy the same billets as when the Battalion was last in RIDGEWOOD.
5. O.C.Companies will hav e complete lists of Trench Stores ready for the incoming unit.
   The signed portion will be sent to the Bn. O.R. within two hours of arrival at RIDGEWOOD. A copy of this list will be sent to the Bn. O.R. by 9 am. 28/2/17.
6. Tables of"work done" and "work in hand and proposed" should be made out and handed over for the information of the incoming unit.
7. The Intelligence Officer will arrange to provide the Intelligence Officer of the incomingunit with a copy of his reports for the past week and give him all possible information.
8. c O.C.Companies are responsible that the trenches, dugouts and latrines are left scrupulously clean.
9. O.C.Companies will make their own arrangements for getting cooking utensils, trench bundles etc. to RIDGEWOOD.
   No one is to pass the BRASSERIE before 11.30 a.m. unless they have been relieved.
10. The Transport Officer will arrange to have Officers kits and all blankets for men br ought up tomorrow.
    Rations will be brought up to the ration dump as usual and O.C.Companies will make necessary arrangements for distribution.
11. Completion of relief will be wired to Bn.O.R. as follows:-
    "COUGH" (time).

(sgd) A.R.Mackay,
Lieut & Adjutant,
26th.Royal Fusiliers

<u>27/2/17.</u>

Copy No. 1 Filed.
2 124th. Infantry Brigade.
3 Adjutant.
4 21st.Bn.K.R.R.C.
5 O.C."A"Coy.
6 O.C."B" "
7 O.C."C" "
8 O.C."D" "
9 O.C.Headquarters & Signalling Officer.
10 Intelligence Off icer & Sniping Officer
11 Transport Officer & Quartermaster.
12 Lewis Gun Officer & Bombing Officer.
13 18th K R R C

Ref Para 10 - Rations [illegible] will be at RIDGEWOOD (Traffic Guard) at 7pm.

[illegible]

Instructions regarding War Diaries and Intelligence Summaries are contained in F. S. Regs., Part II. and the Staff Manual respectively. Title Pages will be prepared in manuscript.

# WAR DIARY of 26th Battn Roy Fus.
or
~~INTELLIGENCE SUMMARY~~
(Erase heading not required.)

March 1917

Vol XI

Army Form C. 2118

| Place | Date | Hour | Summary of Events and Information | Remarks and references to Appendices |
|---|---|---|---|---|
| RIDGEWOOD | 1/3/17 | | Training of Lewis gunners, signallers and men was continued. The usual working parties for the line, were found and parties for R E fatigues. Baths were obtained for the men also clean changes of underclothing. There were heavy falls of snow on the night 4th/5th and during the morning and afternoon of the 5th. Casualties on the 3rd one wounded | CMK |
| DIEPENDAAL SECTOR | 6th to 9th/3/17 | | The battalion relieved the 21st K.R.R's in the line on the afternoon of the 6th and carried on with the usual trench routine. Patrolling during this tour in the trenches, was rendered difficult by the snow | Ref. O.O. No 38<br>CMK |

1875 Wt. W593/826 1,000,000 4/15 J.B.C. & A. A.D.S.S./Forms/C. 2118.

11.K. (10 sheets)

2

Instructions regarding War Diaries and Intelligence Summaries are contained in F. S. Regs., Part II. and the Staff Manual respectively. Title Pages will be prepared in manuscript.

# WAR DIARY of 26th Battalion Roy. Fus
or
~~INTELLIGENCE SUMMARY~~ March 1917

(Erase heading not required.)

Army Form C. 2118

| Place | Date | Hour | Summary of Events and Information | Remarks and references to Appendices |
|---|---|---|---|---|
| DIEPENDAAL SECTOR | 9th/10/3/17 | | The daily trench routine and work on the trenches was continued. The wiring of the front line, New Reserve and S.P.7 was carried on. Patrols were sent out each night and useful information with regard to enemy working + wiring parties was obtained. These parties were dealt with by the artillery. | CPM |
| | 11/3/17 | | There was increased artillery activity by the enemy. The C.T's and back areas being treated intermittently during the day with 4.2. Gas shells were dropped in the region of N.6a.5.9 The enemy appeared to concentrate his aerial activities to the Wytschaete area, on this day. Several engagements took place between British and German machines. Casualties one wounded. | CPM |
| LA CLYTTE | 12.3.17 | | The Battalion was relieved by the 21st K.R.R's at 3.30 pm and went into Brigade Reserve at La Clytte. Working parties were supplied day and night for work in the trenches. The training of the men and specialists was also continued. Casualties on 12th one wounded " 13th 2 Sgts. D. of W. | Ref. O.O No. 39 CPM |

1875 Wt. W593/826 1,000,000 4/15 J.B.C. & A. A.D.S.S./Forms/C. 2118.

Army Form C. 2118

# WAR DIARY of 26th Battn. Roy. Fus.

or

~~INTELLIGENCE SUMMARY~~ March 1917.

(Erase heading not required.)

Instructions regarding War Diaries and Intelligence Summaries are contained in F. S. Regs., Part II. and the Staff Manual respectively. Title Pages will be prepared in manuscript.

| Place | Date | Hour | Summary of Events and Information | Remarks and references to Appendices |
| --- | --- | --- | --- | --- |
| DIEPENDAAL SECTOR | 18/3/17 | | The Battn. relieved the 21st K.R.R.'s in the line at 11.30 am and continued the work of wiring, repairing trenches, dugouts etc. With the exception of the first day the enemy artillery was quieter than usual but increased movement was observed behind the German lines especially about Lounvaege Farm, the St. Eloi Rd. in the region of Onraet Wood and Zero House. Casualties on 19th one wounded. | Ref. O.O. No. 40 |
| RIDGEWOOD + STEENVOORDE | 22.3/17 | | The Battalion was relieved in the trenches by the 8th Battalion North Staffordshire Regt. at 10.15 am and went into Brigade Support in Ridgewood. At 1.0 pm the 10th Battn. Worcester Regt. commenced to relieve the Battn. The Battalion assembled at Hallebast Corner on completion of relief and marched to La Clytte where motor lorries awaited to convey the Battn. to Steenvoorde at which place they arrived at (the) about 8.30 pm having travelled via Poperinghe which was being shelled. Heavy falls of snow occurred intermittently during the afternoon. A hot meal was waiting for the men on arrival at Steenvoorde | Ref. O.O.'s Nos. 41, 42, 43. |

1875 Wt. W593/826 1,000,000 4/15 J.B.C. & A. A.D.S.S./Forms/C. 2118.

4

Instructions regarding War Diaries and Intelligence Summaries are contained in F. S. Regs., Part II. and the Staff Manual respectively. Title Pages will be prepared in manuscript.

# WAR DIARY of 26th Battn. Roy. Fus
or
~~INTELLIGENCE SUMMARY~~ March 1917
(Erase heading not required.)

Army Form C. 2118

| Place | Date | Hour | Summary of Events and Information | Remarks and references to Appendices |
|---|---|---|---|---|
| STEENVOORDE | 23/3/17 | | The Battalion was inspected by the Army Commander, General Sir Herbert C. O. Plumer, G.C.M.G., K.C.B at 2.40 pm. The rest of day was spent in cleaning up the billets | Cr |
| " | 24th – 29th 3.17 | | The Battalion commenced training under company arrangements. Bombing practice, bayonet fighting, physical training, platoon drill, and company drill was carried out. Baths and clean changes of underclothing were obtained at the baths in Steenvoorde. | Cr |
| " | 30/3/17 | | A route march with [illegible] advance guard ~~thrown out~~ was done by 'A' and 'D' Coys. They marched to Watou, at which place outposts were going to be put out, but this was rendered impossible by the town being full of troops. accordingly, a rear-guard action was done, back to billets | Cr |
| " | 31/3/17 | | The Battalion carried out a Bn practice attack, on this day. | Cr |

G Gwyn Thomas Lt. Col
Comdg 26th Royal Fusiliers

1875 Wt. W593/826 1,000,000 4/15 J.B.C. & A. A.D.S.S./Forms/C. 2118.

File for war diary

SECRET. H.W. Copy No. 12....

26th. BN. ROYAL FUSILIERS.

Operation Order No. 38.

1. The Battalion will relieve the 21st. Bn. K.R.R.C. in the line tomorrow 4th. March, 1917, relief to commence at 4 pm.

2. Companies will be disposed as follows :-

"A" Coy. Front Line.
"B" " Reserve Line.
"C" " Sleepy Hollow.
"D" " Redoubts.

3. Order of relief, times at which relieving sections and Companies will be at LA BRASSERIE and routes to be taken will be as follows :-

Snipers, Lewis Gunners and C/S.Ms 4 pm.
"D" Coy. 3.30 pm. CHICORY LANE
"A" " 4.0 pm. 2 Platoons CHICORY LANE & 2 Platoons P & O TRENCH
"B" " 4.30 pm. 2 " " " & 2 " " " "
"C" " 5.0 pm. CHICORY LANE.
Headqu arters 4.30 pm.

4. O.C.Companies must ensure that the return of Trench Stores taken over is despatched to Bn.O.R. immediately after takingover.

5. The camp, dugouts etc. in RIDGEWOOD must be left scrupulously clean and O.C.Companies must see that this order is carried out, also that all latrine buckets are emptied.

6. Each man will take with him one blanket to the t renches.

The remainder will rolled in to bundles of 10, lab elled and taken by rail to the point where the HALLEBAST line meets the road to be ready for collection by Transport at 2 pm.

Officers valises and other boxes that are beingreturn ed to the Transport Lines will be at the same place at the same hour.

7. O.C.Companies will make their own arrangements for taking trench bundles, mess boxes, cooking utensils etc. to the trenches.

8. Rations will be brought up to LA BRASSERIE as usual when the Bat talion is in the line.

9. Completion of relief will be wired to the Bn.O.R. as follows:-

"[redacted]" (time).

'TINA'

(sgd) A. T. Mackay,
Lieut. & Adjutant,
26th. Royal Fusiliers.

3/3/17.

Copy No. 1 Filed.
2 124t h. Infantry Brigade.
3 Adjutant,
4 21st. K.R.R.C.
5 O.C."A" Coy.
6 O.C."B" "
7 O.C."C" "
8 O.C."D" "
9 O.C.Headquarters & Signalling Officer.
10 Transport Officer & Quartermaster.
11 Lewis Gun Officer & Bombing Officer.
12 Intelligence & Sniping Officer.

SECRET. Copy No. 11.

# 26th. BN. ROYAL FUSILIERS.

## Operation Order No. [illegible].

---

1. The Battalion will be relieved in the line tomorrow 12/3/17 by the 21st. Bn.K.R.R.C., relief tocommence at 9 pm.
2. Order of relief, times at which relieving sections and Companies will be at LA BRASSERIE and routes to be taken will be as follws:-
   Lewis Gunners, Snipers and C.S.Ms 11 am.
   Redoubts 1.30 pm. Chicory Lane.
   Front Line 2.0 pm. 2 Platoons Chicory Lane, 2 Platoons F & C.
   Reserve Line 2.30 pm. 2 " " " 2 " " "
   SleepyHollow 3.0 pm. Chicory Lane.
   Headquarters 3.30 pm.
3. Companies and Specialists will occupy the same billets as when the Battalion was last at LA CLYTTE.
4. O.C.Companies will have complete lists of trench stores ready for the incoming unit and the signed portion will be rendered to Bn.O.R. immediately on arrival at LA CLYTTE.
   Alist of the the stores to be handed over will be rendered to the Bn.O.R. by 9 am. tomorrow morning.
5. O.C.Companies are responsible thatthe dugouts and latrines are left scrupulously clean.
6. Tables of "work done" and "work in hand and proposed" should be made out and handed over for the information of the incoming unit.
7. The Intelligence Officer will arrange to provide the Intelligence Officer of the incoming unit with a copy of his reports for the past week and give him all possible information.
8. All trench bundles, cooking utensils etc. will be taken to the junction of the Hallebast Rail with the road by 1.30 pm. ready for collection by the Transport.
9. The Transport Officer will arrange to have Officers kits, blankets etc. taken to MURRUMBIDGEE CAMP.
   Officers horses to be at the junction of the cross roads one hour later than times mentioned in para. 2.
10. Completion of relief will be wired to Bn.O.R. as follows :-

"CARROTS". (time).

(sgd) A.W.Mackay,
Lieut. & Adjutant,
26th. Royal Fusiliers.

11/3/17.

Copy No. 1 Filed.
2 124th. Infantry Brigade.
3 Adjutant.
4 21st. Bn.K.R.R.C.
5 O.C."A"Coy.
6 O.C."B" "
7 O.C."C" "
8 O.C."D" "
9 O.C.Headquarters & Signalling Officer.
10. Transport Officer & Quar termaster.
11 Lewis Gun Officer & Bombing Officer.
12 Intelligence & Sniping Officer.

SECRET. Copy No. 12.

# 26th. BN. ROYAL FUSILIERS.

## Operation Order No. 40.

1. The Battalion will relieve the 21st. Bn. K.R.R.C. in the line tomorrow 18/3/17, relief to commence at 10 am.
2. Order of relief, times at which relieving sections and Companies will be at LA BRASSERIE and routes to be taken will be as follows:-

Snipers, Lewis Gunners and C.S.Ms 9 am.
Redoubts 9.30 am. Chicory Lane.
Front Line 10.0 am. 2 Platoons Chicory Lane and 2 Platoons P & O
Reserve Line 10.30 am. P & O Trench.
Sleepy Hollow. 11.0 am. Chicory Lane.
Headquarters 10.30 am.

3. Companies will be disposed as follows :-

"A" Coy. Redoubts.
"B" " Front Line.
"C" " Reserve Line.
"D" " Sleepy Hollow.

4. Each man will take one blanket to the trenches. The remaining blankets will be rolled into bundles of 10, tallied and stacked outside Bn.O.R. by 7.30 am. Also Officers valises and boxes that are being returned to the Transport Lines.

Officers trench bundles, boxes, cooking utensils etc. will be stacked outside Bn.O.R. by 7.30 am. for collection by Transport.

The Transport Officer will arrange to have horses at the Camp two hours before times mentioned in para. 2.

5. O.C.Companies will be responsible that the camp and huts are left scrupulously clean.
6. O.C.Companies will render to Bn.O.R. immediately on taking over signed list of trench stores.
7. Rations will be at LA BRASSERIE as usual when the Battalion is in the line.
8. Completion of relief will be wired to Bn.O.R. as follows :-

"FINE" (time).

(sgd) A.W.Mackay,
Lieut. & Adjutant.
26th. Royal Fusiliers

17/3/17.

Copy No. 1 Filed.
2 124th. Infantry Brigade.
3 Adjutant.
4 21st. Bn.K.R.R.C.
5 O.C."A"Coy.
O.C."B" "
7 O.C."C" "
8 O.C."D" "
9 O.C.Headquarters and Signalling Officer.
10 Transport Officer & Quartermaster.
11 Lewis Gun Officer & Bombing Officer.
12 Intelligence & Sniping Officer.

SECRET.

Copy No..../...

26th. BN. ROYAL FUSILIERS.

Preliminary Operation Order No. 41.

1. The 124th. Infantry Brigade will be relieved byth 57th. Infantry Brigade on 21/22 nd. instant, relief to be completed by midnight 22/23rd. instant.

2. The Battalion will be relieved by the 8th. BN. NORTH STAFFORDSHIRE REGIMENT on the 22nd.instant, relief to commence at 9 am. Detailed orders will be sent later. On completion of relief the Battalion will proceed to RIDGEWOOD.

3. The Battalion will be relieved at RIDGEWOOD by the 10 th. BN. WORCESTER REGIMENT, relief to commence at 1 pm. On completion of relief the Battalion will assemble at HALLEBAST CORNER where lorries will be waiting to take the Battalion to the training area at STEENVOORDE.

4. The Transport will move on the same day as the Battalion is relieved so as to arrive at STEENVOORDE training area before the Battalion.

The Transport Officer will arrange to leave a small guard to take charge of and hand over the Transport Lines to the incoming unit.

5. Battalion and Company Commanders of the 8th. Bn. North Staffordshire Regiment will visit the trenches on the 20th. inst. A guide from each Company will report to Battalion Headquarters at a time to be notified later, in order to direct the incoming Company Commanders to the respective Company Headquarters.

6. All information likely to be of assistance to the incoming unit must be handed over including all maps in possession. Carefully prepared inventories of trench stores to be made out; a copy of these must be sent to the Battalion Orderly Room by noon 21st. instant.

Deficiencies in establishments of S.A.A., Grenades, Very lights, Iron Rations and Water must be reported immediately in order that indents can be submitted to complete.

Log Books must be written up to date.

The system of "Work done" and "Work in hand and proposed" to be ~~fu~~ fully explained to the incoming unit.

7. Attention is again drawn to the necessity of keeping the trenches thoroughly c lean and in good order during the next two or three days, vide this office letter No.376 of yesterday's date.

8. Acknowledge by wire as follows :-

"O.O.4 1 O.K."

(sgd) A.W.Mackay,
Lieut. & Adjutant,
26th. Royal Fusiliers.

19/3/17.

Copy No. 1 Filed.
2 Adjutant,
3 1 24th. Infantry Brigade.
4 O.C."A" Coy.
5 O.C."B" "
6 O.C."C" "
7 O.C."D" "
8 O.C.Headquarters and Signalling Officer.
9 Transport Officer.

SECRET. Copy No. 2

## 26th. BN. ROYAL FUSILIERS.

### Operati on Order No. 42.

1. The Battalion will be relieved in the line by The 8th. Bn. North Staffordshir Regt. on Thursday 22nd. instant, relief to commenece at 9 am.

2. The following are particulars of relief, times at which Companies will be at LA BRASSERIE and routes to be taken :-

(a) "C" Coy. NORTH STAFFORDSHIRE REGT. will relieve "A" Coy. in the REDOUBTS ( S.P.7, Eastern, Western and Southern Redoubts, 1 Platoon in each).
Company to be at LA BRASSERIE at 8.30 am.
Route - M & N Trench and Chicory Lane.

(b) "A" Coy. N.S.R. will relieve "B" Coy. in the FRONT LINE.
Company to be at LA BRASSERIE at 9 am.
Route - 2 Platoons vi a F & O Trench and 2 Platoons via Chicory.

(c) "B" Coy. N.S.R. will relieve "C" Coy. in the NEW RESERVE LINE.
Company to be at LA BRASSERIE at 9.15 am.
Route - F & O Trench.

(d) "D" Coy. N.S.R. will relieve "D" Coy. at SLEEPY HOLLOW.
Company to be at LA BRASSERIE at 9.30 am.
~~(e)~~Route - M & N Trench.

(e) Headquarters at 9.30 am.

3. O.C.Companies will arrange for 1 guide per Platoon to be at LA BRASSERIE at the hours above mentioned to guide the incoming Platoons. Each guide is to be given full and clear written instructions so as to avoid any mistakes.

4. Signallers, Lewis Gunners, Snipers and Observers of the incoming Unit will be at LA BRASSERIE at 8 am. where guides will be provided to guide them to our Signal Stations, Lewis Gun positions and Snipers' Posts respectively.

5. O.C.Companies will make it their special duty to see that the trenches, dugouts are left scrupulously clean and also that all latrine buckets are emptied.

6. All maps, documents, Log Books and any other articles which will prove to be of assistance to the incoming Unit are to be handed over and receipts obtained.

O.C.Companies, Platoon Commanders, Lewis Gunners, Snipers and Observers will furnish the incoming Unit with all possible information regarding our own line and the enemys.

7. Trench Stores should as far as possible be collected together in the respective Company Dumps and handed over.

Complete lists of Trench Stores will be made out on A.F.3405 1 copy of which will be retained by Companies and the other handed over to the relieving Company.

A complete list of Trench Stores to be handed over will be rendered to Bn. O. R. by 12 noon tomorrow 21st. instant.

8. In order to facilitate Transport, Officers kits and surplus stores which are to be t aken out of the line should be reduced as far as possible and dumped by Companies at LA BRASSERIE before 5 pm. on the 21st. instant.

Each Company will detail one man to hand over these stores to the C.Q.M.Ss and they will be despatched by the empty ration limbers returning on the night of the 21st.

Only the stores actually required for the 22nd. should be left in the line on the night of the 21st.

All remaining Trench Bundles, Cooking Utensils, Dixies etc. must be at the railhead dump by 8 am. prompt on the 22nd. instant where Transport will be waiting to remove same.

9. O.C.Companies are requested to see that all receptacles for water are handed over full and that as much fuel as possible should be left in the trenches for the incoming Unit.

10. Completion of relief will be wired to BN.O.R. as follows :-
"42 O.K. (time)".

11. Acknowledge.

(sgd) A.W.Mackay,
Lieut. & Adjutant,
26th. Royal Fusiliers.

20/3/17.

SECRET. Copy No. 11

**10th. BN. ROYAL FUSILIERS.**

Operatio n Order No.43.

---

1. Upon completion of Operation Order No.42 the Battalion will proceed to RIDGEWOOD and occupy the same billets as usual.
   C.C.Companies will report to the Bn. H.Q. when ~~all~~ their Companies are all present.
2. The Battalion will be relieved in RIDGEWOOD on the 22nd. inst. by the 10th. BN. WORCESTER REGIMENT, relief to commence at 1 pm
3. C.O.Headquarters and C.C.Companies will detail [illegible] guide each to be at HALLEBAST CORNER at 1 .15 pm. on the 22nd. inst. to guide the incoming Headquarters and Companies respectively to the Headquarter and Company Billets at RIDGEWOOD.
4. C.C.Companies will make it their special duty to see that during the short stay in RIDGEWOOD dugouts and surroundings, latrines and urinals are kept in a scrupulously clean condition.
5. All information as to the source of Water, Bomb and S.A.A. Stores, Gas Alarm appliances should be given to the incoming Unit.
6. Receipts for Stores handed over should be obtained; a duplicate of which will be sent to the Bn.O.R. in RIDGEWOOD.
7. Completion of relief will be reported to the Battalion Orderly Room in RIDGEWOOD.
8. On comple tion of relief Companies will proceed, on instructions from the Bn.O.R., to HALLEBAST CORNER where Motor Lorries will be waiting to convey them to STEENVOORDE.
   C.C.Companies are reminded that all movements east of the LA CLYTTE - DICKEBUSCH Road must be by Sections of 100 yards interval.
9. __RATIONS.__ The only rations that will be brought up to LA BRASSERIE tonight will be the ordinary Breakfast Ration for the morning of the 22nd. inst. and haversack rations consisting of - Preserved Meat, Cheese and Biscuits.
   Arrangements have been made for each man to be provided with a hot cup of Cocoa, Tea or Coffee at the Y.M.C.A. Hut RIDGEWOOD and Companies will parade at the Y.M.C.A. at the following hours :-

"A" Coy. 11.15 am.
"B" " 11.45 am.
"C" " 12.15 pm.
"D" " 12.45 pm.
Headquarters 1.15 pm.

   C.C.Companies will arrange this by Platoons.
   The remainder of tomorrows rations will be carried by Transport to STEENVOORDE where a hot meal will be prepared before the arrival of the Battalion.
10. 1 cook from Headquarters and [illegible] cooks per Company are to be sent to the Transport Lines with the ration limbers tonight and they will proceed to STEENVOORDE with the Transport tomorrow morning and prepare the hot meal. The remainder of the cooks will proceed direct to the Transport Lines on relief from the line and will be conveyed to STEENVOORDE by lorries at [illegible] pm.
11. Lorries are allotted as follows :-

| | |
|---|---|
| Officer s | 1 |
| Headquarters | [illegible] |
| Companies | [illegible] per Company |
| Spare | [illegible] |

each lorry carries [illegible] men with equipment.
   Lewis Gun Hand Carts will be loaded on the Company and Spare lorries.
12. On arrival at STEENVOORDE the billeting ~~parties~~ representatives at present there, will meet and guide their respective Companies to their billets.
13. Details left behind at the Transport Lines, *adjacent* will assemble at Headquarters, [illegible] CAMP at [illegible] pm. on 22nd. inst.
   The Transport Officer will detail 1 man to take charge of each lorry containing baggage with written instructions as to his destination.
14. C.C.Companies will see that all Water Bottles are filled before the Battalion leaves RIDGEWOOD.

15 *Acknowledge*

(sgd) A.P.Mackay. . . . .

*File*

SECRET
41ST DIVISIONAL FRONT
LEFT SECTOR
SCALE 1:10.000
Northern Boundary
King's Way
Voormezeele
Batn. H.Q.
Comp. H.Q.
Compy. H.Q.
Lane
late Voormezeele
Ex.th
OLD FRENCH TRENCH
White Horse Cellars
St. Eloi
Battn. Boundary
32
33
41ST DIVISION
30-3-17

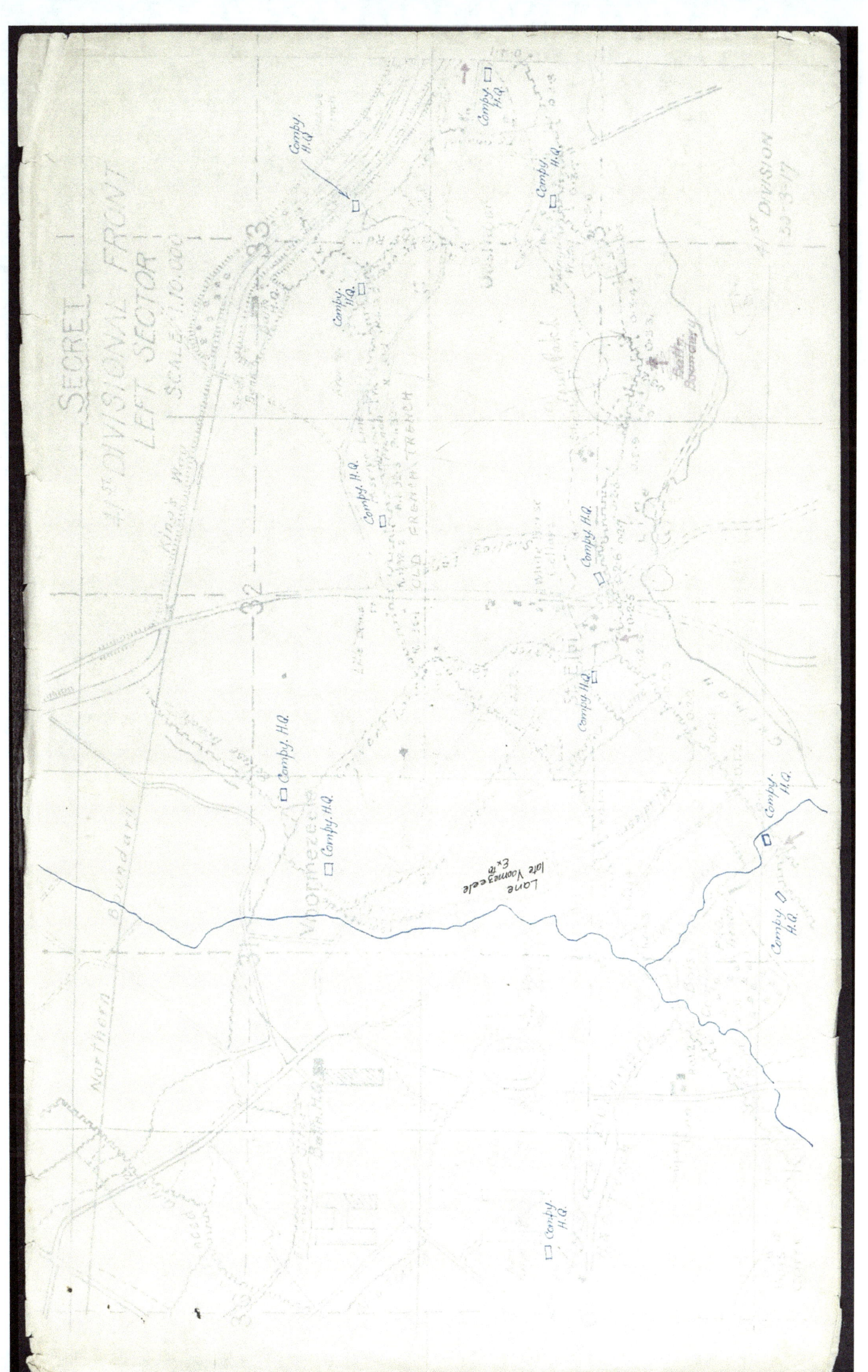

26th Royal Fusiliers

Instructions regarding War Diaries and Intelligence Summaries are contained in F. S. Regs., Part II. and the Staff Manual respectively. Title Pages will be prepared in manuscript.

# WAR DIARY

~~or~~

~~INTELLIGENCE SUMMARY~~

(Erase heading not required.)

Army Form C. 2118

26 R Fus Vol 12

Apr 17

| Place | Date | Hour | Summary of Events and Information | Remarks and references to Appendices |
|---|---|---|---|---|
| STEENVOORDE | 1/4/17 | | The Battalion had been taken in lorries to and billeted in the village of Steenvoorde on 25/3/17 and Battalion training was carried out. A Horswell Capt | |
| – do – | 2/4/17 | | Battalion training was carried out. A Horswell Capt | |
| | 3/4/17 | | The Battalion took part in a Brigade attack over taped trenches, the objective of the Battalion being the first system of trenches. Following our attack the 21st K.R.R.C. passed through our lines to attack the second system of trenches. A Horswell Capt | |
| – do – | 4/4/17 | | The same operations were carried out as on the 3rd inst. A Horswell Capt | |
| – do – | 5/4/17 | | These operations were again repeated. A Horswell Capt | |
| | | | During our rest at Steenvoorde the Battalion was innoculated against typhoid. A Horswell Capt | |

12.K (16 sheets)

1875 Wt. W593/826 1,000,000 4/15 J.B.C. & A. A.D.S.S./Forms/C. 2118.

26th Royal Fusiliers

# WAR DIARY

~~or INTELLIGENCE SUMMARY~~

(Erase heading not required.)

April 1917.

Army Form C. 2118

Instructions regarding War Diaries and Intelligence Summaries are contained in F. S. Regs., Part II. and the Staff Manual respectively. Title Pages will be prepared in manuscript.

| Place | Date | Hour | Summary of Events and Information | Remarks and references to Appendices |
| --- | --- | --- | --- | --- |
| Steenvoorde | 4/4/17 | 9.45 am | The Battalion marched from Steenvoorde to Alberta Camp Reninghelst on 6th April 1917. Dinners were cooked on the march and were served out on arrival at Reninghelst. Route taken Steenvoorde – Abeele – Reninghelst | Reference O.O. No1. A Maxwell Capt |
| Reninghelst | 11/4/17 | | The Battn provided the Guard of Honour on the occasion of the visit of H.M. the Queen of the Belgians. The Queen of the Belgians regretted she was unable to inspect the Guard owing to the weather. The appearance of the men evoking her further admiration of the British Army an admiration which was strongly felt by the King of the Belgians [illegible]. The Divisional and Brigadier Generals expressed their pleasure with the very smart Guard of Honour, the turnout handling of arms and general soldierlike appearance could not have been better, showing a very [illegible] state of efficiency in this Battalion. The Band was in attendance and played the Belgian National Anthem. | Reference letter [illegible] |
| TRENCHES ST ELOI SHEET 28 S.W. SQUARE O.2 | 21/4/17 | 8.30 am | The Battalion relieved the 15th H.L.I. (?) in the line. The Companies were disposed as follows:- | A Maxwell Capt. O.O. No2. |
| | | | "A" Company Right of Old French Trench | Note: This relief took place by day beginning at 8/30 am & was complete by 2/30 pm. Casualty 1 OR |
| | | | "B" " 2 Platoons in Voormezeele Switch | |
| | | | 2 " " Eclusé Trench | |
| | | | "C" " Front Line (Trenches O.2.5 to ~~O.2.5~~ O.2.8. | Vide attached map [illegible] of Batt Sector [illegible] |
| | | | "D" " 3 Platoons on Left of Old French Trench | |
| | | | 1 Platoon in Bluff Patch with 2 additional Lewis Guns from "B" Co. (Trenches O.3.1/O.3.2/O.3.3) | |

1875 Wt. W593/826 1,000,000 4/15 J.B.C. & A. A.D.S.S./Forms/C. 2118.

(3) 26th Royal Fusiliers

Instructions regarding War Diaries and Intelligence Summaries are contained in F. S. Regs., Part II. and the Staff Manual respectively. Title Pages will be prepared in manuscript.

# WAR DIARY
*or*
~~INTELLIGENCE SUMMARY~~
*(Erase heading not required.)*

Army Form C. 2118

April 1917.

| Place | Date | Hour | Summary of Events and Information | Remarks and references to Appendices |
|---|---|---|---|---|
| Trenches ST ELOI | 15/4/17 | 9 am | On the 15th there was an inter-change of Companies A Co. went up in the front line to Company taking the Right of Old French Trench. During this time it rained & snowed incessantly. The trenches are in a very bad state. Large fighting patrols were sent out but no encounter took place. Sniping was very prevalent when we first entered the trenches but this was considerably abated by the time we left. During this tour large working parties were provided nightly & the trenches were greatly improved before the Battalion was relieved. During this tour total casualties amounted to 1 OR killed & 4 OR wounded. 1 Officer wounded Captain W. F. MACDONALD 2nd in Command. A Maxwell Capt | |
| Trenches ST ELOI | 18/4/17 | 8.30 am | The Battalion was relieved in the line today (Bn) by the 15th Bn. Hampshire Regt and proceeded to Alberta Camp Reninghelst. All maps, aeroplane photographs, defence schemes, trench stores & dumps were taken over by the relieving Battalion. Hot tea was served out to all parties at Hallebast Corner. A Maxwell Capt | Ref. Battalion Orders No. 3. |
| Reninghelst | 18/4/17 to 22/4/17 | [illegible] | ~~[illegible]~~ YMCA Reninghelst ~~[illegible]~~ A Maxwell Capt | |

1875 Wt. W593/826 1,000,000 4/15 J.B.C. & A. A.D.S.S./Forms/C. 2118.

(14) 26th Royal Fusiliers

Instructions regarding War Diaries and Intelligence Summaries are contained in F. S. Regs., Part II. and the Staff Manual respectively. Title Pages will be prepared in manuscript.

# WAR DIARY
or
~~INTELLIGENCE SUMMARY~~
*(Erase heading not required.)*

Army Form C. 2118

April 1917.

| Place | Date | Hour | Summary of Events and Information | Remarks and references to Appendices |
|---|---|---|---|---|
| Alberta Camp Reninghelst | 23/4/17 | 8.30 am | The Battalion relieved the 10th Hants in the line on the 23rd the relief being duly completed at 1.30 pm. The distribution of the Companies was as follows:- "A" Co. Reserve line (Voormezeele Switch); "B" " Right of Old French Trench; "C" " Left of Old French Trench; "D" " Front line. } Distribution as on 12/4/17 | Reference O.O. No 4 |
| | | | The day was very suitable for observation and our aeroplanes were very active. Enemy shelling continued during the day which was very effectively replied to by our Artillery. The night passed fairly quietly. Working parties were supplied for [illegible] the trenches also for the usual R.E. fatigues. | |
| St Eloi | [illegible] | | [illegible] fairly heavy shelling by the enemy. About 150 rounds were fired falling mostly to the right of the Batn. No casualties [illegible] out of action. A patrol went out [illegible] in front of trenches [illegible]. Enemy [illegible] apparently lightly held. | Artillery [illegible] |
| | [illegible] | | [illegible] throughout the day [illegible] was heavily shelled. The [illegible] were [illegible] the [illegible]. Observation was very good throughout the day. At 7.30 pm [illegible] enemy aeroplanes were over our lines [illegible] by [illegible] and driven back. | |

1875 Wt. W593/826 1,000,000 4/15 J.B.C. & A. A.D.S.S./Forms/C. 2118.

(5) 26th Royal Fusiliers

Instructions regarding War Diaries and Intelligence Summaries are contained in F. S. Regs., Part II. and the Staff Manual respectively. Title Pages will be prepared in manuscript.

# WAR DIARY
or
# ~~INTELLIGENCE SUMMARY~~
*(Erase heading not required.)*

April 1917

Army Form C. 2118

| Place | Date | Hour | Summary of Events and Information | Remarks and references to Appendices |
|---|---|---|---|---|
| TRENCHES ST. ELOI | 26/4/17 | | Hostile artillery was fairly active during the day. Voormezeele, Dickebusch and Café Belge all received attention. At 3.30 am the enemy shelled our front + support lines near the Craters. Our artillery retaliated on the enemy's front and support lines. The day was very good for observation and our aeroplanes were very active. The [illegible] patrol was sent out to gain further information regarding the enemy Crater and saps and found them both unoccupied. Enemy wire in very poor condition. Working parties were supplied to repair trenches, the R.E. fatigue parties were also found. The night was very quiet. A Maxwell Capt | Intelligence Summary No. 185 |
| — do — | 27/4/17 | 9 a.m. | On the 27th an interchange of Companies took place "B" Company relieving "D" Company in the front line. "D" Company occupying the Right of Old French Trench. A Maxwell Capt. Patrols were sent out but no enemy encounters took place. The night was very quiet. A Maxwell Capt | |
| — do — | 28/4/17 | | The day was very good for observation and aeroplanes were very active on both sides. Hostile artillery was fairly active which was effectively replied to by our artillery. The usual working parties and R.E. fatigue parties were found. Patrols were sent out but no enemy encounters took place. The night was very quiet. A Maxwell Capt | |
| — do — | 29/4/17 | | Hostile artillery was quiet during the day apart from the usual attention paid to Voormezeele, Scottish Wood, Café Belge. Fighting patrols were sent out & thoroughly explored No Man's Land without encountering any hostile parties. The night was very quiet. Two enemy planes were seen to drop | |

1875 Wt. W593/826 1,000,000 4/15 J.B.C. & A. A.D.S.S./Forms/C. 2118.

(6) 2/6th Royal Fusiliers

Instructions regarding War Diaries and Intelligence Summaries are contained in F. S. Regs., Part II. and the Staff Manual respectively. Title Pages will be prepared in manuscript.

# WAR DIARY

~~or~~

~~INTELLIGENCE SUMMARY~~

(Erase heading not required.)

April 1917.

Army Form C. 2118

| Place | Date | Hour | Summary of Events and Information | Remarks and references to Appendices |
|---|---|---|---|---|
| TRENCHES ST. ELOI | 29/4/17 | | in the rear of enemy's lines apparently out of control after being fired on by A.A. Guns. Patrols were sent out but no enemy encounter took place. The usual working parties were found. A Maxwell [illegible] | |
| — do — | 30/4/17 | | The day was very good for observation & our aeroplanes were very active. Hostile artillery has been fairly active in the vicinity of Lockhart Wood [illegible] & Dickebusch. | |
| | | 6-0 pm | A small camouflet was blown in our front today by our Miners, no activity followed. The enemy during the night was exceptionally quiet. Large patrols were sent out but no enemy patrols were encountered. | |

A Maxwell [illegible]

George Gwyn-Thomas [illegible]
[illegible] 2/6th Royal Fusiliers

[illegible]

1875 Wt. W593/826 1,000,000 4/15 J.B.C. & A. A.D.S.S./Forms/C. 2118.

26th Royal Fusiliers

Instructions regarding War Diaries and Intelligence Summaries are contained in F. S. Regs., Part II. and the Staff Manual respectively. Title Pages will be prepared in manuscript.

# WAR DIARY
~~or~~
~~INTELLIGENCE~~ SUMMARY
*(Erase heading not required.)*

April 1917.

Army Form C. 2118

| Place | Date | Hour | Summary of Events and Information | Remarks and references to Appendices |
|---|---|---|---|---|
| | | | Casualties for month :- | |
| | | | 1 Killed 15th inst | |
| | | | 1 do 26th | |
| | | | 1 Wounded 12th | |
| | | | 1 do 15th | |
| | | | 1 Officers do 14th | |
| | | | 1 Or. Rank do 17th | |
| | | | 1 " 24th | |
| | | | 1 Died of Wounds 24th | |
| | | | 2 Wounded 24th | |
| | | | 1 do 25th | |
| | | | 1 Officer accidently wounded 29th | |
| | | | 1 Or Rank 30th | |
| | | | Summary | |
| | | | 1 Officer wounded | |
| | | | 1 do accidently wounded | |
| | | | 2 Other Ranks Killed | |
| | | | 1 Died of Wounds | |
| | | | 8 Wounded. | |

1875 Wt. W593/826 1,000,000 4/15 J.B.C. & A. A.D.S.S./Forms/C. 2118.

26th Royal Fusiliers

Instructions regarding War Diaries and Intelligence Summaries are contained in F. S. Regs., Part II. and the Staff Manual respectively. Title Pages will be prepared in manuscript.

# WAR DIARY
~~or~~
~~INTELLIGENCE SUMMARY~~
*(Erase heading not required.)*

April 1917.

Army Form C. 2118

| Place | Date | Hour | Summary of Events and Information | Remarks and references to Appendices |
|---|---|---|---|---|
| | | | List of Officers at present with the Battalion 30/4/17:– | |
| | | | Colonel | |
| | | | Captain Maxwell | |
| | | | Lieut Mackay | |
| | | | Lieut Backworth | |
| | | | 2/Lieut Pemberton | |
| | | | " Gill | |
| | | | Captain Ovey | |
| | | | 2/Lieut Mason | |
| | | | Lieut Blount | |
| | | | 2/Lieut Pagebrown | |
| | | | Lieut Meinders | |
| | | | " Firth | |
| | | | 2/Lieut Addel | |
| | | | " Denny | |
| | | | Lieut Bach | |
| | | | 2/Lieut Bradford | |
| | | | " Corben | |
| | | | Lieut Biggins | |
| | | | RSM Barnett | |

1875 Wt. W593/826 1,000,000 4/15 J.B.C. & A. A.D.S.S./Forms/C. 2118.

SECRET. COPY NO...... .

# ROYAL FUSILIERS.

## OPERATION ORDER No. 1

1. The Battalion will march to RENINGHELST, distance 10 miles, on Friday, 6th April, 1917, in accordance with attached march table. On arrival it will be accommodated in the ONTARIO GROUP of Huts.

2. The First Line Transport will move with the Battalion, and will return the same day to STEENVOORDE for the men's blankets. Baggage Waggons will be at the Transport Lines tomorrow night.

3. The Billeting Officer (2nd Lt. L. G. Muller) 1 N.C.O. per Company, 1 N.C.O. for Headquarters, and 1 N.C.O. for Quartermasters Stores and Transport, will report, with bicycles, at 124th Infantry Brigade Headquarters at 10 am tomorrow 5/4/17.

4. All Officers Valises, mess boxes and Orderly Room Boxes will be stacked outside the various Headquarters by 6.30.a.m. on 6/4/17, when they will be collected by the Transport.
The mens blankets will be rolled into bundles of 10, and stacked in the same place under a guard of 1 N.C.O. and 3 men

5. O/C Companies will be held responsible that all billets are left in a perfectly clean and sanitary condition, and all latrines filled in.

6. All waterbottles will be filled on the night of [illegible]/4/17.

7. Dinners will be cooked on the march to be ready on arrival at RENINGHELST.

(Sgd) C. L. Mumdey
Lt. &. A/Adjutant.
26th Bn. Royal Fusiliers.

## MARCH TABLE.

| Unit. | Starting Point. | | Time. | Route. | Remarks. |
|---|---|---|---|---|---|
| Band. | K.31.d.4.4½ "D" Coy Billets. | 9·40 | 9.40.a.m. | STeenvoorde Church-Abeele | |
| Headquarters | do. | | 9.43.a.m. | Station- | |
| "D" | do. | 9·41m | 9.46.a.m. | Reninghelst. | |
| "B" | do. | 9·42m | 9.49.a.m. | do. | |
| "C" | do. | 9·43m | 9.52 a.m. | do. | |
| "A" | do. | 9·44m | 9.55 a.m. | do. | |
| Transport | | 9·45m | | | |

1. File.
2. 124th Infantry Brigade.
3. Adjutant
4. O/C "A" Coy.
5. O/C "B" COY
6. O/C "C" Coy.
7. O/C "D" Coy.
8. O/C Headquarters.
9. Transport Officer & Quartermaster.
10. L. G. O. and Bombing Officer.
11. Sniping & Intelligence Officer.

SECRET.                                                                 Copy No....

ROYAL FUSILIERS.

Operation Order No. 2.

---

1. The Battalion will relieve the 10th. Bn. K.R.R.C. in the line tomorrow 12/4/17, the leading platoon to pass DICKEBUSCH at [illegible] am.

2. Companies will be disposed as follows :-

| | |
|---|---|
| "A" Company | Right of OLD FRENCH TRENCH. |
| "B" " | 2 Platoons in VOORMEZEELE SWITCH |
| | 2 Platoons in [illegible] |
| "C" " | FRONT LINE. |
| "D" " | 3 Platoons on left of OLD FRENCH TRENCH |
| | 1 Platoon in RED PATCH with 4 additional Lewis Guns from "B" Company. |

3. Order of relief and times at which leading Platoon is to pass DICKEBUSCH is as follows :-

| | |
|---|---|
| C.S.M's and Drivers | [illegible].30 am. |
| "C" Company | [illegible].30 am. |
| "D" " | [illegible].30 am. |
| "A" " | 10.30 am. |
| "B" " | 11.40 am. |
| Headquarters | 11.[illegible] am. |

All movements between [illegible] and DICKEBUSCH will be by Platoons at 100 yards interval, and East of DICKEBUSCH by sections at 100 yards interval.

4. Each man will take one blanket to the trenches on his pack. The remainder will be rolled in bundles of 10 tied with wire and labelled; these, together with all cooking utensils and kit that is not being taken to the trenches, will be collected by C.Q.M.Ss before 8.30 am. 12/4/17 close to Company Store Rooms. Orders as to disposal will be given to C.Q.M.S. of each Company.

Headquarters will be stacked with their Companies.

5. One limber per Company will be at Bn. H.Q. at 5 pm tonight for the transport of Lewis Guns. These limbers will be loaded immediately with Lewis Guns and ammunition and sent to the Transport Lines with one Lewis Gunner in charge of each limber. These limbers will proceed to VOORMEZEELE tonight.

Officers trench bundles, cooking utensils, mess boxes and Orderly Room boxes that are to go to the trenches willbe stacked outside B. O.R. before [illegible].30 am. tomorrow 12/4/17 when they will be conveyed to the Transport Lines and proceed to the Trenches with the rations at night. These stores together with rations will reach the trenches about midnight and O.C.Companies will arrange to have their parties of 10 at Bn. H.Q. when notified to collect their respective stores. "B"Company will arrange for "A" Company's carrying party.

6. O.C.Companies are responsible that the Camp is left in a perfectly clean and sanitary condition, and all latrine buckets emptied.

7. Trench maps and all documents relating to the line will be taken over on relief.

8. Complete lists of trench stores taken over will be sent to the Bn.O.R. immediately after taking over.

9. Companies are reminded that the minimum amount of material should be taken on account of the difficultyof taking it up the line.

10. Completion of relief will be wired to Bn. O.R. as follows :- "JAM" (time).

(sgd ) C.L.Munday,
Lieut. & A/Adjutant,
Royal Fusiliers.

11/4/17.

| | | | |
|---|---|---|---|
| Copy No. | 1 Filed | No. 2 | 124th. Infantry Brigade. |
| | 3 Adjutant. | 4 | O.C."A" Coy. |
| | 5 O.C."B"Coy. | 6 | O.C."C" " |
| | 7 O.C."D" " | 8 | O.C. Headquarters. |
| | 9 Transport Officer. | 10 | Lewis Gun Officer. |
| | 11 Intelligence Officer | 12 | Spare. |

SECRET.

Copy No.......2

26th Bn. Royal Fusiliers.
Operation Order No. [illegible].

---

1. All Companies.

The Battalion will proceed by march route tomorrow afternoon, and will billet for the night May 31st/June 1st at ARNEKE. The Billeting Party will meet the Battalion, and conduct Companies to their Billets.

The Battalion will entrain at ARNEKE on 1st June at such hour as will enable trains to leave ARNEKE by 8.5.a.m.; details as to time of parade will be notified later. The Battalion will detrain at POPERINGHE Station, and proceed by march route to MICMAC Camp (Norrth).

2. All Companies.

Companies will parade, and the head of the column will pass the starting point (Q.11.c.5.2. Entrance to French Hospital) at [illegible].40.p.m.

Order of March:- Headquarters C, B, A, D.

Dress:- Full Marching Order.

Teas will be served on route during the march.

3. Sanitation.

All Billets will be left thoroughly clean, and all latrine buckets emptied.

4. Transport.

The Transport (less Officers Horses, Mess Cart, Cookers, and Water Carts) will leave MOULLE at 10.a.m. and proceed to Brigade Headquarters, GANSPETTE, and will move off under the orders o the Brigade Transport Officer.

If will halt for the night May 31st/June 1st at NOORDPEENE. The Horses and Vehicles accompanying the Battalion to ARNEKE must be sent back to rejoin the Transport on the evening of the 31st May.

All Officers kits, baggage, surplus kit etc. must be dumped at the various Company Headquarters by 8.30.a.m. tomorrow morning. The Transport Officer will arrange to send Transport to collect same at that hour.

One lorry will be placed at the disposal of the Battalion which will take any surplus kit for which there is no room on the Transport.

Mess Boxes will be carried on the Mess Cart.

5. Rations.

Rations will be drawn from WATTEN for the last time on the 31st May, and from OUDERDOM for the first time on 1st June.

Transport marching by road on the 31st May will carry rations for consumption on that day on the man and horse, and will draw rations for consumption on the 1st June at GANSPETTE.

ACKNOWLEDGE.

(Sgd) A. [illegible]. MACKAY.
LT. & Adj.

Copy No.1. File.
2. War Diary.
3. Adjutant.
4. O/C "A"
5. "B"
6 "C"

Copy No. 7. O/C "D"
8. Headquarters
9. Medical Off.
10. Transport
11. Quartermaster
12. 124th I. B.

[illegible]

April 13th 19[illegible]

My dear Clemson.

Would you please let the O.C. 26th Royal Fusiliers know [illegible] pleased I [illegible] with the very smart Guard of Honour provided by his Battalion on the occasion of the visit of H.M. the Queen of the Belgians. The turn out, handling of arms and general soldierlike appearance could not have been better, [illegible] a very high state of efficiency in that Battalion, which you may well be proud of.

I have been so busy the last 2 days so had not time to write before.

Yours

Sgd. [illegible] Lawford

13th April

Dear [illegible] Thomas

I am very pleased to send you the enclosed letter and to say that I think your men thoroughly deserve to get it - they were splendid. My best congratulations to you all.

Yours sincerely

Sgd. M. F. Clemson

April 4th

Headquarters

41st Division

B.E.F.

My dear Clemson,

The Queen of the Belgians wishes me to convey to the Officer Commanding the Guard of Honour her regret that she was unable to inspect the Guard owing to the weather. The appearance of the men only [illegible] further [illegible] of the [illegible] [illegible] [illegible] which [illegible] [illegible] [illegible] as well.

Yours

Sgd. [illegible] Lawford

SECRET. Copy No. 13

Roal Fsiliers.

## Operation Order No.3.

1. The Batalion will be relievad in th line tomorrow 18/4/17 by the 15th. Battn. Hampshire Regt. and proceed to ALBERTA CAMP the leading platoon will be at DICKEBUSCH at 8. 30 am.
2. Order of relief and times at which relieving companies etc. will arrive at Dickebusch will be as follows :-

| | |
|---|---|
| Snipers and Lewis Guners | 8.30 am. |
| Company occupying RESERVE LINE | 9.0 am. |
| " " FRONT LINE | 10.0 am. |
| Companies occupying FRENCH TRENCH | 11.0 am. |
| Headquarters | 10.30 am. |

All movements East of a North and Soth line through RENINGHELST will be byplatoons at 100 yards interval.
Troops are not to halt in DICKEBUSCH.
3. Companies will occupy exactly the same billets as when last at ALBERTA CAMP.
4. All maps, aeroplane photographs, Defence schemes, trach stores and dmps will be taken over bythe relievig Battalion.
~~All Gum Boots will be collected together at the respective CompanyHeadquarters and handed over to the incoming Companies.~~
5. O.C.Companies are responsible that the trenches and dugouts are handed over in a perfectly clean and snaitary condition; all latrine bukets must be emptied.
6. The Transport arrangments are as follows :-
(a) The breakfast rations only will be ~~bought~~ brought up to the trenches tonight th remainder beingdelivered to the C.Q.M.S. at ALBERTA CAMP.
(b) One Cook and one boiler per Company will go to the Transport lines tonight, and the Transport Officer will arrange for one Kitchen and one watercart to be at HALLEBAST CORNER to spply hot tea for all ranks.
(c) Riding horsesto be at DICKEBUSCH two hours later than times mentioned in para.2.
(d) The Transport Officer will arrange to have two G.S.Wagons at the Ration Dump tonight These will be loaded wih all surpls kits, stores, cooking utensils etc. which must be brought down bythe Ration parties. tonight.
The stores sentaway tonight should not iterfere wih the fighting efficiency of the Battalion.
(e) Any remaining stores and kits will be dumped at the Ration Dump tomorrow and will be brought away tomorrow night by the Transportof the 15th Hants. Regt.
(f) Lewis Gun chests will be sent back by the empty Ration Limbers retuning tonight.
Lewis Guns and drums will be carried ouof the line tomorrow as far as DICKEBUSCH where the Lewis Gun limbers will be waiting to conveythem to Camp.
7. The Platoon in MUD PATCH will be relieved as soon as it is dusk and Transport will be at the Ration Dump for packs etc.of the men.
8. Completion of relief will be wired to Bn.H.Q. as follows :-
"RAIN" (time).

(sgd) A.W.Mackay,
Lieut.& Adjutant,
"B" Bn.Royal Fusiliers

17/4/17

War Diary

SECRET. "B" BN. ROYAL FUSILIERS. Copy No. 13.

OPERATION ORDER No. 4.

1. The Battalion will relieve the 16th Hants in the line tomorrow 23/4/17, the leading platoon to pass DICKEBUSCH at 8.30 a.m.

2. Companies will be disposed as follows:

| | |
|---|---|
| "A" Coy. | [illegible] line [illegible] VORMEZEELE SWITCH & [illegible] |
| "B" " | Right of Old French Trench |
| "C" " | Left of Old French Trench. |
| "D" " | Front line. |

3. Order of relief is as follows:

| | | |
|---|---|---|
| Lewis Gunners & Snipers | leave ALBERTA CAMP at | 5 a.m. |
| S. S. Ms and Signallers | do. | 6 a.m. |
| "A" Coy. Leading platoon | passes DICKEBUSCH at | 8.30 a.m. |
| "D" " | do. | 9.30 a.m. |
| "B" " | do. | 10.30 a.m. |
| "C" " | do. | 11.30 a.m. |
| Headquarters | do. | 11.30 a.m. |

All movement east of a [illegible] line through RENINGHELST will be by platoons at 100 yards interval. Troops will not halt in DICKEBUSCH.

4. Each man [illegible] one blanket [illegible] on his back. The remainder will be rolled [illegible] bundles of 10 [illegible] and labelled, these together with all cookers [illegible] not being taken to the trenches will be collected by Q.M.S. and stored in the company store rooms.

[illegible] will be stored with their Companies.

5. One limber per Coy will [illegible] at 8 p.m. tonight for the transport of Lewis guns. These will be [illegible] at the transport [illegible] tonight and [illegible] in DICKEBUSCH [illegible] morning with the [illegible]. [illegible] will proceed with each Lewis Gun limber.

One Cook, one [illegible] and [illegible] for each Coy. and Headquarters will be [illegible] tonight & proceed to VORMEZEELE.

[illegible] bombs, [illegible] utensils [illegible] boxes and [illegible] to the [illegible] will be [illegible] at 9.30 a.m. where they will be [illegible] to the transport [illegible] the [illegible] [illegible] will [illegible] [illegible] tonight & O.C. [illegible] [illegible].

6. O.C. Companies [illegible] [illegible] and sanitary [illegible] and all [illegible] [illegible].

7. All maps, [illegible] photographs [illegible] [illegible] will be taken over.

Receipts for [illegible] will be sent to the O.C. immediately relief is completed.

8. Completion of relief will be wired to Bn. O.R. as follows:

"FINE" (time)

O.C. Companies are requested to [illegible] [illegible] when up to the [illegible] of a [illegible] or transport is [illegible].

(Sgd) A. W. MURRAY.
Capt. & Adjutant
"B" Bn. Royal Fusiliers

22/4/17

Copy No. 1. [illegible]
2. [illegible]
3. [illegible]
4. [illegible]
5. [illegible]
6. [illegible]
7. [illegible]
8. [illegible]
[illegible]

Dome House.
41st Division
26·4·17

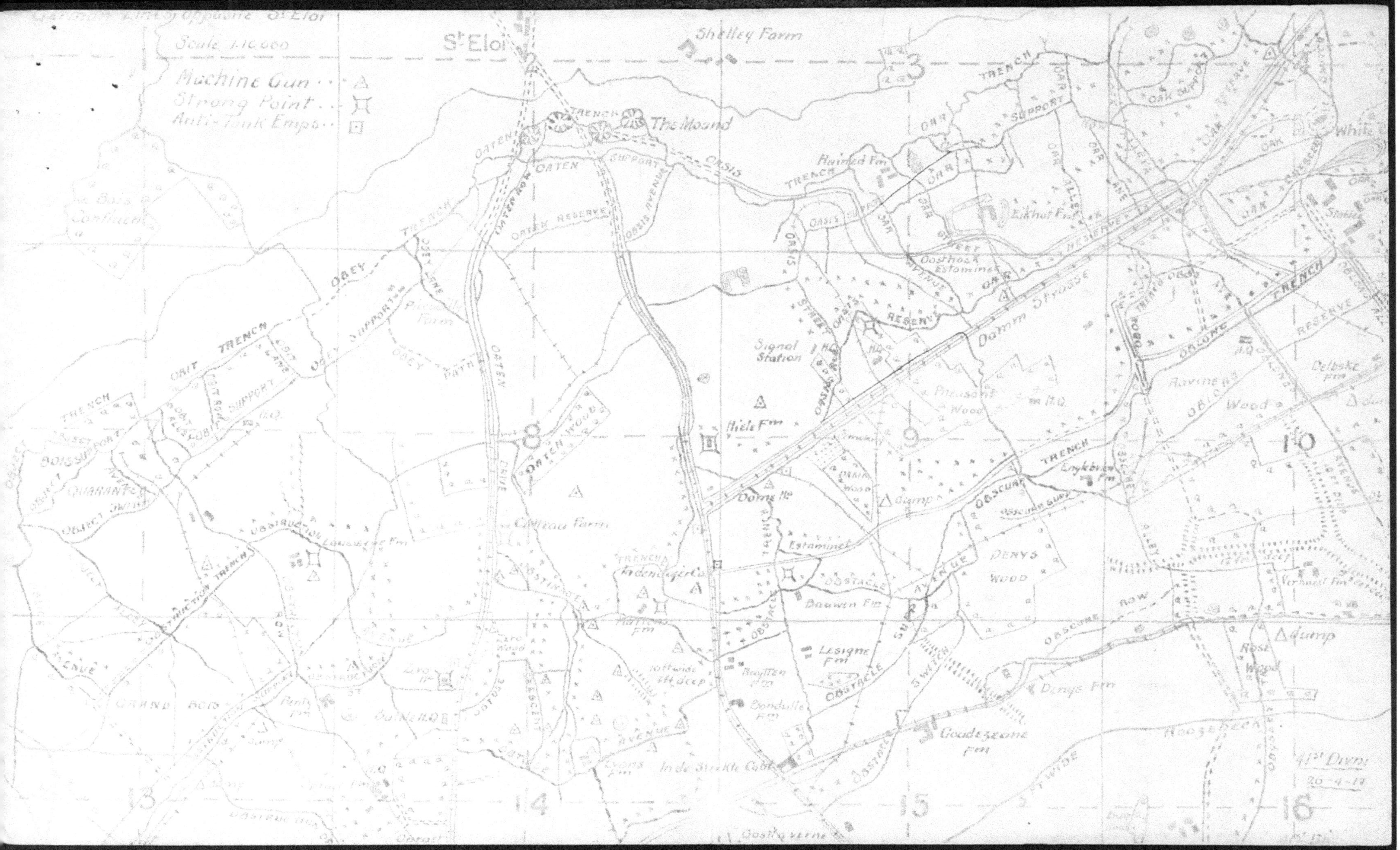
Scale 1:10,000
St Eloi
Shelley Farm
Machine Gun
Strong Point
Anti-Tank Emps
The Mound
Bois Confluent
OBEY
OBIT TRENCH
OATEN
OASIS
OAR
OAK SUPPORT
Raimed Fm
Eikhof Fm
Oosthoek Estaminet
Damm Strasse
Signal Station
Hiele Fm
Pheasant Wood
Oaten Wood
Obscure
Obstacle
Denys Wood
Oblong
Ravine
Wood
Rose Wood
Dump
Estaminet
Bauwin Fm
Lesigne Fm
Goudezeeuwe Fm
Denys Fm
Hoozebeek
Grand Bois
Quarante
Oblique
Obstruction Trench
Cotteau Farm
In de Sterkte Cabt
Oosttaverne
41st Divn
20-4-17
3
8
9
10
13
14
15
16

26th Royal Fusiliers

Instructions regarding War Diaries and Intelligence Summaries are contained in F. S. Regs., Part II. and the Staff Manual respectively. Title pages will be prepared in manuscript.

# WAR DIARY
*or*
~~INTELLIGENCE~~ SUMMARY.
(*Erase heading not required.*)

26 R F
Vol 13

Army Form C. 2118.

| Place | Date | Hour | Summary of Events and Information | Remarks and references to Appendices |
|---|---|---|---|---|
| Trenches [illegible] Sector [illegible] Map O.2. | 1st | | Artillery was fairly active on both sides during the day. Our Artillery had a practice Barrage on enemy front commencing about [illegible]. The enemy retaliated on our Reserve & Support lines but did little damage to our trenches. Our casualties were 1 Killed 1 Died of Wounds [illegible] Wounded. The day was good for observation and our aeroplanes were active. The usual Working parties and R.E. fatigue parties were found. The night was quiet. | A Maxwell Capt |
| Trenches [illegible] | 2nd | | The Battalion was relieved in the line by the 11th Royal West Kents the relief being completed by 12 noon, and proceeded to Chippawa Camp A. On completion All maps, aeroplane photographs, Defence schemes and trench stores and Dumps were taken over by the relieving Battalion. Hot tea was served out to all ranks at Hallebast Corner. The casualties during our tour were 1 Killed 1 Died of Wounds [illegible] Wounded. During the tour working parties were provided nightly and the trenches were greatly improved before the Battalion was relieved. | O.O. [illegible] A Maxwell Capt |
| Chippawa Camp [illegible] Sheet 28 S.W. | 3rd | | Baths were obtained also complete changes of underclothing. Battalion training was carried out and fatigue parties supplied. | A Maxwell Capt |

13-K (17 [illegible])

A6945 Wt. W11422/M1160 350,000 12/16 D. D. & L. Forms/C./2118/14.

26th Royal Fusiliers

Instructions regarding War Diaries and Intelligence Summaries are contained in F. S. Regs., Part II. and the Staff Manual respectively. Title pages will be prepared in manuscript.

# WAR DIARY

or

~~INTELLIGENCE SUMMARY.~~

*(Erase heading not required.)*

May 1917

Army Form C. 2118.

| Place | Date | Hour | Summary of Events and Information | Remarks and references to Appendices |
|---|---|---|---|---|
| Chippewa | 4th | | Battalion training was carried out and fatigue parties supplied. A Maxwell Capt | |
| Camp A | 5th | | Early in the morning the Battalion transport left for Moulle billeting at | O.O. 6 |
| Sheet 28 S.W. | | | Nordpeene for the night. A dinner was provided at Reninghelst to celebrate | |
| | | | the anniversary of the Battalion's arrival in France. This was part taken | |
| | | | by some 230 of the original men and 5 of the original officers – the Transport was unavoidably absent which would have made the numbers | |
| | | | ~~[illegible]~~ Dinner | |
| | | | [illegible] by 41 officers + 49 ORs | |
| | | | The Evening the Band gave an anniversary concert in the YMCA at Reninghelst. A Maxwell Capt | |
| do | 6th | 6.20 am | The Battalion marched from Chippewa Camp A to Abeele Station | O.O. 6 |
| | | | where they entrained for ~~[illegible]~~ WATTEN. Tea was provided at Abeele before | |
| | | | entraining. Entraining commenced at 11 am and was completed | |
| | | | by 11.15 am. At St Omer the Battalion had to vacate the coaches to | |
| | | | enable enemy prisoners to be entrained; this was done in about | |
| | | | 20 minutes. On arrival at Watten (2.30 pm) the Battalion detrained in | |
| Moulle | | | 10 minutes and marched to Moulle where they were billeted. The billets were | |
| Sheet 27th S.E. | | | good. The Battalion was billeted by 5 pm. Packs were carried throughout | |
| | | | the day for the men. The day was hot. Mounted Officers' horses met | |
| | | | the Battalion soon after the march to Moulle had commenced. A Maxwell Capt | |

26th Royal Fusiliers

# WAR DIARY
*or*
~~INTELLIGENCE SUMMARY.~~
*(Erase heading not required.)*

May 1917

Army Form C. 2118.

Instructions regarding War Diaries and Intelligence Summaries are contained in F. S. Regs., Part II. and the Staff Manual respectively. Title pages will be prepared in manuscript.

| Place | Date | Hour | Summary of Events and Information | Remarks and references to Appendices |
|---|---|---|---|---|
| Moulle Ref. Sheet 27A S.E. [illegible] | 7th | 7.30 am | The Battalion marched to A Range Moulle and carried out two practices at 200x of a General Musketry Course returning at 1.30 pm. The afternoon was taken up with Lewis Gun practice, Live Bomb throwing. During the evening the Battalion Band played in the Square. A Maxwell Capt | |
| do | 8th | 6.30 am | Battalion training was carried out viz Physical Drill, Musketry, Route March, Lewis Gun practice, Rifle Grenade and Live Bomb throwing. During the evening the Battalion Band played in the Square. A Maxwell Capt | |
| do | 9th | 7.15 am | The Battalion marched to A Range Moulle and completed two practices at 300x of a General Musketry Course returning at 1.30 pm. A Battalion Route March to Eperlecque took place in the afternoon. At Eperlecque the Battalion played the 21st London T.F. at Rugby and Association ~~[illegible]~~ ~~[illegible]~~ A Maxwell Capt | |
| do | 10th | 7.15 am | The Battn marched to A Range Moulle and completed two practices of a General Musketry Course returning at 6.30 pm. Dinners were served on the range. A Maxwell Capt | |

26th Royal Fusiliers

# WAR DIARY
or
~~INTELLIGENCE SUMMARY.~~
(Erase heading not required.)

Instructions regarding War Diaries and Intelligence Summaries are contained in F. S. Regs., Part II. and the Staff Manual respectively. Title pages will be prepared in manuscript.

Army Form C. 2118.

May 1917

| Place | Date | Hour | Summary of Events and Information | Remarks and references to Appendices |
|---|---|---|---|---|
| Moulle Sheet 27a S.E. [illegible] | 11th | 7.15 am | The Battalion marched to [illegible] Range Moulle and completed the General Musketry Course with a field firing scheme from 600 to 200 [illegible] firing from the hip. A Maxwell Capt | |
| do | 12th | 7.0 am | The Battalion marched from Moulle to Watten where they entrained for Abeele at 10.39 a.m. arriving at 1 p.m. The Battalion then marched to Micmac Camp and relieved the 32nd Battn Royal Fusiliers at [illegible] Battalion arriving at 6 p.m. The Transport spent the night of the 12/13th at Noordhene and proceeded to Brigade Transport Lines | O.O. 8. |
| Sheet 28 S.W. | | | G 34 d 1.3 on the 13th. Packs were carried throughout the day for the men. Hot tea was served on arrival at Micmac Camp. Working parties were supplied up the line. A Maxwell Capt | A Maxwell Capt |
| Micmac Camp Sheet 28 S.W. | 13th | | Working parties were supplied up the line. Reinforcements of 15 joined the Battalion | A Maxwell Capt |
| | 14th | | Reinforcements of 115 joined the Battalion and remained at Chippawa Camp as there was not sufficient accommodation at Micmac till the morning of 17th when they moved off with the Battalion to Bousbecque. Day and night working parties were supplied | A Maxwell Capt |
| | 15th | | The Officers Commanding Companies attended a [illegible] demonstration | |

26th Royal Fusiliers

Instructions regarding War Diaries and Intelligence Summaries are contained in F. S. Regs., Part II. and the Staff Manual respectively. Title pages will be prepared in manuscript.

# WAR DIARY
*or*
~~INTELLIGENCE SUMMARY.~~
*(Erase heading not required.)*

May 1917

Army Form C. 2118.

| Place | Date | Hour | Summary of Events and Information | Remarks and references to Appendices |
|---|---|---|---|---|
| Micmac Camp | 15th | | at the 2nd Army School of Cookery, Hazebrouck. The Battalion Band proceeded to the 2nd Army School, Wisques. The usual working parties were supplied. A Maxwell Capt | |
| do | 16th | | A lecture was given by Lt. Col. [illegible] Thomas D.S.O. to the Officers & Sergeants of the 12th Brigade at the Theatre, Reninghelst. The usual working parties were supplied. A Maxwell Capt | |
| do Sheet 28 N.W. | 17th | | The Battalion (less day working parties) moved to Bivouacs at Busseboom G.21.a.2.7 on the 17th inst. The Battalion was relieved at Micmac by the 12th East Lancs Regt. The head of column passed Ouderdom at 2 p.m. all troops were clear of camp by 2.30 p.m. Route taken Micmac, Ouderdom, Busseboom G.21.a.2.7. The day working parties returned to Micmac Camp where guides awaited them & conducted them to Bivouacs. The packs of the day working parties were carried to Busseboom. First Line Transport marched on the 17th inst under arrangement of Brigade Transport Officer, billeting at Noordpeene on the night of the 17/18th inst and proceeded to Gonnehem on the 18th inst. The Draft at Chippawa Camp / A Maxwell Capt | B.O.1 |

26th Royal Fusiliers

Instructions regarding War Diaries and Intelligence Summaries are contained in F. S. Regs., Part II. and the Staff Manual respectively. Title pages will be prepared in manuscript.

# WAR DIARY

*or*

~~INTELLIGENCE SUMMARY.~~

(*Erase heading not required.*)

May 1917

Army Form C. 2118.

| Place | Date | Hour | Summary of Events and Information | Remarks and references to Appendices |
|---|---|---|---|---|
| Busseboom [illegible] G.21.a.27 | 17th | Aft. | marched to Micmac Camp for breakfast on the morning of the 17th and remained there till the Battalion moved. A Maxwell Capt. | |
| | 18th | 5.30am | On the morning of the 18th inst the Battalion paraded at 5.30 am and moved from Bivouacs at G.21.a.27 and proceeded to Poperinghe Main Station and entrained at 7.45 am for the Gonsiette Area detraining at 10.45 am. The Battalion marched from Watten to billets at Moulle arriving at Moulle at 1.0 pm. A Maxwell Capt. | |
| Moulle [illegible] | 19th | 9.0 am | The Battalion marched to the training area at Moringhem and there commenced a General Course of Training (Musketry, Bayonet Fighting, Physical Drill, Extended Order Drill, Bombing) and returned at 3.0 pm. | A Maxwell Capt. |
| Training Area Sheet 27 S.E. P.20.30.36 Q.31 | 20th | | Divine Service was held at the Transport Lines. A Maxwell Capt. | |
| do | 21st | | Breakfast was served at 6.30 am the Battalion paraded by Companies at 7.20 am and marched to the training area at Moringhem and carried out a General Course of Training by Platoons returning at 3.30 pm. Dinners were served on the training ground. A lecture on formations and the various duties of the tactical Platoon was given in the evening. A Maxwell Capt. | |

26th Royal Fusiliers

Instructions regarding War Diaries and Intelligence Summaries are contained in F. S. Regs., Part II. and the Staff Manual respectively. Title pages will be prepared in manuscript.

# WAR DIARY
*or*
# INTELLIGENCE SUMMARY.
*(Erase heading not required.)*

May 1917

Army Form C. 2118.

| Place | Date | Hour | Summary of Events and Information | Remarks and references to Appendices |
|---|---|---|---|---|
| Training Area Squares P29.30 36 & Q31 Sheet 27 SE | 22nd | 5.20 am | The Battalion continued its training by Companies. Platoons in close order drill. Extended order drill. Platoon Drill special attention was paid to direction and moving behind a barrage marked by flags. Tactical schemes with platoons. Demonstrations with flares and smoke bombs. The Battalion returned at 12 pm. A lecture on fire discipline was given in the evening. A Maxwell Capt | |
| do Sheet 27 SE. Squares P29 30 36 & Q31 | 23rd | 5.20 am | Training by Companies was continued in the Aeroplane Sheds. Arm Drill. Physical Drill. Demonstrations with flares and smoke bombs were carried out. A Maxwell Capt | |
| do | 24th | 5.20 am | The Battalion paraded by companies at 5.20 am and marched to the training area and carried out Battalion formations drill on arriving in drill area. Deploying from column of Route to Artillery & wave formation and vice versa. The Battalion in attack on position and advancing with moving barrage was also carried out. A Maxwell Capt | |
| do | 25th | 5.20 am | The Battalion marched to Training Area and carried out Battalion in advanced Guard formation meeting enemy opposition | |

A6945 Wt. W11422/M1160 350,000 12/16 D. D. & L. Forms/C./2118/14.

26th Royal Fusiliers

Instructions regarding War Diaries and Intelligence Summaries are contained in F. S. Regs., Part II, and the Staff Manual respectively. Title pages will be prepared in manuscript.

# WAR DIARY
*or*
~~INTELLIGENCE SUMMARY.~~
*(Erase heading not required.)*

May 1917

Army Form C. 2118.

| Place | Date | Hour | Summary of Events and Information | Remarks and references to Appendices |
|---|---|---|---|---|
| Training Area Squares 29.30 36 & 31 Sht 27 S.E. | 25th | | obtaining superiority of fire and building up firing line. A rehearsal of Brigade Scheme of an attack on hostile trenches was carried out. A lecture was given in the evening by the Commanding Officer on the days work, emphasising violation of principles in F.S.R. | A Maxwell Capt |
| Moulle. | 26th | | A lecture was given at 6.30 am by the Commanding Officer to the Officers of the Battalion. Rapid wiring and Lewis Gun practice was carried out by the Battalion. | A Maxwell Capt |
| | 27th | | Divine Service was held. Cricket was played during the afternoon. | A Maxwell Capt |
| Training Area | 28th | | A rehearsal of Brigade Scheme of an attack on hostile trenches was carried out in the new formation. | A Maxwell Capt |
| | 29th | | The scheme was again carried out slight alterations being made on the previous days scheme. | A Maxwell Capt |
| | 30th | | The scheme was again carried out. Dinners were taken on the Training Ground. The Battalion marched back arriving at billets at 3.30 pm. | A Maxwell Capt |

26th Royal Fusiliers

Instructions regarding War Diaries and Intelligence Summaries are contained in F. S. Regs., Part II. and the Staff Manual respectively. Title pages will be prepared in manuscript.

# WAR DIARY
or
~~INTELLIGENCE SUMMARY.~~
*(Erase heading not required.)*

May 1917

Army Form C. 2118.

| Place | Date | Hour | Summary of Events and Information | Remarks and references to Appendices |
|---|---|---|---|---|
| Moulle | 31st | 2.40pm. | The Battalion marched from Moulle to billets for the night May 31/June 1st at Arneke. Tea was provided on the march. The Transport (less Officers Horses, Mess Cart, Cookers and Water Carts) left Moulle at 8 a.m. & proceeded to Brigade Headquarters [illegible] and moved off under orders from the Brigade Transport Officer. The Transport halted for the night May 31st/June 1st at Noordpeene. The horses & vehicles accompanying the Battalion to Arneke rejoined the Transport | 10.2. |
| | | 10pm | on the evening of the 31st May. The Battalion was billeted at Arneke by 10 p.m. | |
| | | | A Maxwell Capt. | |
| | | | George [illegible] Lt Col<br>Cmdg 26th Royal Fusiliers | |

A6945 Wt. W11422/M1160 350,000 12/16 D. D. & L. Forms/C./2118/14.

26th Royal Fusiliers

Instructions regarding War Diaries and Intelligence Summaries are contained in F. S. Regs., Part II. and the Staff Manual respectively. Title pages will be prepared in manuscript.

# WAR DIARY

*or*

~~INTELLIGENCE SUMMARY.~~

*(Erase heading not required.)*

May 1917.

Army Form C. 2118.

| Place | Date | Hour | Summary of Events and Information | Remarks and references to Appendices |
|---|---|---|---|---|
| | | | Casualties for month ending 31st May. | |
| | | | 1 Killed. 1 Died of Wounds. 5 Wounded. A Maxwell Capt. | |
| | | | Officers at present with the Battalion | |
| | | | Lt. Col. Gwyn Gwyn-Thomas D.S.O. | |
| | | | Captain Allen Maxwell | |
| | | | Lt. A.W. Mackay | |
| | | | Captn. Berry | |
| | | | Lt. C.G. Birch | |
| | | | Lt. R.C. Barkworth M.C. | |
| | | | 2/Lt. A.C. Chambers | |
| | | | 2/Lt. Barnett | |
| | | | 2/Lt. Pemberton | |
| | | | " McWhirter | |
| | | | " [illegible] | |
| | | | " Mason | |
| | | | " Denny | |
| | | | " J.V. Hall | |
| | | | " Page-Green | |
| | | | " Cole | |
| | | | " Bradford | |
| | | | " Ford | |
| | | | " Eddis | |
| | | | " Hamilton | |
| | | | " Adams | |
| | | | " Cookers | |

A6945 Wt. W11422/M1160 350,000 12/16 D. D. & L. Forms/C./2118/14.

SECRET

Copy No. 3

"8" BN. ROYAL FUSILIERS

OPERATION ORDER No 3.

1. The Battalion less Transport will entrain at ABEELE on 6th inst, entrainment to be complete by 10 am.

2. The Battalion will detrain at WATTON and billet at MOULLE

3. The Transport will march on 5th inst. stopping the night of 5th/6th at NORDPEENE and arriving at MOULLE on the 6th.

4. Transport will be available on the 6th for the carriage of packs one blanket per man.
Officers trench bundles, one Mess Box, two Boilers and two frying pans per Company. One boiler, one Camp kettle and one frying pan for Headquarters will also be taken to the station of entrainment.

5. Officers kit, other than trench bundles, must be ready for loading by 5 am. tomorrow 5/5/17 outside Church Army Hut
Kit may be dumped outside Church Army Hut tonight when a Battalion Guard will take charge of same.
No surplus kit going to England will be dealt with before 10 am. tomorrow.

6. Every man without exception will proceed with the Battalion on Sunday to MOULLE.

7. Times of parade on Sunday will be notified later

8. O.C. Companies will be responsible that the Camp is left in a perfectly clean and sanitary condition and that all latrine buckets are emptied.

(Sgd) R.C. BARKWORTH, Lieut
for Capt & Adjutant.
"8" BN. ROYAL FUSILIERS.

4/5/17.

Copy No. 1. Filed.
2. 124th Infantry Brigade
3. Adjutant.
4. O.C. "A" Coy.
5. O.C. "B" Coy
6. O.C. "C" Coy.
7. O.C. "D" Coy.
8. O.C. Headquarters.
9. Transport Officer & Quartermaster.
10. War Diary
11. Spare.

Copy No. 14.

5th Royal [illegible]

Operation Order No. [illegible]

The [illegible] ved in [illegible] 2nd

[illegible]

(1 + 2) A 3U RF

[illegible]

Headquarters

[illegible]

[illegible] R.C.M.P. [illegible]

[illegible] makes [illegible]

[illegible]

All [illegible]

Lewis [illegible]

7 am. on morning of relief.

[illegible]

be [illegible]

[illegible]

P.10.

7. The Platoon in MUD PATCH will be relieved as soon as it is dusk.

8. Completion of relief will be wired to Bn.H.Q. as follows:

"BLUE" (time).

(Sgd.) A.W. MACKAY.
Lieut and Adjutant.
3 Bn. Royal Fusiliers.

30/IV/17.

Copy No. 1. Filed.
2. Adjutant.
3. 12th Infantry Brigade.
4. 10th Bn. R.W.K. Regt.
5. O.C. "A" Coy.
6. O.C. "B"
7. O.C. "C"
8. O.C. "D"
9. O.C. Headquarters & R.S.M.
10. O.C. Signals.
11. Transport Officer and Quartermaster.
12. Intelligence and Sniping Officer.
13. O.C. Lewis Gunners.
14. War Diary.

Cop. 10

[illegible] Orders [illegible]

[illegible] will [illegible] at 6.40 am [illegible] on the road [illegible] on [illegible] [illegible] D Company. Rations will be [illegible]

2. Blankets will be rolled [illegible] by ten.

[illegible] blankets, [illegible] on the compound by 6 am.

A loading party of 20 O.R. will be detailed by O.C. D Company.

3. Two cooks have been [illegible] will be [illegible]

[illegible]

H.Q. [illegible]

[illegible]

26th Bn. Royal [illegible]

Operation Order No. 8.

1. The Battalion will entrain at WATTEN at 10.30 am tomorrow 12/5/17 & arrive at ABEELE at 1 pm. on the same day, and will march from there to MICMAC CAMP where it will [illegible] the 32nd Bn. Royal Fusiliers as "Works Battalion".

2. The Transport will proceed to NOORDPEENE tomorrow 12/5/17 and spend the night of 12/13th there obtaining billets from the MAIRE; proceeding to the Brigade Transport lines at G36 d1.3 on the 13th.

3. Supplies. [illegible] will be issued from ST. OMER for the last time on the [illegible] for consumption on the 12th inst.

Transport moving by road will draw rations on the 11th inst for consumption on both the 12th & 13th inst. and will carry these with it.

Personnel entraining will draw rations on the 11th inst. for consumption on the 12th inst. and carry them on the man.

Rations for [illegible] for consumption on 13th inst. will be [illegible] Officer [illegible] train from WIPPENHOEK on the [illegible] at MICMAC CAMP on the 12th inst.

124th Infantry Brigade are arranging (I) a guard for these rations to take charge until the arrival of the Battalion and (II) necessary transport for packs and 1 blanket per man to [illegible] personnel at ABEELE Station.

4. All Officers [illegible], 1 Coy. Mess Box, packs & Blankets, 2 Boilers and 2 frying pans per Coy, one [illegible], one Camp kettle and one frying [illegible] will be [illegible] outside the various Coy. Headquarters by 6 am ready for [illegible] by Transport. These will be carried [illegible]

Officers valises [illegible] will be stacked outside Coy. Headquarters by 5 am [illegible] with the Bn. Transport.

5. The Battalion will parade at [illegible] the [illegible] of the [illegible] and march to WATTEN. Order of March; Band, HQ, "A" "B" "C" "D" Companies.

6. O.C. Companies will please see that all billets are left in a clean and sanitary condition, and that all latrine buckets are emptied.

7. Blankets will be [illegible] on to the pack by the blanket [illegible]

(Sgd) D. MAXWELL
Capt & a/Adjutant
26th Royal Fusiliers

11/5/17

Copy No.

| | | | |
|---|---|---|---|
| 1 File | 4 O.C. "B" Coy | 7 Quartermaster | 10. Band |
| 2 Adjutant | 5 O.C. "C" Coy | 8 Transport Officer | 11. [illegible] |
| 3 O.C. "A" Coy | 6 O.C. "D" Coy | 9 Headquarters | 12. Spare |

# 26th Bn Royal Fusiliers

SECRET

## Battalion Order No. 1.

Copy No. ......

Map ref.
Sheet 28 N.W.

1. MOVE 17/5/17. (a) The Battalion (less day working parties) will move to Bivouacs at G21 a 2.7. on the 17th inst.
Order of March: H.Q. A. B. C. D Companies.
Companies will march by Platoons at 100 paces interval. Head of column to pass Q.M. Stores at 2 pm. All troops to be clear of Camp by 2.30 pm.
Route - MICMAC - OUDERDOM - BUSSEBOOM - G21 a 2.7.

18/5/17. (b) On the morning of the 18th inst. the Battalion will parade at 5.30 am and move from bivouacs at G21 a 2.7 and proceed to POPERINGHE MAIN STATION where it will entrain for the GANSPETTE Area.
Order of March as in para. (a).

2/Lt Chambers. 2/Lt. CHAMBERS will precede the battalion by ½ an hour and make arrangements for entraining.
(c) The Battalion will detrain at WATTEN and march to billets at MOULLE.

2. WORKING PARTIES. All day working parties will be found on the 17th inst., all work to finish at 4.30 pm (or sooner). Working parties will return to MICMAC CAMP where guides will await them and conduct them to bivouacs.
The packs of men on day working parties will be stacked outside the Q.M. Stores by 11.30 am. on the 17th inst and will be loaded on Transport and taken to bivouacs. Each Company will supply a loading party of 3 men, who will unload at G21 a 2.7.

3. TRANSPORT. First line Transport will march on the 17th inst. under arrangements of Brigade Transport Officer, billeting at NOORDPEENE on the night of the 17/18th inst. and proceeding to GANSPETTE on the 18th inst.

4. BAGGAGE. All Officers kits, baggage and other articles to be conveyed by transport will be dumped at the Q.M Stores NOT LATER THAN 5 am. on the morning of the 17th inst.

5. SUPPLIES. (a) Rations for the Transport will be drawn at WIPPENHOEK on the 17th for consumption on the 18th & 19th and at WATTEN on the 19th for consumption on the 20th inst and subsequently.
(b) Rations for personnel entraining will be drawn at WIPPENHOEK for the last time on the 18th inst. and at WATTEN for the 1st time on the 19th.

COOKERS 2 Cookers of the 123rd Infantry Brigade will be attached to the Battalion up to the morning of the 18th.
Fuel for cooking will be supplied by the Battalion.
Cookers must be returned complete and clean to the 123rd Infantry Brigade.
The Battalion has the use of a water cart at G21 a 2.7 loaned by No. 2 or 3 Coy. A.S.C. whose lines adjoin the field.

6. CAMP (sanitation). The Huts and Tents now occupied must be left perfectly clean.
All latrine buckets etc. must be emptied and the camp generally left in a clean condition.
The bivouacing ground will similarly be left clean.

7. AREA STORES. Area Stores will be handed over to the Camp Warden by the Quartermaster Sergeant and receipt obtained.

8. BILLETING PARTY. 2/Lt Barnett and 5 O.R. — 2/Lt. Barnett and 1. O.R. each Coy. and Transport will move at 9.30 am. on the 17th inst. by lorry to the billeting area. Instructions as to arrangements of billets have been given to 2/Lt. Barnett.
The party will take bicycles with them.

9. DRAFT at CHIPPEWA. The draft at present at CHIPPEWA CAMP will march to MICMAC CAMP tomorrow morning for breakfast.
They will take full kit and will remain at MICMAC until the Battalion moves.

10. BIVOUACS. O/c. "A" Coy. — O/c "A" Coy. will detail 1 N.C.O. and 2 men to report at D.A.D.O.S. Office RENINGHELST. at 9 a.m. tomorrow. They will draw Bivouacs and will act as a guard over bivouacs and rations until arrival of Battalion.

11. Acknowledge.

(Sgd) A.W. MACKAY
Lieut & Adjutant
26th Bn. Royal Fusiliers

16/5/17.

Copy No. 1 Filed.
2. Adjutant.
3. O.C. "A" Coy.
4. O.C. "B" Coy.
5. O.C. "C" Coy.
6. O.C. "D" Coy
7. O.C. Headquarters
No. 8. Quartermaster
9. Transport Officer
10. 124th Infantry Brigade
11. War Diary.
12. Medical Officer
13. O.C. Draft.
14. Billeting Officer.

Instructions regarding War Diaries and Intelligence Summaries are contained in F. S. Regs., Part II. and the Staff Manual respectively. Title pages will be prepared in manuscript.

# WAR DIARY
*or*
# INTELLIGENCE SUMMARY.
*(Erase heading not required.)*

Army Form C. 2118.

| Place | Date | Hour | Summary of Events and Information | Remarks and references to Appendices |
|---|---|---|---|---|
| Arnecke | 1/4/17 | | After spending the night in billets at ARNECKE the Battalion entrained at ARNECKE Station at 9.15 am and detrained at POPERINGHE Station about 11.45 am and proceeded to the Camp at MICMAC NORTH taking over from 20th Bn Durham Light Infantry | [initials] |
| MICMAC CAMP NORTH | 2/4/17 – 7/4/17 | | There is nothing of importance to record during this ~~[illegible]~~ period. The Battalion furnished a large number of working parties for the front line system of trenches preparing for the offensive operations. Casualties 1 OR killed | [initials] |

A6945 Wt. W11422/M1160 350,000 12/16 D. D. & L. Forms/C./2118/14.

Instructions regarding War Diaries and Intelligence Summaries are contained in F. S. Regs., Part II. and the Staff Manual respectively. Title pages will be prepared in manuscript.

# WAR DIARY
*or*
# INTELLIGENCE SUMMARY.
*(Erase heading not required.)*

Army Form C. 2118.

| Place | Date | Hour | Summary of Events and Information | Remarks and references to Appendices |
|---|---|---|---|---|
| Micmac Camp. (East) | 5th | 6am | At this hour in accordance with March Table (Exhibit 1) Battalion HQrs B & D Coys moved from Micmac Camp E up into the trenches. B Coy occupied front line trenches O 25 O 26 and O 27 with two platoons & had two platoons in the support line within the same limits. D Coy occupied the Reserve line, Crater Lane to Bus House Road (Exclusive) & Voormezeele Switch from Junction with Middlesex Lane to Voormezeele St Eloi Road | March Table Exhibit 1 |
| | | | Battalion Headquarters were in dug outs in Convent Lane. (Map ~~Attached~~ 1) | Map 1 Attached |
| | | | ~~Yesterday p.m.~~ The remaining two Companies moved from Micmac Camp E to Micmac Camp South. | (Map from Our Records) |
| | | | The day passed uneventfully in the line. There was heavy Artillery fire on both sides, but there is nothing of importance to record. | |
| | | | Patrols were sent out by B Coy at night. They found the Enemy wire thoroughly cut & no obstacle. Owing to a bright moon one of the patrols which got almost up to the enemy parapet was bombed and the officer was slightly wounded. | |
| | | 11pm | At this hour A & C Coys left Micmac Camp East & proceeded to | |

T2134. Wt. W708—776. 500000. 4/15. Sir J. C. & S.

Instructions regarding War Diaries and Intelligence Summaries are contained in F. S. Regs., Part II. and the Staff Manual respectively. Title pages will be prepared in manuscript.

# WAR DIARY
*or*
# INTELLIGENCE SUMMARY.
*(Erase heading not required.)*

Army Form C. 2118.

| Place | Date | Hour | Summary of Events and Information | Remarks and references to Appendices |
|---|---|---|---|---|
| | | | occupy G.H.Q. 2nd line which they did at 1.30 am on the 6th June in accordance with March Table (Exhibit 1) | Exhibit 1. |
| In the line | 6th | | The whole battalion was disposed in the line in accordance with March Table (Exhibit 1) The Artillery duel continued throughout the day otherwise there is nothing of importance to record | |
| | | | Orders for moving into assembly positions were issued (Exhibit 2) and notification as to Zero hour was received (Exhibit 3) | × |
| do | 7th | | The day of the attack on the 2nd Army front from Observatory Wood to St Yves. | |
| | | | According to orders issued the Battalion was supposed to be in its assembly position 2 hours before Zero (ie 1.10 am) but owing to considerable traffic in the Communication Trenches and on account of the traffic it was not until 2.35 am that the Battalion was finally ready and the Coys all out in their lines of waves between our own front line trench & the support line. Although a bit tired the men were in splendid spirits. They had been trained up to the | |

Instructions regarding War Diaries and Intelligence Summaries are contained in F. S. Regs., Part II. and the Staff Manual respectively. Title pages will be prepared in manuscript.

# WAR DIARY
*or*
# INTELLIGENCE SUMMARY.
*(Erase heading not required.)*

Army Form C. 2118.

| Place | Date | Hour | Summary of Events and Information | Remarks and references to Appendices |
|---|---|---|---|---|
| | | | minute. Every officer and man knew exactly what was expected of him, knew exactly what the objective was and were ready to gain it. After 6 long weary winter months of waiting in the St Eloi sector, overlooked by the enemy, every movement and turn observed, all ranks were assembled with one thought – to get the Boche out of it – All had complete confidence in our supporting artillery. | |
| | 7th | 2.50am | At this hour the enemy having evidently spotted the Battalions in front assembling in NO MANS LAND began to send up his Stand To signal (A rocket bursting into Golden Red Stars) and his artillery opened a barrage. Luckily however his artillery barrage was weak and it did not disorganise or worry the assembled men | |
| | 7th | 3.10am | Promptly to the second our Artillery opened and our line of waves went forward. About 5 secs after Zero the St Eloi mine went up with a huge blaze and a rocking of the ground. This seemed to startle the men for they seemed to turn left handed | |

Instructions regarding War Diaries and Intelligence Summaries are contained in F. S. Regs., Part II. and the Staff Manual respectively. Title pages will be prepared in manuscript.

# WAR DIARY
*or*
# INTELLIGENCE SUMMARY.
*(Erase heading not required.)*

Army Form C. 2118.

| Place | Date | Hour | Summary of Events and Information | Remarks and references to Appendices |
|---|---|---|---|---|
| | | | Fortunately this Check was only momentary and the men soon settled down and were over the top and following the 32nd Royal Fusiliers who were in front in good order. The enemy defensive barrage came down on NO MANS LAND about 4 minutes after Zero but it only caught our rear waves & caused little damage. | |
| | | | The attack went off exactly as per schedule. The 32nd Royal Fusiliers took the enemy Front & Reserve Trenches and at Zero plus 35 mins this Battalion were ready to advance on their objective the DAMMSTRASSE. This consisted of a sunken road which was strongly fortified and which was supposed to be a bit of a stumbling block. The ground had been thoroughly prepared by our Artillery who maintained a heavy standing barrage on the objective. The Co-operation between Infantry & Artillery was excellent. The advance behind the Creeping barrage was orderly and the men kept their distances & direction admirably. | |
| | | 4 11am | Promptly to time the barrage lifted off the DAMMSTRASSE & our men | |

Instructions regarding War Diaries and Intelligence Summaries are contained in F. S. Regs., Part II. and the Staff Manual respectively. Title pages will be prepared in manuscript.

# WAR DIARY
*or*
# INTELLIGENCE SUMMARY.
*(Erase heading not required.)*

Army Form C. 2118.

| Place | Date | Hour | Summary of Events and Information | Remarks and references to Appendices |
|---|---|---|---|---|
| | | | rushed in and captured it with very little resistance & before large numbers of the enemy who had been sheltering in strong concrete dug outs were able to come out and fight. A large number of prisoners estimated at between 300 & 400 were taken by the Battalion. Those of the enemy who did not choose to evacuate their strongholds were bombed out of it. The enemy, with the exception of one machine gun crew whose was soon knocked out, showed no inclination to fight. He was beaten & demoralised by the intensity of our Artillery fire and the suddenness of the attack. | |
| | | | According to orders a line was immediately dug about 50 to 100 yards in front of the DAMMSTRASSE (BLUE LINE) as close up to our protection barrage as possible and the work of consolidation was carried on with all possible speed. | |
| | | | Enemy artillery fire was ineffective. | |
| | | | According to plan the 3 remaining Battalions of the Brigade came | |

Instructions regarding War Diaries and Intelligence Summaries are contained in F. S. Regs., Part II. and the Staff Manual respectively. Title pages will be prepared in manuscript.

# WAR DIARY
*or*
# INTELLIGENCE SUMMARY.
*(Erase heading not required.)*

Army Form C. 2118.

| Place | Date | Hour | Summary of Events and Information | Remarks and references to Appendices |
|---|---|---|---|---|
| | | | up behind us and formed up ready to advance on to the BLACK LINE which they did. All objectives allotted to the Brigade were taken to the scheduled time and were held. | |
| | 7th | 3.10pm | Exactly 12 hours after Zero at 3.10 pm the 21st Division who had come up across the ground in a magnificent way went through & carried on the advance and by about 5 pm news was received that all objectives had been taken. Meanwhile large numbers of prisoners kept streaming back. | |
| | | | In connection with this fight the following documents maps & photos are attached | |
| | | | 1/ Large Scale Tracing of our own front line system of trenches. | |
| | | | 2/ do map of Enemy Trenches opposite the Brigade Sector showing in colours the various stages of the attack & how it was carried out. | |
| | | | 3/ Map showing Barrage | |
| | | | 4 Map showing Destruction Fire on [illegible] | |

Instructions regarding War Diaries and Intelligence Summaries are contained in F. S. Regs., Part II. and the Staff Manual respectively. Title pages will be prepared in manuscript.

# WAR DIARY
*or*
# INTELLIGENCE SUMMARY.
*(Erase heading not required.)*

Army Form C. 2118.

| Place | Date | Hour | Summary of Events and Information | Remarks and references to Appendices |
|---|---|---|---|---|
| In the line | 8th | 2am | At about this hour orders (Exhibit 4) were received for the relief of the Battalion by the 23rd Middlesex Regiment, and the 20th Durham Light Infantry. This was carried out and completed by 3/30am and the Battalion was withdrawn to GHQ 2nd Line near RIDGE WOOD | Exhibit 4 |
| | | | During the day the Divisional Commander visited the men and heartily congratulated them on their splendid achievement. | |
| | | 4/30pm | The Battalion moved from G.H.Q. 2nd Line to Bivouac in ELZENWALLE where they spent the night. There is nothing of importance to record. [initials] | |
| ELZENWALLE | 9th | – | The day was spent in cleaning up and resting. Small parties were found for burial and salvage purposes on the battlefield. Otherwise there is nothing to record | |
| do | 10th | | There was a Church Parade in the morning and in the afternoon the men had baths at ELZENWALLE CHATEAU. Orders were received for relieving unit in the line and the Intelligence Officer and Company Commanders visited the trenches | |

Instructions regarding War Diaries and Intelligence Summaries are contained in F. S. Regs., Part II. and the Staff Manual respectively. Title pages will be prepared in manuscript.

# WAR DIARY
*or*
# INTELLIGENCE SUMMARY.
*(Erase heading not required.)*

Army Form C. 2118.

| Place | Date | Hour | Summary of Events and Information | Remarks and references to Appendices |
|---|---|---|---|---|
| In the line | 11th | | The Battalion took over from the 10th Royal West Kents, the 2 [illegible] and a small portion of the line held by the 20th Durham Light Infantry. | O.O No 3. |
| | | | Companies were disposed as follows:- | |
| | | | D Company from O 3 c 9 3 to O 3 d 4 5 | |
| | | | A Company " O 9 a 9 0 " O 10 a 0 5 BLUE LINE | |
| | | | B & C Companies held a line from O 10 b 2 7 to O 10 c 2 9 BLACK LINE | |
| | | | Battalion Headquarters were disposed in a trench leading off to right and left from OAR AVENUE (O 9 b 5 5) in front of the DAMMSTRASSE | |
| | | | A strong concrete dugout a few yards behind the DAMMSTRASSE was used as R.A.P. and as Battalion Battle Headquarters. | |
| | | | The lines taken over in most cases required considerable consolidation | |
| | | | Casualties O.R. 5 Killed 2 Wounded | |
| | 21/6/17 | | In the [illegible] of an advance by the Division on our left, the Battalion stood to all night and during the retaliatory bombardment, suffered 6 casualties amongst other ranks. | |
| | | | Casualties 1 OR Died of Wounds 5 OR Wounded | |

Instructions regarding War Diaries and Intelligence Summaries are contained in F. S. Regs., Part II. and the Staff Manual respectively. Title pages will be prepared in manuscript.

Army Form C. 2118.

# WAR DIARY
*or*
# INTELLIGENCE SUMMARY.
*(Erase heading not required.)*

| Place | Date | Hour | Summary of Events and Information | Remarks and references to Appendices |
|---|---|---|---|---|
| In the line | 13/4/17 | | In expectation of counter attack the Battalion stood to all night. Nothing occurred however except heavy shelling by the enemy. | |
| | | | Casualties OR 7 killed 11 wounded | [illegible] |
| do | 14/4/17 | | The Battalion relieved the 21st Bn Kings Royal Rifle Corps who were holding the front and BLACK LINES. | Exhibit No 5 [illegible] |
| | | | Dispositions. | |
| | | | C Company OLIVE TRENCH and OLIVE SWITCH O 10 d 1.7 to O 10 [illegible] | |
| | | | D Company FRONT LINE Approximately O 10 d 8.8 to O 11 c 2.2 | |
| | | | A & B Companies BLACK LINE | |
| | | | Battalion Headquarters DELBSKE FARM | |
| | | 9 pm | During the relief the enemy barraged the front and support lines and and we suffered casualties as follows: | |
| | | | Killed NIL OR 5 | |
| | | | Wounded 2/Lt R C BARKWORTH MC and 23 OR | |

A6945 Wt. W11422/M1160 350,000 12/16 D. D. & L. Forms/C./2118/14.

Army Form C. 2118.

Instructions regarding War Diaries and Intelligence Summaries are contained in F. S. Regs., Part II. and the Staff Manual respectively. Title pages will be prepared in manuscript.

# WAR DIARY
*or*
# INTELLIGENCE SUMMARY.
*(Erase heading not required.)*

| Place | Date | Hour | Summary of Events and Information | Remarks and references to Appendices |
|---|---|---|---|---|
| In the Line | 17/1/17 | | A Communion Service was held in Battalion Headquarters dugout by Padre Walker. Most of Headquarters attended. | [illegible] |
| | | | Casualties OR ~~killed~~ Nil killed 4 OR Wounded | |
| do | 18/1/17 | 1/30 am | During the early morning we bombarded the enemy's front system with 5.9s and 15 pounders. He sent up rockets descending in GOLDEN RAIN which seem to have produced artillery retaliation. | [illegible] |
| | | 5 pm | ENEMY MOVEMENT was observed opposite O.10.d.7.7. A small party of men, about six in number, were observed moving between shell holes about 800 yards away. They were fired on by our Lewis Guns and disappeared. | |
| | | | A patrol of 1 Officer & 6 OR left our front line this night moving forward about 400 yards. They encountered none of the enemy. | |
| do | 19/1/17 | | With the exception of the usual shelling nothing of importance occurred. DELESKE FARM an old GERMAN DUGOUT which was used as our Battalion Headquarters suffered heavy bombardments. Being of reinforced concrete and being 3 or 4 seven feet thick, it withstood the effect of | [illegible] |

A6945 Wt. W11422/M1160 350,000 12/16 D. D. & L. Forms/C./2118/14.

Instructions regarding War Diaries and Intelligence Summaries are contained in F. S. Regs., Part II. and the Staff Manual respectively. Title pages will be prepared in manuscript.

# WAR DIARY
*or*
# INTELLIGENCE SUMMARY.
*(Erase heading not required.)*

Army Form C. 2118.

| Place | Date | Hour | Summary of Events and Information | Remarks and references to Appendices |
|---|---|---|---|---|
| In the line | 19/4/17 | | direct hits even with 15 cm howitzers | |
| | | | Today two enemy BIPLANES flew very low over my FRONT & SUPPORT TRENCHES | |
| | | | they fired MACHINE GUNS into our trenches without effect and were finally driven off | |
| | | | by our VICKERS GUN fire. | |
| | | | The continuous enemy line of defence has been discovered on the slope of the | |
| | | | hill in front of us. The defences appear to be behind the ridge. | |
| | | | Casualties OR. 2 killed 9 Wounded | [illegible] |
| do | 20/4/17 | | Nothing of special importance to record. The work of the RUNNERS both | |
| | | | of Companies and Headquarters has been worthy of special note during this | |
| | | | tour in the line. The utmost difficulty is often found in approaching | |
| | | | Battalion Headquarters owing to the shelling of the FARM LOCALITY and RAVINE | |
| | | | WOOD. Nevertheless these runners have always gone about their duties with | |
| | | | great courage as have the LINESMEN attached to the Signal Section. There | |
| | | | has been great difficulty in maintaining the lines unbroken during shell fire | |
| | | | and the linesmen have always gone out even during heavy shelling to | |
| | | | repair breakages. | |

A6945 Wt. W11422/M1160 350,000 12/16 D. D. & L. Forms/C./2118/14.

Army Form C. 2118.

Instructions regarding War Diaries and Intelligence Summaries are contained in F. S. Regs., Part II. and the Staff Manual respectively. Title pages will be prepared in manuscript.

# WAR DIARY
*or*
# INTELLIGENCE SUMMARY.
*(Erase heading not required.)*

| Place | Date | Hour | Summary of Events and Information | Remarks and references to Appendices |
|---|---|---|---|---|
| [illegible] | [illegible] | | Nothing of importance to record, beyond the usual heavy shelling of RAVINE WOOD and DELBSKE FARM. From 11/30 am three bodies of 30 of the enemy were seen at intervals of half an hour moving along HOLLEBEKE ROAD from N to S. | |
| | | [illegible] pm | A hostile AEROPLANE flew over our lines, down the RAVINE, turned NORTH along our FRONT LINE firing a machine gun all the way, and then leisurely flew off towards his own lines. | |
| | | | An M.T.M. battery (FISHTAIL) was this morning located as firing from FERRET FARM (O 11 b 2.1). It was silenced by our 75 Pounders. | |
| | | | Casualties OR 1 killed 3 wounded | |
| [illegible] | [illegible] | | Hostile Guns could be seen in action this morning by our Observers. Flash bearings were taken wherever possible, and reported to Brigade. | |
| | | | Today we suffered casualties to 3 Officers and 2 OR killed 1 OR wounded | |
| | | | 2nd Lt R. S. PAGE-GREEN 2nd Lt E. F. ADAMS | |
| | | | 2nd Lt H. H. H. BOND | |

Instructions regarding War Diaries and Intelligence Summaries are contained in F. S. Regs., Part II. and the Staff Manual respectively. Title pages will be prepared in manuscript.

# WAR DIARY
*or*
# INTELLIGENCE SUMMARY.
*(Erase heading not required.)*

Army Form C. 2118.

| Place | Date | Hour | Summary of Events and Information | Remarks and references to Appendices |
|---|---|---|---|---|
| In the line | 22/6/17 | | These constituted all the Officers of D Company holding the FRONT LINE | |
| | | | and 2/Lts WOODVILLE-MORGAN and STOYLE were sent to replace them. | |
| | | | Tonight the Battalion was relieved in the line by the 10th Bn QUEENS | |
| | | | Royal West Surrey Regiment | O.O. B32. |
| | | | In our turn we replaced the 21st Bn Kings Royal Rifle Corps who were | |
| | | | in dugouts in our old RESERVE LINE from BUS HOUSE to P.E.O TRENCH. | |
| | | | The relief was successfully carried out without casualties. Companies were | |
| | | | disposed along the whole length of the trench, with Battalion Headquarters | |
| | | | in two Kapola dugouts just inside of BOIS CONFLUENT | |
| Old Reserve line | 23/6/17 to 24/6/17 | | There is nothing of importance to record during this period. | |
| | | | The Battalion furnished working parties for the front line each night and | |
| | | | the remainder of the time was spent in cleaning up and resting. | |
| | | | Casualties 5 OR Wounded. | |

A6945 Wt. W11422/M1160 350,000 12/16 D. D. & L. Forms/C./2118/14.

Instructions regarding War Diaries and Intelligence Summaries are contained in F. S. Regs., Part II. and the Staff Manual respectively. Title pages will be prepared in manuscript.

Army Form C. 2118.

# WAR DIARY
*or*
# INTELLIGENCE SUMMARY.
*(Erase heading not required.)*

| Place | Date | Hour | Summary of Events and Information | Remarks and references to Appendices |
|---|---|---|---|---|
| OLD | 26/4/17 | 8.45pm | The Battalion proceeded to relieve the 21st Bn LRRC in the FRONT, BLACK | OO No 5 |
| RESERVE | | | BLUE LINES. Companies were disposed as follows:- | |
| LINE | | | FRONT LINE & IMMEDIATE SUPPORT — "C" Company | |
| | | | BLACK LINE — "B" " | |
| | | | BLUE LINE RIGHT — "D" " | |
| | | | LEFT — "A" " | |
| Front Line | 27th | | During this period the Battalion remained in the front | |
| System | 28th | | line system. There is no incident of any note to | |
| | 29th | | record. The work of consolidation & improvement | |
| | | | of the trenches was proceeded with. Wiring was | |
| | | | done. | |
| | | | There was considerable artillery activity on both sides | |
| | | | during the period. | |
| | | | On the 28th the Commanding Officer & O/c Coys of the | |
| | | | 24th London Regiment visited the trenches prior to taking | |

A6945 Wt. W11422/M1160 350,000 12/16 D. D. & L. Forms/C./2118/14.

Instructions regarding War Diaries and Intelligence Summaries are contained in F. S. Regs., Part II. and the Staff Manual respectively. Title pages will be prepared in manuscript.

# WAR DIARY
*or*
# INTELLIGENCE SUMMARY.
*(Erase heading not required.)*

Army Form C. 2118.

| Place | Date | Hour | Summary of Events and Information | Remarks and references to Appendices |
|---|---|---|---|---|
| | | | over the line. They were well satisfied with the state of the trenches | |
| | | | On the same day Major General Gorringe visited the trenches | |
| | | | On the evening of the 29th we were relieved by the 1st Batt London Regiment. The relief was carried out in a remarkably quick time and the Battalion returned to ONTARIO CAMP REMINGHELST | OO no 6 |
| | | | It is a remarkable fact that during the whole of this period in the front line trenches, the Battalion suffered no casualties and not a man even went sick, in spite of the fact that they had been up in the trenches & support for almost three weeks. | |
| | | | AW | |
| ONTARIO CAMP | 30th | | The day was spent resting & cleaning up. The Battalion paraded at [illegible] and marched to | OO. no 7 |

A6945 Wt. W11422/M1160 350,000 12/16 D. D. & L. Forms/C./2118/14.

Army Form C. 2118.

Instructions regarding War Diaries and Intelligence Summaries are contained in F. S. Regs., Part II. and the Staff Manual respectively. Title pages will be prepared in manuscript.

# WAR DIARY
*or*
# INTELLIGENCE SUMMARY.
*(Erase heading not required.)*

| Place | Date | Hour | Summary of Events and Information | Remarks and references to Appendices |
|---|---|---|---|---|
| | | | the METEREN TRAINING area. The Battalion was peaceably down in camp by 10 pm at 1 X 8 central! | |
| | | | JHB | |
| | | | A Maxwell<br>Major Commdg<br>26th Royal Fus. | |
| | | | 1/7/17 | |

Instructions regarding War Diaries and Intelligence Summaries are contained in F. S. Regs., Part II. and the Staff Manual respectively. Title pages will be prepared in manuscript.

# WAR DIARY
*or*
# INTELLIGENCE SUMMARY.
*(Erase heading not required.)*

Army Form C. 2118.

| Place | Date | Hour | Summary of Events and Information | Remarks and references to Appendices |
|---|---|---|---|---|
| | | | 5/ Copy No 4. of 1st I B. Op. O No 111 date 23/5/17 | |
| | | | 6/ 2 16. R.F. O.O No 3 date 2/6/17 | |
| | | | 7/ 2 16 R.F. Admin. Order date 5/6/17 | |
| | | | 8/ Copy Code of Signals used | |
| | | | 9/ Copy of Lieut Col. G. [illegible] despatch of the fight. | |
| | | | | [illegible] |
| | | | Casualties. Officers / O.R. | |
| | | | Killed nil 25 | |
| | | | Wounded 5 161 | |
| | | | Missing nil 7 | |

APPENDIX. II

SECRET. File. Copy. No. 1

26th. BN. THE ROYAL FUSILIERS.

OPERATION ORDER No.6.

Maps Sheet 27 S.E. & 28.

Orderly Officer for to-morrow: 2nd.Lieut. N. L. CORBEN.

1. The Battalion will move to the WESTOUTRE AREA to-morrow 18th.July 1917 and will be accommodated at KEMPTON CAMP (M 14 B 9.8)

2. The Battalion will parade in close column of Companies at 5.30 a.m. ready to move off. Revielle will be at 4.30 a.m. and Breakfast at 5.30 a.m.
ORDER OF MARCH: Headquarters, Band, C.A.B.D. Companies, Transport.
DRESS:- Battle Order, Steel Helmets to be carried on RIGHT shoulder.
The usual hourly halts will be adhered to.
ROUTE:- X roads X 4 c - SCHAEXKEN - LA MANCHE - R 24 c - M 26 a M 21 a - WESTOUTRE - VEMPTON PARK M 14 b 9.8.

3. All Officers Kits, men's packs, surplus baggage, mess boxes, Orderly Room Boxes etc. will be stacked at the entrance to the Camp by 6.30 a.m.
O/C. "B" Company will detail 1 N.C.O. & 6 men to act as laoding party, and 2nd.Lieut. W.H.COLE will be in charge of this party.
2 Motor Lorries will report at 7.15 a.m. and will make three trips each. The loading party will proceed with the last load.

4. 2nd.Lieut. W.H.COLE will hand over the camp to the Unit of the 23rd.DIVISION taking over, and obtain a receipt for all tents and utensils handed over and also a Certificate thatthe Camp is in a thoroughly clean condition.
He will also obtain a Certificate from the Owner at all Billets ~~of~~ that no claims are outstanding against the Battalion.

5. The Transport will move with the Battalion and the Transport Officer will make the necessary arrangements for loading up and moving off.
All practice ammunition, bombs etc, will be taken with the Battalion, by the motor lorries.

6. On arrival in the HESKEN AREA 2nd.Lieut. MASON will report to the AREA COMMANDANT, WESTOUTRE and arrange for the drawing of tents. He will arrange with the Transport Officer for the necessary Transport and O/C. "C" Company will detail a loading party of 1 N.C.O. and 6 men to report to the Transport Officer for loading immediately on arrival.

(Signed) D.M.C.GILL
2nd.Lt. for.
Lieut. & Adjutant.,
26th.Bn. The Royal Fusiliers.

Copy No.1 File.
2 War Diary.
3 Adjutant.
4 124th.Infantry Bde.
5 "A"
6 "B"
7 "C"
Copy. No.8 "D"
9 Headquarters.
10 Transport Officer.
11 Quartermaster.
12 Medical Officer.
13 2nd.Lt.Cole.
14 2nd.Lt.Mason.

APPENDIX III

26th. Bn. The Royal Fusiliers.

OPERATION ORDER FOR PRACTICE ATTACK.

1. INTENTION. A Brigade has carried out an attack, and the enemy has proved himself to be demoralised. In order to exploit a success a Reserve Brigade is called upon to pass through the Brigade that has carried out the attack and advance to the next series of trenches on the line of the main road from BERTHEN to WESTOUTRE.

2. DISPOSITION OF BRIGADE MAKING ATTACK.

| | |
|---|---|
| On the RIGHT. | 26th.Bn. Royal Fusiliers. |
| On the LEFT. | 21st.Bn. K. R" R. Corps. |
| In SUPPORT | Two Companies of 10th.Bn. "Queens" R" W" S" Regt. |

3. DISPOSITION OF BATTALION.

| | |
|---|---|
| On the RIGHT, | "B" Company on two platoon frontage. |
| On the Left. | "D" " do. |
| In SUPPORT | "C" " |
| In Reserve. | "A" " |

The Three platoon system will be used.

4. ASSEMBLY POSITIONS.
On the Road between M 20 d 1.1. and M 20 d 9.7.

5. OBJECTIVES.
First Objective. The line of the road from R 17 c 7.7. to R 18 a 6.7.
Second Objective. The Road from R 11 c 2.3. to R 11 c 9.6.

6. METHOD OF ATTACK.
At 8 a.m. the 21st. K. R". R. C. and 26th.Bn. Royal Fusiliers will move off in a N.-W. direction in Artillery Formation on a frontage of about 500 yards each. On reaching the BLUE LINE shown on the map they will deploy into waves, and continue the advance through the GREEN LINE. The creeping barrage which had been halted 400 yards beyond the GREEN LINE will advance at 25 yards per minute when the leading waves arrive within 100 yards of it, and halt 200 yards beyond the line of the first objective which will be captured and mopped up.
As soob as the 10th.Bn. "Queens" R"W.S. Regt. have passed through, the 21st.Bn. K. R. R. C. and 26th.Bn. R. F. will form up and march back to billets the latter leading.

7. MARKINGS.
The RED, BLUE, and GREEN LINES; the flanks of attacking Battalions; and the first and second objectives will be marked by flags on the ground.

8. BARRAGE.
25 flag men (detailed by Signalling Officer) will parade outside Marquee, under 2nd.Lt. A. E. CHAMBERS at 6.50 a.m. and proceed to report to Brigade Intelligence Officer at M 20 c 9.8. 7.30 a.m.

9. TRENCH MORTARS.
One Trench Mortar from 124th. L.T.M.B. will be attached to the Battalion, and will move forward with Battalion Headquarters.

(Signed) D. M. C. GILL, 2nd.Lt. for
Lieut. & Adjutant.,
26th.Bn. The Royal Fusrs.

23rd.July 1917.

APPENDIX IV.

War Diary

SECRET. COPY No: 2

26th. Bn. THE ROYAL FUSILIERS.

OPERATION ORDER No.7.

Maps Sheet 28. S.W.

1. INTENTION:
The Battalion will move Camp, this afternoon and proceed to Camp at M.6 d and take over from 23rd.Bn.MIDDLESEX REGIMENT.

2. PARADE.
The Battalion will parade at 4 p.m. this afternoon on the road outside the Camp facing N. W.
DRESS:- Marching Order.
ORDER of MARCH:- Band: Headquarters: "C". "D" "A". "B".

3. ROUTE.
IF DRY: M 9 c 46 - W & Y Track to M 5 a 31 - Overland track to LA CLYTTE - RENINGHELST-ROAD.

IF WET: WESTOUTRE - HYDE PARK CORNER - LA CLYTTE.

4. SANITATION:
The Camp will be left in a perfectly clean & sanitary condition.

5. M 6 d CAMP:
2nd. Lt. W. H. COLE will arrange to take over the Camp from 23rd. Bn. MIDDLESEX REGIMENT prior to the arrival of the Battalion. His party of Bombers will form the advance party & they will report at the Camp before 4 p.m. C. Q. M. S. or representatives will proceed to the Camp, to be there before 4 p.m.

6. KEMPTON CAMP:
2nd.Lt. R. BULLOCH will be responsible for this Camp and will obtain Certificate from the Camp Warden to the effect that it has been left in a thoroughly clean condition. He will also obtain a Receipt for all Stores handed over.

7. TRANSPORT:
The TRANSPORT OFFICER will arrange for the Transport of all Stores.
All Officers Kits, Boxes and surplus Stores will be dumped at the MARQUEE ready for collection before 2 p.m. to-day.

8. ACKNOWLEDGE.

(Signed) D. M. C. GILL, 2nd.Lt.for
Lieut. & Adjutant.,
26th.Bn. The Royal Fusilier

25th.July 1917.

COPY No. 1. File.
2. War Diary.
3. Adjutant.
4. 124th. I. B.
5. "A" Company.
6. "B" "
7. "C" "

COPY No.8. "D" Company.
9. Headquarters.
10. Transport Officer.
11. Quartermaster.
12. Medical Officer.
13. Spare.
14. Spare.

War Diary

APPENDIX V.

SECRET. COPY No. 9

26th. Bn. THE ROYAL FUSILIERS.

OPERATION ORDER No.8.

Maps Sheet 28 S.W. & 28 N.W.

1. INTENTION.

The Battalion will move on "X/Y" night from its Camp at M 6 d to RIDGEWOOD, and take over tents & bivouaes from Guard of 32nd.Bn. THE ROYAL FUSILIERS.

2. PARADE.

The Battalion will parade at 8 p.m. ready to move off.
ORDER of MARCH: "D". "B". "C". "A". Headquarters.
DRESS: Battle Order.

3. ROUTE:

IF FINE: LA CLYTTE - HALLEBAST ROAD to N 2 d 0.7 - track via N 2 d 9 7 - N 3 a 3 9 - N 3 d 5.9 - by southern end of DICKEBUSCH LAKE.

IF WET: LA CLYTTE - HALLEBAST CORNER - VIERSTRAAT ROAD and southern end of DICKEBUSCH LAKE.

O/C. "D" Company will detail an Officer to reconnoitre the former, and O/C. "B" Company an Officer to reconnoitre the latter during the day.

All movements will be by platoons at 50 yds. interval and the Battalion must be clear of the point N 3 d 5.9 by 10.30 p.m.

4. PACKS & OVERCOATS:

All packs will be carefully stacked by 10 a.m. to-morrow 26/7/17; they must be marked on the back with the No. RANK, NAME of Owner, and also the Company & Battalion.

All overcoats will be fastened together by sections and stacked by the same time; they will be tied together with rope and labelled with the number of the section and a roll of the men. The Quartermaster will supply the rope and wooden labels.

The Transport Officer will arrange to deliver the packs and overcoats to 41st. DIVISIONAL KIT STORE RENINGHELST at 2 p.m. on 26/7/17.

6. RATIONS:

Rations for consumption on "Y" day will be carried to RIDGEWOOD by Transport which will accompany the Battalion.
Three Kitchens will also accompany the Battalion to RIDGEWOOD and remain there until the Battalion moves.
Rations for consumption on "Z" day will be sent to RIDGEWOOD on "Y" day and carried up to the line on the man.
Rations for "Z" + 1 day will be drawn from IMP DUMP (O 4 a 8.8)

6. DETAILS.

Details of 124th. INFANTRY BRIGADE will remain at DEZON CAMP on the move of the Brigade into the Forward Area.

7. BRIDGE:

A Pontoon Bridge will be constructed at dusk on Y/Z night at O 4 a 7.7.
Infantry must break step when crossing the Bridge.
Horsed Transport will proceed at a walk.

8. ASSEMBLY:

The Battalion will move from RIDGEWOOD on Y/Z night to assembly positions. The head of the column to reach Bridge at I 33 a 22 at 2 a.m. on "Z" day.

/ROUTE.-

ROUTE:

Overland Track from RIDGEWOOD - BRASSERIE - BUG HOUSE - CANAL BRIDGE (I 33 a 22).

If I 33 a 22 is under shell fire, alternative Bridges will be available as follows:-

1. NORFOLK BRIDGE I 33 d 22 55.
2. PONTOON BRIDGE O-4 a 25-75.

O/C. Companies will each detail one guide to reconnoitre the route with alternatives as stated above.

All moves will be by Platoons at 100 yards interval.

O/C. Companies will advise Battalion Orderly Room immediately they are in position. Headquarters will advise 124th. INFANTRY BRIGADE.

(Signed) D. M. C. GILL, 2nd.Lt. for
Lieut. & Adjutant.,
26th.Bn. The Royal Fuse,

26th. July 1917.

COPY No.
1. File.
2. War Diary.
3. The Adjutant.
4. 124th.Infy.Bde.
5. "A" Company.
6. "B" do.
7. "C" do.
8. "D" do.
9. Headquarters.
10. Medical Officer.
11. Transport Officer.
12. Quartermaster.
13. Spare.
14. Spare.

War Diary APPENDIX VI

SECRET. **26th. BN. THE ROYAL FUSILIERS.** COPY No. 2

## OPERATION ORDER No.7.

Maps. 1/10.000 HOLLEBEKE.

1. INTENTION: The 41st. DIVISION will attack on a date to be notified later in conjunction with the 19th.DIVISION of the IXth.CORPS on the RIGHT and the 24th.DIVISION of the IInd. CORPS on the LEFT.

The front of attack for the 41st.DIVISION will be from FORRET FARM on the RIGHT to the KLEIN ZILLEBEKE ROAD on the LEFT.

The objectives are as shown on attached map.

The 122nd. INFANTRY BRIGADE will attack SOUTH and the 123rd. INFANTRY BRIGADE-NORTH of the YPRES-COMINES CANAL.

The 72nd. INFANTRY BRIGADE will be on the RIGHT of the 24th.DIVISION with Headquarters in LARCH WOOD.

2. DISPOSITION OF DIVISION: Prior to X/Y night units of the Division will be disposed as follows:-

Divisional Headquarters: WESTOUTRE.
On the RIGHT. 122nd.Infy.Bde. SPOIL BANK I 33 d 0.2.
" LEFT. 123rd.Infy.Bde. BLUFF SUBWAY I 33 d 28.
124th.Infy.Bde. RENINGHELST.

X/Y NIGHT: 26th.Bn.Royal Fusiliers will move to RIDGWOOD AREA where they will remain under cover on Y day and come under the orders of G.O.C. 123rd. INFANTRY BRIGADE who will issue orders for the move to assembly positions via BRASSERIE, BUSS HOUSE, and CANAL BRIDGE at SPOIL BANK.

All movements will be by platoons at 50 yards interval and no movement will take place before 10 p.m.

3. DISPOSITIONS of 123rd. INFANTRY BRIGADE: Dispositions of 123rd. INFANTRY BRIGADE one hour before ZERO, Hqrs Boundaries, Overland Tracks, Tramway Tracks, R.A.P's Objectives & Barrage lines are given on attached map.

The ground shaded in green is allotted to 24th.DIVISION for assembly prior to the attack.

The 21st. Bn. K. R. R. C. will be in support and the 26th.Bn. Royal Fusiliers in Reserve.

4. PREVIOUS to ATTACK: There will be a preliminary bombardment lasting several days.

On the return of the Battalion to the line all Officers and runners will carefully reconnoitre the various routes to FRONT LINE, BATTN. & BRIGADE HEADQUARTERS etc.

5. METHOD OF ATTACK: All troops will be in position by ZERO minus ½ hr.

The Battalion will be ready to move on receipt of orders from the Brigade Commander, from ZERO hour onwards.

ZERO: The barrage will come down on to the RED LINE.

ZERO + 4 minutes: do. pile on to the BLUE LINE whilst the Infantry mops up the RED LINE.

ZERO + 28 minutes: The barrage will lift off the BLUE LINE and creep forward to its final protective position, some 400 yards beyond the GREEN LINE, which is the final objective, except for the LEFT FLANK, where it will pivot about J 34 c 5.9 remaining there until

ZERO + 48 minutes: The barrage will advance in conjunction with 24th.DIVISION.

The GREEN LINE, when completed will become the OUTPOST line. The creeping barrage will advance at 100 yds /in

in 4 minutes.
The general direction of attack is 127 degrees T.B.

6. STRONG POINTS: Strong Points will be established as under:-
(a) In front of RED LINE.-
about:- Railway Embankment O 6 a 4.4½.
Corner of Wood. O 6 a 9.7.
1.36 d 2.0.
1.36 d 5.5.

(b). In front of BLUE LINE.-
about O 6 c 30.42.
D 6 d 25.80.
D 6 d 50.50.
O 6 b 30.90.
1.36 d 90.50.

7. MACHINE GUNS: There will be a Machine-gun barrage under arrangements to be made by the CORPS M. G. O.

8. STOKES GUNS: Stokes Guns will be allotted to Battalions and these will be placed in defensive position under instructions of O/C.Battalion.

9. SIGNAL COMMUNICATIONS: The arrangements for Signalling Communications will be issued later.
The Code of Signals used on 7th. June 1917 will be used on this occasion and should be practised by all Signallers.
The arrangements for the BRIGADE FORWARD PARTY will be the same as on 7th.June 1917.

10. DRESS: Dress and equipment to be worn by all ranks will be as laid down in section XXXI of S.S.135 paras 1 & 2 with the following exceptions.-
(a) Every third man will carry an entrenching tool (1 pick to 3 shovels)
(b) 150 rounds of SAA will be carried except by Bombers, Signallers, Scouts, Runners, Lewis Gunners and carrying parties who will only carry 50 rounds.

(Signed) D.M.C.GILL, 2nd.Lt.for
Lieut. & Adjutant.,
26th.Bn. The Royal Fusiliers.

20th.July 1917.

| | | | |
|---|---|---|---|
| Copy No.1 | File. | Copy No.8. | "D" Company. |
| 2. | War Diary. | 9 | Headquarters. |
| 3. | Adjutant. | 10 | Transport Officer. |
| 4. | 124th. I.B. | 11 | Quartermaster. |
| 5. | "A" Company. | 12 | Medical Officer. |
| 6. | "B" Company. | 13 | Spare. |
| 7. | "C" Company. | 14 | Spare. |

"A" Form

Army Form C. 2121 (in pads of 100).

## MESSAGES AND SIGNALS.

No. of Message..............

| Prefix........Code........m. | Words. | Charge. | This message is on a/c of: | Recd. at........m. |
|---|---|---|---|---|
| Office of Origin and Service Instructions. | Sent | | ..................Service. | Date........ |
| | At........m. | | Appendix VII | From........ |
| | To........ | | (Signature of "Franking Officer.") | By........ |
| | By........ | | | |

TO O/C A.T.C. Coy. Hdqrs.

| Sender's Number. | Day of Month. | In reply to Number. | AAA |
|---|---|---|---|
| C3K. | 31 | | |

O/C A T Co. Coy T Hdqrs. will move at once to IMPACT SUPPORT and IMPACT TRENCH.
C Coy in IMPACT SUPPORT
A " " IMPACT TRENCH

C Coy will move from the TUNNELS at 12 30 pm
A Coy also will move from the TUNNELS at 1 30 pm
ROUTE: Duckboard track from I 33 d 36 heading through O H a 9 9 thence along IMPUDENCE SUPPORT
Guides will be sent to meet Companies as soon as they can be allowed.

From

Place

Time 12 noon

The above may be forwarded as now corrected. (Z)

Censor. Signature of Addressor or person authorised to telegraph in his name. 2/Lt [illegible]

* This line should be erased if not required.

(18965.) Wt. W12952/M1294. 187,500 Pads. 1/17 McC. & Co., Ltd. (E. 818.)

War Diary

**SECRET.** COPY No 2.

## 26th. BN. THE ROYAL FUSILIERS.

### ADMINISTRATION ORDERS.

1. **Personnel to be left behind.**-
As per Appendix "A" attached.
O/C. Companies will render to Battalion Orderly Room within 24 hours a nominal roll of those to be left behind in accordance with Appendix "A" and a Daily Return, due at 9 a.m., of any alteration in the Nominal Roll.

2. **RATIONS & WATER:**
Rations for "Z" day (700) will be dumped in the immediate vicinity of IMP DUMP O 4 a 8.8.
Water in Petrol Tins (1/3rd. gallon per man per diem) will be dumped at the same place (approximately) 100 tins).
Instructions for Companies to draw from above dump will be issued later.
Rations for "Z" plus 1 and subsequent days will be delivered by pack transport and the Transport Officer will arrange point for handing over.

3. **WATER:**
1. Water-Cart Refilling Point. I.31 d 2.4.
2. Water Tanks & Stand Pipes. I.33 a 5.1 )
3 I 33 c 8.7 ) SUPPLY
I 33 c 50.45) UNRELIABLE.
I.33 d 3.5.)
O 4 a 75.60)

3 Wells I.31 c 4.6. )
I.31 c 3.4. )
O 2 a 6.7. ) NOTICE BOARDS ERECTED SHOW
I.33 a 80.85.) AMOUNT OF CLORINATION REQUIRED.
I.32 d 85.20 )

Companies will be issued with petrol tins which will be filled from dump at NORFOLK LODGE BRIDGE I 33 d 3.6. should the pipe line break down.
The greatest care will have to be exercised with these tins.

4. **AMMUNITION.**
Divisional Dump will be at N 4 c 5.2.
Left Bde.Dump. do. I 34 c 5.0.

2nd.Lt. NEWMAN, 23rd.Bn. Middlesex Regiment will be in charge of the Left Infantry Brigade Dump, from which Battalion will draw any ammunition required.
Every man will carry one aeroplane flare.
"B" & "D" Companies will have 2 S.O.S. Rockets & H.Q. 1.

5. **R. E. STORES:**
Divisional R. E. DUMP at LA BRASSERIE N 6 a 1.1.
Advanced R. E. DUMP: IMP DUMP O 4 a 8.8. (Old-German Crater).

6. **MEDICAL:**
The MEDICAL OFFICER will remain with the Battalion unless otherwise ordered.

/REGIMENTAL

REGIMENTAL AID POSTS:

Left Brigade Sector: O 4 b 2.9.
I.34 d 6.8.

Collecting Post. SPOIL BANK I 33 d 32.
A. D. S. VOORMEZEELE. I.31 c 4.6.
Collecting Station, Walking Wounded, BRASSERIE N 6 a 22.
Main Dressing Station, Seriously Wounded. M 6 a 8.6.
Do. Walking Wounded. N 7 c 4.5.

7. PRISONERS OF WAR:
These will be collected together and sent back to Divisional Cage and a receipt obtained from the Officer i/c Cage at N 3 a Central, under an escort not exceeding 5% of Prisoners.

8. BATTLE STRAGGLERS POSTS:
A line of Divisional Straggler Posts will be at.-
O 2 a 4.6 (BUS HOUSE), I 32 d 4.4., I 33 a 2.3 (BRIDGE).

Stragglers arrested by Divisional Posts will be handed over to First Line Transport and sent back to the line at first opportunity.

9. RE-INFORCEMENTS:
Personnel left behind (para 1) will be accommodated at the Transport Lines where any Drafts which may arrive will also be sent.
No Personnel will be sent to join the Battalion without orders from DIVISIONAL HEADQUARTERS.

10. PACKS & SURPLUS KIT.
Packs and surplus kit will be stored in the BARN at RENINGHELST (G 35 d 65.80).
In order to facilitate rapid issue should the opportunity occur, greatcoats will be rolled into bundles separate from the packs and labelled with the number of the Platoon and a roll of the men.
No personal PROPERTY should be left in the pockets ofthe greatcoat.
All packs must be marked in indelible pencil with No. Rank, & Name of Owner; also Company & Battalion.

11. SALVAGE:
All Salvage will be collected by Companies to facilitate return to dump. All parties proceeding to the Dump will carry some salvaged article.

12. A Revised map showing tramways, overland tracks, dumps etc., will be issued shortly.

ACKNOWLEDGE.

(Signed) D. M. C. GILL, 2nd.Lt. for
Lieut. & Adjutant.,
26th.Bn.The Royal Fusiliers.

23rd.July 1917.

COPY No.1. File.
2 War Diary.
3 Adjutant.
4 124th. I. B.
5. "A" Company.
6. "B" Company.
7 "C" Company.

COPY No.8. "D" Company.
9 Headquarters.
10. Transport Officer.
11 Quartermaster.
12 Medical Officer.
13 Spare.
14 Spare.

# A P P E N D I X "A"

## DETAILS TO BE LEFT BEHIND.

| | | OFFICERS. | O.R. |
|---|---|---|---|
| Transport. | | 1 | 46 |
| Q.M. Stores. | | | 4 |
| Orderly Room Personnel. | | | 2 |
| Officer & Batman: | Capt. Sir.W.A.Blount,Bart. | 1 | 1 (2) |
| Instructors: | Sgt. Warner. / " Thompson / " Wells. / L/C. Allen. | | 4 |
| Signallers: | Detailed by Sigs.Officer. | | 26 |
| Cooks: | Sgt. Howell. / 1 H"Q. / 2 per Coy. / 1 Q.M.Store. | | 11 |
| Sheemakers | | | 3 |
| Shoemakers. | | | 2 |
| Butchers. | | | 3 |
| Tailors. | | | 2 |
| Pioneers. | Sgt. Forster & 1 man. | | 1 |
| Armourers. | A. O. C. & | | 1 |
| Post Corporal. | | | 1 |
| Sanitary Corporal | | | 5 |
| Water Personnel. | | | 8 |
| C. Q. M. S. & Storeman. | | | = |
| Coy. Clerks. | | | 2 |
| C. S. M's. | "A" & "C" Coys. | | 13 |
| Runners. | 5 H.Q. & 2 per Company. | | |

IN EACH COMPANY:-

| | | | |
|---|---|---|---|
| Sergeants. | 1 per Company. | | 4 |
| Corporals. | 1 do. | | 4 |
| L/Corporals. | 1 do. | | 4 |

IN EACH PLATOON:-

| | | | |
|---|---|---|---|
| Rifle Bomber. | 4 per Company. | | 16 |
| Scout & Sniper. | 4 do. | | 16 |
| Lewis Gunners.. | 8 do. | | 32 |

---

23/7/17.

Instructions regarding War Diaries and Intelligence Summaries are contained in F. S. Regs., Part II. and the Staff Manual respectively. Title pages will be prepared in manuscript.

# WAR DIARY

*or*

~~INTELLIGENCE SUMMARY.~~

*(Erase heading not required.)*

26 R.F.

Vol 15

Army Form C. 2118.

| Place | Date | Hour | Summary of Events and Information | Remarks and references to Appendices |
|---|---|---|---|---|
| PHINCBOOM | 1·7·17 | | The Battalion rested during the whole of the day. | |
| " | 2·7·17 to 7·7·17 | | During this period parades consisted of Physical training from 6·30 AM – 7·15 AM and from 9 am – 12·30 pm training in Musketry, Bayonet Fighting, close order Drill, Bombing and Lewis Gun work. The Band played daily from 12 PM – 12·30 PM and from 4 pm – 5 pm. The afternoons were devoted to cricket and other recreations. A Batt<sup></sup>n concert was held on the evening of the 6th inst. A draft of 104 N.C.O's and men arrived on the 5th inst. The Divisional Concert Party gave a performance for the 26TH Bn Royal Fusiliers in the Y.M.C.A. Hut at METREN on the 4th inst. | D McGie |
| " | | | | D McGie |
| " | 8·7·17 | 11·30 AM | Divine Service was held on the Battn Parade ground, which was attended by the G.O.C. 124TH INFY. BDE | D McGie |
| " | 9·7·17. | | Parades consisted of Physical Training from 6·30 AM to 7·15 AM and Infantry Training under Company arrangements from 9 am to 1 pm. A draft of 69 N.C.O's and men arrived in the evening. A cricket match was played against the A.S.C. at FLETRE, | |

Army Form C. 2118.

Instructions regarding War Diaries and Intelligence Summaries are contained in F. S. Regs., Part II, and the Staff Manual respectively. Title pages will be prepared in manuscript.

# WAR DIARY
*or*
~~INTELLIGENCE SUMMARY.~~
*(Erase heading not required.)*

| Place | Date | Hour | Summary of Events and Information | Remarks and references to Appendices |
|---|---|---|---|---|
| PHINCBOOM | 9.7.17 | | contd. which resulted in a win for the Battn. | Sh C Guest |
| " | 10.7.17. | | 6.30 - 7.15 AM. Physical Training. 9 AM - 1 pm. Infantry Training under Company arrangements. All specialists paraded under specialist Officers. The G.O.C. 124th INFY BDE inspected all drafts which had arrived during the last few days. He also, on conclusion of the parade addressed a few words to them, and the Commanding Officer inspected the Battn at 2 p.m. Dress - Battle order. A draft of 120 N.C.O's and men arrived at 1 p.m. | Sh C Guest |
| " | 11.7.17 | | Reveillé sounded at 4.30 A.M. and the Battn paraded in battle order at 5.50 AM. and proceeded to view the trenches which had been marked out in R 17 and 18 (Sheet 27 S.E.). On its return the Battn was met by the band at BERTHEN, and was treated to a selection of new tunes on the march to Camp. The Battalion Sports were held in the afternoon commencing at 1 p.m. Amongst the many visitors was the Staff of the 124th INFY BDE. | APPENDIX 1. |

A6945 Wt. W11422/M1160 350,000 12/16 D. D. & L. Forms/C./2118/14.

Instructions regarding War Diaries and Intelligence Summaries are contained in F. S. Regs., Part II. and the Staff Manual respectively. Title pages will be prepared in manuscript.

# WAR DIARY
*or*
~~INTELLIGENCE SUMMARY.~~
*(Erase heading not required.)*

Army Form C. 2118.

| Place | Date | Hour | Summary of Events and Information | Remarks and references to Appendices |
|---|---|---|---|---|
| PHINCBOOM | 11.7.17 contd | | The Sports proved a great success. Amongst the many interesting events were the obstacle race, the Officers' and Senior N.C.O's' race in walking out dress, the musical chairs for Officers (mounted) and wrestling on horseback. The G.O.C, who had previously judged the tug-o'-war contests, presented prizes to the successful competitors. In the evening a concert was held which was attended by some of the afternoon's visitors. The Band played selections during the afternoon and evening. | |
| Do | 12.7.17 | | The morning was spent in cleaning up. The Battalion & Transport paraded at full strength at 1/15 pm for inspection by the Divisional Commander. After the inspection, the Companies did Company Drill, Bayonet Fighting, Musketry etc. The Battalion was then formed into a hollow square and Medal Ribbons were presented to the undermentioned for deeds performed on June 7th 1917.<br>Bar to M.C. Lieut R. C. BARKWORTH M.C<br>M.C Lieut & Adjutant A. W. MACKAY. M. C. | Dm C Gilesh |

A6945 Wt. W11422/M1160 350,000 12/16 D. D. & L. Forms/C./2118/14.

Army Form C. 2118.

Instructions regarding War Diaries and Intelligence Summaries are contained in F. S. Regs., Part II. and the Staff Manual respectively. Title pages will be prepared in manuscript.

# WAR DIARY
or
# INTELLIGENCE SUMMARY.
(*Erase heading not required.*)

| Place | Date | Hour | Summary of Events and Information | Remarks and references to Appendices |
|---|---|---|---|---|
| PHINEBOOM | 12/4/17 | (Contd) | D.C.M. CSM. SIMPSON J. | |
| | | | M.M. 4441 Cpl STEVENS J.W. | |
| | | | 19416 L/c SAVILLE A.E. | |
| | | | 19707 " WALTERS E.A. | |
| | | | 20284 " WATERHOUSE R.V. | |
| | | | 19623 Pte SPRING S. | |
| | | | 60026 " BURGESS J. | |
| | | | The Divisional Commander also expressed his satisfaction at the training he had seen during the afternoon. | DMC Gieen |
| do | 13th/14th/4/17 | | Infantry Training under Company and Specialist Officers | DMC Gieen |
| do | 15/4/17 | 11/30am | Divine Service was held on the Battalion Parade Ground. | DMC Gieen |
| do | 16/4/17 | 6/30am | The Battalion paraded at 6/30 am and proceed to R.H.C. central (Sheet 27 SE) for a practice attack in advancing and reinforcing over open ground. | DMC Gieen |

Instructions regarding War Diaries and Intelligence Summaries are contained in F. S. Regs., Part II. and the Staff Manual respectively. Title pages will be prepared in manuscript.

# WAR DIARY
*or*
# INTELLIGENCE SUMMARY.
*(Erase heading not required.)*

Army Form C. 2118.

| Place | Date | Hour | Summary of Events and Information | Remarks and references to Appendices |
|---|---|---|---|---|
| PHINEBOOM | 16/7/17 | 10/30 am | The Band joined the Battalion at LA MANCHE and played them to billets. | |
| | | | The remainder of the day was spent in Recreational Training. | |
| | | | | D.McC Sieur Lt |
| do | 17/7/17 | | Infantry Training under Company & Specialist Officers during the morning. All recent drafts attended a demonstration and lecture in Gas and had their Box Respirators fitted in Lachrymatory Gas. | |
| | | | The Superintendent of Physical Training and Bayonet Fighting in the Second Army visited the Battalion and inspected the various squads whilst Bayonet Fighting. | |
| | | | | D.McC Sieur Lt |
| do | 18/7/17 | | The Battalion paraded at 6/30 am and proceeded to KEMPTON CAMP M.16.b.9.5 (Sheet 28 S.W.) in accordance with attached Operation Order. | APPENDIX II. |
| | | | At the 41st Divisional Horse Show held at BERTHEN the Battalion obtained First Prize for both the following:- | |
| | | | G S Limber & pair of Mules. | |
| | | | Field Kitchen & pair of H D Horses. | |

A6945 Wt. W11422/M1160 350,000 12/16 D. D. & L. Forms/C./2118/14.

- Instructions regarding War Diaries and Intelligence Summaries are contained in F. S. Regs., Part II. and the Staff Manual respectively. Title pages will be prepared in manuscript.

# WAR DIARY
*or*
# INTELLIGENCE SUMMARY.
*(Erase heading not required.)*

Army Form C. 2118.

| Place | Date | Hour | Summary of Events and Information | Remarks and references to Appendices |
|---|---|---|---|---|
| [illegible] | 18/7/17 | | Gees to all units of the Division. This is the first time that a First Line Transport has been successful in obtaining these prizes. | D.M.C. Green |
| WESTOUTRE | 19/7/17 | | Infantry training under Company & Specialist Officers during the morning. The Rifle Grenadiers had the use of the T.M. Range at R 23 c (Sheet 27 SE) for the purpose of firing Rifle Grenades. During the afternoon the Battalion used the Rifle Range at R33a (Sheet 27 SE) when all Companies fired 200 yards Application and 200 yards Rapid. | D.M.C. Green |
| do | 20/7/17 | | Infantry training under Company & Specialist Officers. Officers & NCO's of the Battalion visited the model of the trenches at RENINGHELST (M 4 & 5 Sheet 28 SW) during the day. | D.M.C. Green |
| do | 21/7/17 | | Infantry training under Company & Specialist Officers. | D.M.C. Green |

A6945 Wt. W11422/M1160 350,000 12/16 D. D. & L. Forms/C./2118/14.

Instructions regarding War Diaries and Intelligence Summaries are contained in F. S. Regs., Part II. and the Staff Manual respectively. Title pages will be prepared in manuscript.

# WAR DIARY
*or*
# INTELLIGENCE SUMMARY.
*(Erase heading not required.)*

Army Form C. 2118.

| Place | Date | Hour | Summary of Events and Information | Remarks and references to Appendices |
|---|---|---|---|---|
| WESTOUTRE | 22/4/17 | 11/15am | Divine Service was held in the Transport Field. | |
| | | | The Corps Commander inspected the Camp and gave a very favourable report. He was very pleased with the condition of the Field Kitchens. | |
| | | | | D McGill[illegible] |
| do | 23/4/17 | | Baths at MURRUMBIDGEE CAMP, LA CLYTTE, were allotted to the Battalion during the whole of the day, and every man had a bath and a clean change of under clothing. | |
| | | | | D McGill[illegible] |
| do | 24/4/17 | | The Battalion paraded at 6/45am and proceeded to the road between M 20 d 1.1 and M 20 d 9.7 (Sheet 28 SW) for practice attack as per attached Operation Order | APPENDIX III |
| | | | The afternoon was spent in the reorganization of Companies into the three Platoon system for active warfare. | |
| | | | | D McGill[illegible] |

Instructions regarding War Diaries and Intelligence Summaries are contained in F. S. Regs., Part II. and the Staff Manual respectively. Title pages will be prepared in manuscript.

# WAR DIARY
*or*
# INTELLIGENCE SUMMARY.
*(Erase heading not required.)*

Army Form C.

| Place | Date | Hour | Summary of Events and Information | Remarks and references to Appendices |
|---|---|---|---|---|
| WESTOUTRE | 25/7/17 | | No training was done in the morning. It was very wet and the time was spent in cleaning up the camp and preparing to move in the afternoon. | |
| | | 4 pm | The Battalion paraded at 4 pm and proceeded to camp at M6d (Sheet 28 S.W.) in accordance with attached Operation order. Owing to the very greasy nature of the ground the wet weather route had to be used | APPENDIX. 1 |
| | | | | Wm C Gi[illegible] |
| LA CLYTTE | 26/7/17 | | The morning was spent in cleaning up and resting under Company arrangements. The Battalion paraded at 2pm in full Battle Order and Steel Helmets for inspection by the Commanding Officer. | Wm C Gi[illegible] |
| LA CLYTTE | 27/7/17 – 29/7/17 | | The day was spent in training. The morning from 9am to 12/30 pm being devoted to Deploying from Artillery Formation, Bayonet Fighting & Physical Training, the afternoon from 2pm to 4 pm to Fire Discipline, Fire Control and Firing Exercises. | |

[illegible signature]

Instructions regarding War Diaries and Intelligence Summaries are contained in F. S. Regs., Part II. and the Staff Manual respectively. Title pages will be prepared in manuscript.

# WAR DIARY
*or*
# INTELLIGENCE SUMMARY.
*(Erase heading not required.)*

Army Form C. 2118.

| Place | Date | Hour | Summary of Events and Information | Remarks and references to Appendices |
|---|---|---|---|---|
| LA CLYTTE | 29/7/17 | | Divine Service which should have been held at 11/30 am was cancelled owing to the inclemency of the weather. Holy Communion was, however, celebrated in the YMCA Hut at 3/30 pm | |
| | | 8 pm | The Battalion paraded at 8 pm and proceeded to the Camp at RIDGEWOOD in accordance with Operation Order No 8. The weather being very wet, the dry weather route had to be followed. On arrival at RIDGEWOOD CAMP the Battalion came under the Orders of the G.O.C. 123rd Infantry Brigade. | APPENDIX V. |
| | | | [signature] | |
| RIDGEWOOD | 30/7/17 | | The whole of the day was spent in resting and drawing implements &c. [illegible] for the coming offence. | [signature] |
| | | 10 pm | The Battalion paraded and proceeded to take up assembly positions in the BLUFF TUNNELS in accordance with Operation Order No 8 ready for | APPENDIX V |
| BLUFF TUNNELS | 31/7/17 | | the Offensive Operations detailed in Operation Order No 7. In position at 2/50 am | APPENDIX VII |
| | | 3/50 am | ZERO hour was at 3/50 am and at this moment the Barrage commenced. | |
| | | 6/45 am | About 6/45 am orders were received that two Companies would take | – |

A6945 Wt. W11422/M1160 350,000 12/16 D. D. & L. Forms/C./2118/14.

Instructions regarding War Diaries and Intelligence Summaries are contained in F. S. Regs., Part II. and the Staff Manual respectively. Title pages will be prepared in manuscript.

# WAR DIARY
*or*
# INTELLIGENCE SUMMARY.
*(Erase heading not required.)*

Army Form C. 2118.

| Place | Date | Hour | Summary of Events and Information | Remarks and references to Appendices |
|---|---|---|---|---|
| B. LUFF TUNNELS | 31/7/17 | 6/45 am | over IMPACT & IMPERIAL SUPPORT trenches from the 21st Bn KRRC who had been sent forward to reinforce the 20th Bn Durham Light Infantry who were meeting with some resistance on the right of the Brigade Front. 'B' & 'D' Companies were therefore ordered forward. | [signature] Major |
| | | 12 noon | A & C Coys & H.Qrs moved forward in accordance with attached APPENDIX Battalion Headquarters being situated at I 34 d 5.6 (Sheet 28 N.W.) | APPENDIX VII |
| | | 1.30 pm | On completion of this move the Battalion was disposed as follows:- | |
| | | | 2 Companies in IMPERIAL SWITCH | |
| | | | 2 " " OLD BRITISH FRONT LINE | |
| | | | Bn. H.qrs at I 34 d 5.6. | |

J. Maxwell
Major
26th Royal Fusiliers

APPENDIX. 1

26th. BN. THE ROYAL FUSILIERS.

*=*=*=*=*=*=*=*=*

P R O G R A M M E

-* of *-

REGIMENTAL SPORTS MEETING TO BE HELD ON

THE BATTALION PARADE GROUND

AT

P H I N E B O O M

on

WEDNESDAY, the 11th. JULY, 1917

COMMENCING AT 1.30 pm.

*O*O*O*O*O*O*O*O*O*O*O*

R.H.

## -*.PROGRAMME.*-

| No. | EVENT. | No. of ENTRIES | PRIZES 1st. Frs. | 2nd. Frs. | 3rd. Frs. |
|---|---|---|---|---|---|
| 1. | 100 yds. Handicap | 3 per Company | 15 | 5 | |
| 2. | Sack race | 6 " " | 10 | | |
| 3. | Lewis Gun Team Race | Team of 6 per Coy. (32 magazines per team.) | 30 | 15 | |
| 4. | Pick-a-back Wrestling | 4 pairs per company | 15 | 10 | |
| 5. | Half mile race | 2 per company | 30 | 15 | 5 |
| 6. | Reville & Stand To race | 2 per company | 10 | | |
| 7. | Bombing event Individual | distance. 2 per coy. 3 throws each-each man throws three bombs. | 15 | 5 | |
| 8. | Bombing " Team of four | One team per Coy. | 20 | | |
| 9. | Inter-Company Relay Race | (4 men per team) 1 Team per Coy. | 40 | 10 | |
| 10. | Potato race | 4 per Coy. | 10 | | |
| 11. | 220 yds. Handicap | 3 per Coy. | 20 | 10 | 5 |
| 12. | V.C. Race (dismounted) | 2 pairs per Coy. | 15 | | |
| 13. | Tug-of-war (8 men per team) | 1 Team per Coy. | 40 | | |
| 14. | Obstacle Race | 4 per Coy. | 25 | 10. | |

**- * * INTERVAL OF 15 MINUTES * * -**

*-*-*-*-*-*-*-*-*-*-*-*-*-*-*

| No. | EVENT. | No. of ENTRIES | 1st. Frs. | 2nd. Frs. | 3rd. Frs. |
|---|---|---|---|---|---|
| 15. | 100 yds. (open) | 3 per Unit | 30 | 15 | 5 |
| 16. | High jump (open) | 4 per Unit | 10 | | |
| 17. | Long Jump (open) | 4 per Unit | 10 | | |
| 18. | Wrestling on Horseback | Officers only. | - | - | - |
| 19. | 440 yds. race (open) | 2 per Unit | 30 | 15 | 5 |
| 20. | Three legged race | 2 pairs per Company | 15 | 10 | |
| 21. | One mile race (open) | 2 per Unit | 30 | 15 | |
| 22. | 100 yds. Race-walking out dress. | Officers and Senior N.C.Os. only. | - | - | |
| 23. | Mule race (open) | | 15 | 5 | |
| 24. | Tug-of-war (open) 8 men per team | 1 team per Unit | 40 | 20 | |
| 25. | Musical chairs (mounted) | Open to officers only | - | - | |
| 26. | Band race (handicap) | | 15 | 5 | |
| 27. | V.C. Race (Mounted) | Open to officers only | - | - | |
| 28. | Wrestling for men (6 men per team. | Open - one team per Unit | 30 | - | |
| 29. | Obstacle race (open) | | 30 | 15 | 5 |
| 30. | Musical chairs for N.C.Os. and men | | 25 | 10 | |

********************

ALL ENTRIES FOR OPEN EVENTS FROM OTHER UNITS SHOULD BE

SENT IN TO THE SECRETARY by 6 pm. 10th. July, 1917.

********************

Secretary:- Sir W.A. BLOUNT, Bart.,
26th. Bn. The Royal Fusiliers.

Instructions regarding War Diaries and Intelligence Summaries are contained in F. S. Regs., Part II. and the Staff Manual respectively. Title pages will be prepared in manuscript.

# WAR DIARY
or
# INTELLIGENCE SUMMARY.
(*Erase heading not required.*)

26 RF

174/41

Vol 16

Army Form C. 2118.

| Place | Date | Hour | Summary of Events and Information | Remarks and references to Appendices |
|---|---|---|---|---|
| [illegible] | 27.7.17 | 8 P.M. | [illegible] | [illegible] |
| [illegible] | 29.7.17 | | [illegible] 11.30 P.M. [illegible] | [illegible] |
| [illegible] | 31.7.17 | | [illegible] 3.50 A.M. [illegible] I 36 c 4 4 [illegible] 1.30 P.M. [illegible] I 36 c 2 8 | [illegible] |
| | 1.8.17 | | Two Coys attacked at 4 AM - lost direction, enemy put down heavy barrage inflicting casualties. these Coys afterwards occupied a trench by the KLEIN ZILLEBECK Rd J 31 a 2.0. Heavy rain throughout the day & night weather conditions very bad. Two Coys remained with the 21 KRR. the remainder were withdrawn about 2 PM to IMPACT TRENCH. At about 10.PM | [illegible] |

A6945 Wt. W11422/M1160 350,000 12/16 D. D. & L. Forms/C./2118/14.

16 K

Instructions regarding War Diaries and Intelligence Summaries are contained in F. S. Regs., Part II. and the Staff Manual respectively. Title pages will be prepared in manuscript.

# WAR DIARY
*or*
# INTELLIGENCE SUMMARY.
*(Erase heading not required.)*

Army Form C. 2118.

| Place | Date | Hour | Summary of Events and Information | Remarks and references to Appendices |
|---|---|---|---|---|
| FUSILIER WOOD | 1·8·17 | | The Bn relieved the 11th Royal West Kents in the front line B. H.Q. I 35. 95. 9. Details around that night. Heavy rain. | CAM |
| | 2·8·17 | | D. Coy held the front line A.B. support. C. reserve. Constant enemy barrages were put on the front & support lines. Heavy rain all day. | CAM |
| | 3·8·17 | 10·PM | On the night of 2nd/3rd at 10. 30 PM the 32nd Royal Fusiliers relieved the Bn Coys proceeded to Imperial switch & IMPACT TRENCH. B.H.Q. I 35. c. 44. | CAM |
| | 4·8·17 | | Held the line enemy artillery active all around. | CAM |
| | 5·8·17 | 9·30 | At 9. 30 PM enemy delivered a counter attack on HOLLEBEKE. Bn stood too. enemy driven off suffering heavy losses. | CAM |
| | 6·8·17 | | Bn relieved by 20th D.L.I. & proceeded to SCOTTISH WOOD. under canvas. | CAM |

A6945 Wt. W11422/M1160 350,000 12/16 D. D. & L. Forms/C./2118/14.

Instructions regarding War Diaries and Intelligence Summaries are contained in F. S. Regs., Part II. and the Staff Manual respectively. Title pages will be prepared in manuscript.

# WAR DIARY
*or*
# INTELLIGENCE SUMMARY.
*(Erase heading not required.)*

Army Form C. 2118.

| Place | Date | Hour | Summary of Events and Information | Remarks and references to Appendices |
|---|---|---|---|---|
| SCOTTISH WOOD | 7.8.17 | | Bn rested & cleaned up. | [illegible] |
| " " | 8.8.17 | | 5.30 PM Bn fell in for G.O.C. inspection. at 6. PM. Bn proceeded to WILTSHIRE FARM. Bivd under canvas. | |
| | ~~9.8.17~~ 9. | | ~~B~~ | |
| WILTSHIRE FARM | 9.8.17 | | Bn inspected by Commanding Officer, gas drill etc carried out. | [illegible] |
| " | 10.8.17 | 9.30 PM | Bn moved off to the RAILWAY EMBANKMENT at O.6. to relieve 23rd Bn MIDDLESEX Regt. C Coy front line. A. embankment. D. BATTLEWOOD. B. BLUFF TUNNELS. Relief complete at 1.4 AM. | [illegible] |
| Front line | 11.8.17 | | Bn holding the line shelling normal. Bn dug new Front line trench on the night of 11/12th weather conditions bad rain. | [illegible] |
| | 12.8.17 | | D Coy reinforced front line continued digging front line. | [illegible] |

A6945 Wt. W11422/M1160 350,000 12/16 D. D. & L. Forms/C./2118/14.

Army Form C. 2118.

Instructions regarding War Diaries and Intelligence Summaries are contained in F. S. Regs., Part II. and the Staff Manual respectively. Title pages will be prepared in manuscript.

# WAR DIARY
*or*
# INTELLIGENCE SUMMARY.
*(Erase heading not required.)*

| Place | Date | Hour | Summary of Events and Information | Remarks and references to Appendices |
|---|---|---|---|---|
| Front line | 13.8.17 | | Shelling very heavy during the morning quietened down during the day enemy aeroplanes very active, flying down low & firing at front line. | [illegible] |
| | 14.8.17 | | Day quiet at 1 AM raiding party of 1 officer & 20 men left BHQ to blow up enemy dug outs on sky line at 0.6 & 9.8. this having been done party returned with no loss. front line completed. | [illegible] |
| | ~~15.8.17~~ | | | |
| | 15.8.17 | 9. PM | Bn relieved by 17th KRR. heavy rain, heavy shelling with gas shells. relief completed at 4 AM. Bn proceeded to WILTSHIRE CAMP. at 4 PM Bn moved off to embuss at HALLEBAST CORNER. proceeded to THIESHOUK | [illegible] |
| | 16. | | | |
| | ~~[illegible]~~ | | Casualties during the whole of the operation | [illegible] |
| | | | Killed 3 Officers 22 OR. | |
| | | | Missing 8 OR. | |
| | | | Wounded 3 Officers 114 OR. | |

A6945 Wt. W11422/M1160 350,000 12/16 D. D. & L. Forms/C./2118/14.

Instructions regarding War Diaries and Intelligence Summaries are contained in F. S. Regs., Part II. and the Staff Manual respectively. Title pages will be prepared in manuscript.

# WAR DIARY
*or*
# ~~INTELLIGENCE SUMMARY.~~
*(Erase heading not required.)*

Army Form C. 2118.

| Place | Date | Hour | Summary of Events and Information | Remarks and references to Appendices |
|---|---|---|---|---|
| THILSHOEK | [illegible] | | [illegible] parade. | [initials] |
| | [illegible] | [illegible] | Battalion paraded for inspection by the Commanding Officer previous to General inspection | [initials] |
| | | 3.30 PM | Inspection by Lieut General Sir T L N Morland K.C.B. K.C.M.G. D.S.O. | |
| | [illegible] | [illegible] | Inspection by General Sir Herbert C O Plumer G.C.M.G. K.C.B. A.D.C. | |
| | | [illegible] | Enemy aircraft flew over Camp dropping four bombs. Casualties 2 Officers killed | |
| | | | 1 Officer wounded 1 O.R. killed | [initials] |
| | | | 11 wounded | |
| | [illegible] | | Battalion [illegible] | [initials] |
| | [illegible] | [illegible] | [illegible] 9 AM & 12 noon [illegible] | [initials] |
| | | | with bayonet practice. 2 P.M. [illegible] | |

A6945 Wt. W11422/M1160 350,000 12/16 D. D. & L. Forms/C./2118/14.

Instructions regarding War Diaries and Intelligence Summaries are contained in F. S. Regs., Part II. and the Staff Manual respectively. Title pages will be prepared in manuscript.

# WAR DIARY
or
# INTELLIGENCE SUMMARY.
(Erase heading not required.)

Army Form C. 2118.

| Place | Date | Hour | Summary of Events and Information | Remarks and references to Appendices |
| --- | --- | --- | --- | --- |
| THIEUSHOEK | 21/8 | 8.45 AM | Battalion route march. 2.0 P.M. to 3 P.M. Bayonet practice & physical drill | [illegible] |
| | 22/8 | 8 AM | Battalion route march. 2.0 P.M. Company arrangements. | [illegible] |
| | 23/8 | 6 AM | Battalion parade under R.S.M. for rifle drill. 8.45 AM Inspection by Commanding Officer. Distribution of cards in recognition of work in the field. 2.0 P.M. Company arrangements. | [illegible] |
| | 24/8 | 6 AM | Battalion parade under R.S.M. rifle drill. 8.45 AM Inspection by Commanding Officer of Battalion in full marching order, followed by a route march. | [illegible] |
| | 25/8 | 6.30 AM | Battalion march to STAPLE and resting there for the night. | [illegible] |
| | 26/8 | 6.0 AM | Battalion march to Longuenesse having dinner on the road, arrived there at 1.30 P.M. | |

A6945 Wt. W11422/M1160 350,000 12/16 D. D. & L. Forms/C./2118/14.

# WAR DIARY
*or*
# INTELLIGENCE SUMMARY.
*(Erase heading not required.)*

Army Form C. 2118.

Instructions regarding War Diaries and Intelligence Summaries are contained in F. S. Regs., Part II, and the Staff Manual respectively. Title pages will be prepared in manuscript.

| Place | Date | Hour | Summary of Events and Information | Remarks and references to Appendices |
|---|---|---|---|---|
| LONGUENESSE | 27.8.17 | | General clean up throughout the Battalion during the morning. Company arrangements [illegible] | [illegible] |
| LONGUENESSE | 28.8.17 | | Battalion parade for training area owing to bad weather training could not be carried out. NCO's lectured in billets | [illegible] |
| " | 29.8.17 | | Battalion parade for training area. All companies on the range & Bayonet [illegible] [illegible] arrangements. NCO lectures | [illegible] |
| | 30.8.17 | 9.30am | Battalion parade for inspection by Field Marshal Sir Douglas Haig KT GCB GCVO KCIE Commander in Chief British Army in France | [illegible] |
| | 31.8.17 | 7.15am | Battalion parade for training Area. Companies in Attack formation | [illegible] |

[illegible] Capt & Adjt
26th Royal Fusiliers

A6945 Wt. W11422/M1160 350,000 12/16 D. D. & L. Forms/C./2118/14.

17.K. (Various)

124/41

Army Form C. 2118.

26 R Fus 41/124

Vol 17

# WAR DIARY
*or*
# INTELLIGENCE SUMMARY.

(*Erase heading not required.*)

Instructions regarding War Diaries and Intelligence Summaries are contained in F. S. Regs., Part II. and the Staff Manual respectively. Title pages will be prepared in manuscript.

| Place | Date | Hour | Summary of Events and Information | Remarks and references to Appendices |
|---|---|---|---|---|
| LONGUENESSE Sheet 27A S.E. [illegible] X 15 [illegible] | 1/9/17 | 7am | The Battalion commenced training at 7am daily on the training area near TATINGHEM map reference 27A. S.E. R.31.32.33 and X.1.92. for the future attack on the SOUTHERN SPUR of the TOWER HAMLETS RIDGE. Training [illegible] [illegible] and the rest of the day was devoted to games [illegible] [illegible] the [illegible] at LONGUENESSE [illegible] [illegible] [illegible] [illegible] 46 [illegible] [illegible] [illegible] were taken by [illegible] [illegible] [illegible] [illegible] they [illegible] to attack [illegible] [illegible] [illegible] were taken to [illegible] [illegible] of the ground. | |

[illegible] of 13th [illegible]

D. D. & L., London, E.C.
(A8004) Wt. W1771/M231 750,000 3/17 Sch. 52 Forms/C2118/14

Instructions regarding War Diaries and Intelligence Summaries are contained in F. S. Regs., Part II. and the Staff Manual respectively. Title pages will be prepared in manuscript.

# WAR DIARY
*or*
# INTELLIGENCE SUMMARY.
*(Erase heading not required.)*

Army Form C. 2118.

| Place | Date | Hour | Summary of Events and Information | Remarks and references to Appendices |
|---|---|---|---|---|
| [illegible] | 14th | 7am | The Battalion proceeded by motor march to ST MARIE CAPPELLE where it arrived about 1pm. | [initials] |
| ST MARIE CAPPELLE | 15th | Noon | The Battalion marched to THIEUSHOUK arriving about 4/30pm. | [initials] |
| THIEUSHOUK | 16th | 10am | The Battalion marched to LA CLYTTE where it was accommodated in MURRUMBIDGEE CAMP. arriving at 4/30pm. | [initials] |
| LA CLYTTE | 17th | | The Battalion rested in MURRUMBIDGEE CAMP during the day. At 8pm | |
| | | 8/30pm | paraded and proceeded to RIDGEWOOD where it arrived at 1am on 19/10/17 | [initials] |
| RIDGEWOOD | 18th | | The Battalion rested before proceeding to VOORMEZEELE at about 10pm. Mobilisation stores and all battle necessaries were drawn here. | [initials] |
| VOORMEZEELE | 19th | 4/30pm | The Battalion proceeded to take over assembly positions ready for the attack as per 124th Infantry Brigade Warning Order No 10, Operation Order No 130, and Barrage Map attached. | APPENDIX I II III |
| | 20th | 5/30am | The Battalion took part in an attack on the TOWER HAMLETS RIDGE. Zero hour being 5/30am. A/Col G McNickll DSO. Died of wounds received in action. | [initials] |
| | | | Total Casualties: | |
| | | | | Officers / Other Ranks |
| | | | Killed — 6 / 27 | |
| | | | Died of Wds — 2 / 15 | |
| | | | Wounded — 12 / 246 | |
| | | | Missing — 4 / 45. | [initials] |

D. D. & L., London, E.C.
(A8604) Wt. W1771/M2 31 750,000 5/17 Sch. 52 Forms/C2118/14

Instructions regarding War Diaries and Intelligence Summaries are contained in F. S. Regs., Part II. and the Staff Manual respectively. Title pages will be prepared in manuscript.

# WAR DIARY
*or*
# INTELLIGENCE SUMMARY.
(*Erase heading not required.*)

Army Form C. 2118.

| Place | Date | Hour | Summary of Events and Information | Remarks and references to Appendices |
|---|---|---|---|---|
| IN THE LINE | 21/22nd | | The Battalion continued to hold the line until relieved by a unit of the 39th Division on the night of 22/23rd when the Battalion proceeded to WILTSHIRE CAMP at RIDGEWOOD arriving about 4am on 23/10/17. | PSB |
| WILTSHIRE CAMP | 23rd | 1pm | The Battalion proceeded to OUDERDOM SIDING where it entrained for CAESTRE and marched to Billets at BORRE, near HAZEBROUCK. | PSB |
| BORRE | 24th | | The Battalion rested all day. Lieut Col R.W HAMMOND took over command of the Bn | PSB |
| | 25th | 10am | With the exception of an Inspection by the Commanding Officer there were no parades the time being spent in cleaning up. | PSB |
| | 26th | | Companies were at the disposal of Company Commanders for the purposes of reorganisation. | PSB |
| | 27th | | The whole of the Battalion had baths today. | PSB |
| | 28th | 7.15am | The Battalion paraded and proceeded to the Embussing Point where busses picked up the whole of the Brigade for the GHYVELDE area.<br>About 8 pm hostile aircraft dropped three bombs, one just outside the Headquarters Mess. These exploded and the following casualties resulted:-<br>Lieut Col. R. W. HAMMOND — Died of Wounds.<br>Capt & Adj. A. W. MACKAY — do<br>Major. A MAXWELL — Wounded<br>Capt. C.E. JIGGINS. — do<br>[illegible] Wilson (RAMC) &<br>Lieut F Pyke were both wounded but remained at duty.<br>2 OR were killed & 1 OR Wounded | PSB |

D. D. & L., London, E.C.
(A8004) Wt. W1771/M2 31 750,000 5/17 Sch. 52 Forms/C2118/14

Army Form C. 2118.

Instructions regarding War Diaries and Intelligence Summaries are contained in F. S. Regs., Part II. and the Staff Manual respectively. Title pages will be prepared in manuscript.

# WAR DIARY
*or*
# INTELLIGENCE SUMMARY.
*(Erase heading not required.)*

| Place | Date | Hour | Summary of Events and Information | Remarks and references to Appendices |
|---|---|---|---|---|
| LOYVELDE | 29th | | Major H.W. Tuite assumed command of the Battalion. | |
| | | 10/30am | The Battalion was inspected at 10/30am by Major-General S.T.B. LAWFORD. C.B who congratulated all ranks on the splendid fight they had made during recent operations. | [illegible] |
| | 30th | 10 am | The Battalion paraded with 21st Bn. K.R.R.C. for Church Parade on the Parade Ground. The remainder of the day was spent in resting. | [illegible] |

7th Oct 1917

H.W. Tuite Major,
Comm'dg 26th Royal Fusiliers

D. D. & L., London, E.C.
(A8004) Wt. W1771/M2 31 750,000 5/17 Sch. 52 Forms/C2118/14

26th Bn. Royal Fusiliers

Instructions regarding War Diaries and Intelligence Summaries are contained in F. S. Regs., Part II. and the Staff Manual respectively. Title Pages will be prepared in manuscript.

46

# WAR DIARY
or
~~INTELLIGENCE SUMMARY~~

*(Erase heading not required.)*

Army Form C. 2118.

ORDERLY ROOM 5 OCT 1918 No. A296 26th ROYAL FUSILIERS

Vol 30

| Place | Date | Hour | Summary of Events and Information | Remarks and references to Appendices |
|---|---|---|---|---|
| AMERICA - KRUISEECKE ROAD | 1/10/18 - 7/10/18 | | Battalion engaged in operations as per attached copy of report. | |
| KAIRN CAMP. | 8/10/18 - 13/10/18 | | The Battalion was resting, refitting, and reorganising, at KAIRN CAMP. ABEELE. | |
| | 14/15th | | Active operations as per attached copy of report. | |
| MOORSEELE | 16/20th | | The Battalion was in Rest Billets, reorganising, and refitting. | |
| | 21/26th | | Active operations as per attached copy of report. | |
| COURTRAI AREA | 27/31st | | The Battalion was in Rest Billets, reorganising & refitting. Training took place each day between the hours of 0900 to 1200 and 1400 to 1600. | |

[signature] Major
Commanding 26th (S) Battn. Royal Fusiliers

2449 Wt. W14957/M90 750,000 1/16 J.B.C. & A. Forms/C.2118/12.

30 F.
(6 sheets)

Instructions regarding War Diaries and Intelligence Summaries are contained in F. S. Regs., Part II. and the Staff Manual respectively. Title pages will be prepared in manuscript.



# WAR DIARY
or
# ~~INTELLIGENCE SUMMARY.~~
(*Erase heading not required.*)



26 RE

Army Form C. 2118.

... Batt. Royal Fusiliers

Vol 18

| Place | Date | Hour | Summary of Events and Information | Remarks and references to Appendices |
|---|---|---|---|---|
| Ghyvelde | 1st–4th Oct 1917 | | General refitting and reorganisation of the Battalion | [illegible] |
| | 5/10/17 | | The Battalion proceeded by march route to Coxyde Bains via Adinkerke, La Panne, and St Idesbalde and relieved the 9th Battalion Manchester Regiment on Coast Defence. | [illegible] |
| Coxyde Bains | 6th–14th Oct. | | Dispositions: A and C companies front line, B and D companies support. | [illegible] |
| " | 15/10/17 | | The Battalion relieved the 23rd Battalion Middlesex Regiment in left Battalion front in Nieuport Sector. Dispositions: ~~Front~~ line, Left sector D company, Right sector B company. Support C company, Reserve A company | [illegible] |
| Nieuport Bains | 16/10/17 | | There was no activity on the part of the enemy infantry. Hostile artillery was fairly active shelling back areas. | [illegible] |
| " | 17/10/17 | | Enemy light artillery and trench mortars active against our front line | [illegible] |
| " | 18/10/17 | | Our line was heavily bombarded by artillery and trench mortars during the latter part of the day but no casualties were caused. Our aeroplanes were very active against hostile machine gun and trench mortar emplacements. | [illegible] |
| " | 19/10/17 | | Individual movement behind the enemy line was much more apparent during the day and counter battery work by the artillery was much greater than usual. Atmospheric conditions were rather opposed to good observation work. | [illegible] |
| " | 20/10/17 | | Enemy machine guns and trench mortars more active against our front and artillery counter battery work was again heavy. Several hostile aeroplanes attempted to cross our line but were prevented by machine gun fire. Our patrols were unable to discover any trace of the enemy by night. | [illegible] |

18.K. (5 sheets)

Instructions regarding War Diaries and Intelligence Summaries are contained in F. S. Regs., Part II. and the Staff Manual respectively. Title pages will be prepared in manuscript.

# WAR DIARY
*or*
# ~~INTELLIGENCE SUMMARY.~~
*(Erase heading not required.)*

Army Form C. 2118.

26th Battalion Royal Fusiliers

| Place | Date | Hour | Summary of Events and Information | Remarks and references to Appendices |
|---|---|---|---|---|
| Nieuport Bains | 21/10/17 | | Our artillery carried out an effective bombardment of the enemy back areas causing an explosion. Enemy artillery was generally much quieter. One of our aeroplanes was brought down by machine gun fire and fell behind the enemy lines during the afternoon. | [illegible] |
| " | 22/10/17 | | Hostile artillery and trench mortars active but ceased fire on being engaged by our batteries. During the afternoon our line was shelled by a war vessel which put out from Ostend, slight material damage only was caused. A number of gas shells were thrown into our rear lines but no inconvenience was caused. | [illegible] |
| | 23/10/17 | | Beyond counter battery work by the artillery during the day there was no unusual activity. The Battalion was relieved by the 21st Battalion Kings Royal Rifles and proceeded to Middlesex Camp at Oost-Dunkerque Bains where it was accommodated in hutments. | Appendix I. [illegible] |
| Oost Dunkerque Bains | 24/10/17 to 27/10/17 | | Battalion occupied in refitting and specialist training. During these four days A and C Companies were detached from the Battalion and were attached to the 21st Battalion Kings Royal Rifles as a working party in the line being quartered in the tunnels in the reserve line in the left Battalion sector. | [illegible] |
| " | 28/10/17 | | The Battalion was relieved at Middlesex Camp by the 5th Battalion Cameron Highlanders (9th Division) and proceeded by motor lorry via Coxyde, La Panne, and Adinkerke to Uxem and was accommodated in farm out-buildings in the Ferme Grand Colombier Area. | [illegible] |
| Uxem. | 29/10/17 to 31/10/17 | | Battalion training in Route Marching, Artillery Formations and Extended Order. | [illegible] |

H.W. Tuite ___ COMMANDING,
26th (S) BN. ROYAL FUSILIERS

D. D. & L., London, E.C.
(A6004) Wt. W1771/M2 31 750,000 5/17 Sch. 52 Forms/C2118/14

SECRET. Copy No. 5

"DWINDLE" OPERATION ORDER. No.16.

Reference Maps:-
SHEET 11 S.E. ed.2.
No.4 Ed.1 & No.5.Ed.3.

1. INTENTION. "DWINDLE" will be relieved by "DROSS" in the Left Sector of the Line on 23/10/17.

2. METHOD OF RELIEF. (a) 7 Lewis Gun Teams and 2 Pom pom teams of DROSS will be at junction of BATH AVENUE and BATH ALLEY at 5 a.m. where they will be met by Sgt.Turner and one guide from "B" Company. Sgt.Turner will proceed with the Lewis Gun Officer of DROSS and the Lewis Gun Teams and pom pom teams of the Left Company in Front Line and assist in putting these teams into position. The guide from "B" Company will guide the five teams of DROSS for the Right Front Company to "B" Company Headquarters where they will be met by one guide per team and taken to their respective opposite numbers. O/C."B" Company will see that relief is properly carried out and the teams, when in position, will be visited by the Lewis Gun Officer of DROSS & Sgt.Turner.

(b) Five Lewis Gun teams of "B" Company, made up as follows:- 1 team - 1 N.C.O. and 4 men, and 4 teams - 1 N.C.O. and 2 men, will be detailed to be at junction of BATH ALLEY and BATH AVENUE at 10 a.m. where they will be met by the Lewis Gun Officer of DROSS and proceed to take over 5 Anti-Aircraft posts of DROSS. These men will be rationed by the R.F.A. and come off our ration strength. The remainder of the Lewis Gunners of this relief will assemble immediately after relief at junction of BATH ALLEY and BATH AVENUE and will be taken by 2/Lt.C.Phillips to Cross Roads, OOST DUNKERKE BAINS where a guide will meet them and take them to billets.

(c) At 3 p.m. on 23/10/17, 3 Lewis Gun teams from Support Company, DROSS, will be at junction of BATH ALLEY and BATH AVENUE and will be met by Sgt.Turner who will take them to relieve the one team of "C" Company and 1 team of "D" Company along BATH AVENUE and 1 team of "C" Company on Anti-Aircraft Defence. On relief these teams will assemble at BATH ALLEY and BATH AVENUE and be taken by Sgt.Turner to OOST DUNKERKE BAINS Cross Roads where a guide will meet them and conduct them to billets.

(d) At 12 Noon on 23/10/17, 12 Signallers of DROSS 4 for Battalion Headquarters Signal Station and 2 per Company, Regimental Sergeant Major and Company Sergeant Majors, will report to Battalion Headquarters where a guide will meet them and take them to their various Headquarters to take over.

(e) 4 Snipers of DROSS will report to Sniping Sergeant at Battalion Headquarters at 12 Noon on 23/10/17 and proceed to take over Observation Posts.

(f) At 12 Noon on 23/10/17 the Medical Orderly from DROSS will be at Battalion Headquarters to find out Medical arrangements from the Medical Officer.

(g) At 5.45 p.m. on 23/10/17, two guides per Company, one from Headquarters and Capt.D.N.de Wet will be at junction of BATH ALLEY and BATH AVENUE to take DROSS to their various posts.

(i) "A" Company, DROSS, will relieve "B" Company, DWINDLE. The party will proceed via BATH AVENUE to No.6 entrance BRISTOL TUNNEL where guides will meet and conduct each party to their posts and Company Headquarters

(ii) "D" Company.DROSS, will relieve "D" Company, DWINDLE, and will proceed via BATH AVENUE to BISE HURLE where guides will meet and conduct the various parties to their posts and Company Headquarters.

(iii) "C" Company, DROSS, will relieve "C" Company, DWINDLE, and will proceed via BATH ALLEY and BLIGHTY AVENUE to "C" Company Headquarters where guides will meet and conduct the various parties to their posts.

IV 'B' Coy. DROSS, will relieve our "A" Coy via BATH ALLEY & BLIGHTY AVENUE

(v) ~~(iv)~~ Headquarters, DROSS, will proceed along BATH ALLEY to Battalion Headquarters.

When Relief is complete -

(1) "A" Company will leave via BLIGHTY AVENUE, BATH-ALLEY and BATH LANE.

(2) "B" Company will leave via BRISTOL TUNNEL and BATH AVENUE.

(3) "C" Company will leave via BLIGHTY AVENUE, BATH-ALLEY and BATH AVENUE.

(4) "D" Company will leave via BATH AVENUE.

(5) Headquarters will leave via BATH ALLEY and BATH-AVENUE.

All Companies and Headquarters on relief will proceed to OOST DUNKERKE BAINS Cross Roads where guides will meet them and conduct them to quarters.

(h) 1 runner from "D" Company, 1 runner from "A" Company and 1 runner from Battalion Headquarters will relieve 3 runners of DROSS at Brigade Headquarters at 10 a.m. on 23/10/17.

(i) 1 N.C.O. and 3 men of "A" Company will relieve 1 N.C.O. and 3 men of DROSS on Point Duty at the LAITERIE at 10 a.m. on 23/10/17.

(j) The Provost Sergeant of DROSS will be at Battalion Headquarters at 10 a.m. on 23/10/17 to take over the duties of Provost Sergeant, DWINDLE.

3. OFFICERS VALISES, MESS BOXES etc. Officers valises, Mess Boxes and Orderly Room Boxes, Cooking Utensils etc. will be stacked by Gas Guard outside Battalion Headquarters by 7 p.m.

4. R. S. M. The Regimental Sergeant Major will detail men to act as a Guard over these Stores and load them on to the limbers on their arrival.

5. QUARTERMASTER. The Quartermaster will arrange to have Transport at Battalion Headquarters after dark to take these Mess Boxes, valises etc.

6. TRENCH STORES etc. All Trench Stores, Defence Schemes.etc. will be handed over to the incoming Unit (including the SOYER STOVES).

7. NOTIFICATION OF RELIEF. The Code name of the Company, followed by the time, will be sent through to Battalion Headquarters by telephone when relief is complete.

8. ACKNOWLEDGE.

(Signed) S. H. FIRTH.
Captain & Adjutant,
"DWINDLE"

22/10/17.

124th Inf.Bde.
41st Div.

Battn. with Bde. returned to France from Italy 2/7.3.18.

WAR DIARY

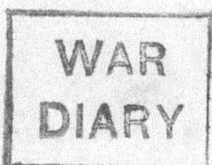

# 26th BATTN. THE ROYAL FUSILIERS.

M A R C H

1 9 1 8

Attached:-

Report on Operations between 22nd March & night 29th/30th March 1918.

Instructions regarding War Diaries and Intelligence Summaries are contained in F. S. Regs., Part II. and the Staff Manual respectively. Title pages will be prepared in manuscript.

Army. Form C. 2118.

# WAR DIARY
*or*
# INTELLIGENCE SUMMARY.
*(Erase heading not required.)*

ORDERLY ROOM 8 MAY. 1918 No. B1941 20th (S) BN. ROYAL FUSILIERS

| Place | Date | Hour | Summary of Events and Information | Remarks and references to Appendices |
|---|---|---|---|---|
| VILLA FRANCA | 1/3/18 | | The Battalion rested during the day preparatory to entraining for France | [illegible] |
| " | 2/3/18 | 17/50 | The Battalion entrained for FRANCE and spent the next six days in the train | [illegible] |
| MONDICOURT PAS | 8/3/18 | 8/30 | Detrained and proceeded by march route to SUS. ST LEGER (LENS 11) arriving about 2/30 pm. | [illegible] |
| SUS. ST. LEGER | 9/3/18 | | The day was spent in the cleaning up of billets, equipment etc. and the whole area generally | [illegible] |
| do | 9/3/18 | | Training on the Battalion Training Area | [illegible] |
| do | 10/3/18 | | Church Parade | [illegible] |
| do | 11th to 14/3/18 | | The whole of this period was spent in Company and Battalion Training – The [illegible] Ranges being used on alternate days. The afternoons were devoted | [illegible] (6 sheets) |

A6945 Wt. W11422/M1160 350,000 12/16 D. D. & L. Forms/C./2118/14.

Instructions regarding War Diaries and Intelligence Summaries are contained in F. S. Regs., Part II. and the Staff Manual respectively. Title pages will be prepared in manuscript.

# WAR DIARY
*or*
# INTELLIGENCE SUMMARY.
*(Erase heading not required.)*

Army. Form C. 2118.

| Place | Date | Hour | Summary of Events and Information | Remarks and references to Appendices |
|---|---|---|---|---|
| SUS ST. LEGER | 11/3/18 to 16/3/18 | | Recreational Training and Games. | [illegible] |
| DO | 17/3/18 | | Church Parade | [illegible] |
| DO | 18/3/18 | | Training on the Battalion Training Area in the morning. | [illegible] |
| DO | | 1.20 pm | Orders were received that the Battalion would move in one hour. This was a practice move and turned out quite satisfactory. The Brigadier General was quite pleased with the Parade, and the troops were lectured on "Bayonet Fighting". | [illegible] |
| DO | 19/3/18 to 20/3/18 | | Training in Company and Battalion work on the Training Area. | [illegible] |
| DO | 21/3/18 | 5.30 am | The Battalion marched to SAULTY STATION under orders to proceed to the BAIZEAUX AREA. The enemy had, however, launched a big attack at 4/50 in the morning, and the whole Division proceeded into the forward zone. | [illegible] |

A6945 Wt. W11422/M1160 350,000 12/16 D. D. & L. Forms/C./2118/14.

Instructions regarding War Diaries and Intelligence Summaries are contained in F. S. Regs., Part II. and the Staff Manual respectively. Title pages will be prepared in manuscript.

# WAR DIARY
*or*
# INTELLIGENCE SUMMARY.
*(Erase heading not required.)*

Army Form C. 2118.

| Place | Date | Hour | Summary of Events and Information | Remarks and references to Appendices |
|---|---|---|---|---|
| ACHIET LE GRAND | 22/3/18 | 4 am | The Battalion detrained at ACHIET LE GRAND and proceeded by march route to No 11 Camp FAVREUIL where we arrived at about 5/30 am | [illegible] |
| | 22/3/18 to 31/3/18 | | The Battalion was engaged in the operations on the River SOMME see Detailed report attached. Casualties:– | [illegible] |
| | | | Officers / Other Ranks | |
| | | | Killed 3 / 38 | |
| | | | Wounded 17 / 127 | |
| | | | Missing 1 / 102 | |

[illegible signature] Major for Lieut Col.
Commanding 26th (S) Battn. Royal Fusiliers

A6945 Wt. W11422/M1160 350,000 12/16 D. D. & L. Forms/C./2118/14.

REPORT ON OPERATIONS between 22nd March 1918 and night 29th/30th March 1918.

26th R. Fusiliers

REPORT ON OPERATIONS BETWEEN 22nd March, 1918 and night 29/30th March, 1918.

REFERENCE MAP:- Sheet 57c.

The Battalion arrived in camp in the concentration area, FAVREUIL, about 5/30.a.m. on 22nd March, 1918.

About 7/30.a.m., the Commanding Officer (Lieut-Col H. M. TUITE) went with the Officers Commanding 10th Bn. "Queens" R. W. S. Regt. and 20th Bn. Durham Light Infantry, and the Brigade Major, to reconnoitre a position North East of BEUGNATRE with a view to forming three lines of trenches which were to be held should the enemy force a withdrawal of our troops from the vicinity of VAUX-VRAUCOURT. The Battalion moved forward about 12 noon, and commenced constructing the third lines of trenches between H.5.a. and H.18.Central. These trenches were occupied during the night 22nd/23rd March. During the night the 6th Division, who were holding the front line, were relieved by the 10th Bn. "Queens" R.W.S. Regt. and 20th Bn. Durham Light Infantry the 26th Bn. Royal Fusiliers being in Support. During the 23rd March the enemy made repeated attacks on the front line, which were all repulsed with rifle and machine gun fire. During the night 23rd/24th March "C" Company of this Battalion was sent to reinforce the 20th Bn. Durham Light Infantry on the left of the Brigade front.

During 24th March, 1918 the enemy repeatedly made strong attacks against our troops on the right, and as it was thought that they might force a withdrawal at this point, "A" Company was sent forward to form a defensive flank on the right. At dusk the 10th Bn. "Queens" R.W.S. Regt. and 20th Bn. Durham Light Infantry were forced to withdraw from the line they had held for two days, and as our troops on the right had by this time given way an order was received from Brigade to retire to the FAVREUIL line. This position was held for some time, but, as the enemy continued to advance on the right, it became necessary to withdraw further

to a line behind the BAPAUME - ARRAS ROAD, which had already been selected by the Brigade. During this time "A" and "B" Companies were on the left of the line of the Brigade front near SAPIGNIES which was held until about midday on the 25th March, 1918.
It had been impossible to get supplies of ammunitions and rations up to the line during the night, and, as the left flank was again exposed, an order was given to withdraw on BIHUCOURT. This was done by half platoons which had been reformed, covering fire being given the whole time. A number of tanks came through at this point, and temporarily held back the enemy's advance. The remainder of these two Companies dug in with troops of another Division between ACHIT LE GRAND and ACHIT LE PETIT, which they held until night of 26th 27th March, 1918

About 3.p.m. on 25/3/18 the whole of the Brigade Details, together with the men who had become detatched from their Battalions and had joined "A" Echelon, were ordered to bivouac at GOMMECOURT. About 5.a.m. on morning 26/3/18 the Brigade occupied a line EAST of GOMMECOURT to support the troops who were holding the front line in the event of a withdrawal becoming necessary.
On 26th March, 1918, the troops who had been fighting from 22nd March were ordered to retire and to rejoin their units in the GOMMECOURT LINE. On the night 26th/27th the Brigade moved from the GOMMECOURT LINE to bivouacs at BIEN VILLIERS.

About noon 28/3/18, the Battalion received orders to move forward to the GOMMECOURT LINE which was occupied about 3.p.m. The Battalion sector being between E.30.central and E.29.d.5.5. (Sheet 57d) During the afternoon two Officers patrols went forward and got in touch with the 185th and 186th Infantry Brigades who were then holding the front line.
About 6.p.m. an order was received signed by G.O.C. 186th Infantry Brigade, ordering the Battalion to move forward and counterattack the enemy who had occupied ROSSIGNAL WOOD, at K.12.a. A copy of this order

was taken to 124th Infantry Brigade Headquarters by an Officer of the 186th Infantry Brigade. At 7.5.p.m. the Battalion moved forward in four waves and had proceeded about 700 yards when orders were received from the 124th Infantry Brigade to "Stand Fast." The Battalion returned to the trenches about 7.30.p.m. At 3/30.p.m. on 29th March, orders were received that the Battalion was to relieve the 1/7th Lancashire Fusiliers, and one Company of the 1/7th Northumberland Fusiliers in the front line East of BUCQUOY (Sheet 57.d.) from F.20.c.8.4. to F.28.b.30.55. The relief commenced about 11/30pm 29/3/18, and was completed about 3.a.m. on 30/3/18.

[signature]

Major,

6/4/18. 26th (S) Bn. Royal Fusiliers.

41st Division.
124th Infantry Brigade

WAR
DIARY

26th BATTALION

THE ROYAL FUSILIERS

APRIL 1918

Instructions regarding War Diaries and Intelligence Summaries are contained in F. S. Regs., Part II. and the Staff Manual respectively. Title Pages will be prepared in manuscript.

7

124/41 Army Form C. 2118

# WAR DIARY
*or*
# INTELLIGENCE SUMMARY
*(Erase heading not required.)*

1918

Vol 24



| Place | Date | Hour | Summary of Events and Information | Remarks and references to Appendices |
|---|---|---|---|---|
| BUCQUOY | 30/31 Mch to 1/2 Apl. | | The Battalion held a sector of the line East of BUCQUOY from the night 30/31st March until the night 1/2nd April 1918 when it was relieved by 1/7th Battalion Manchester Regiment. During this period the enemy shelled our line intermittently, but did not make any definite attack. About 5 am on 31/3/18 the enemy placed a heavy barrage on our front and support lines, under cover of which he moved forward and dug in in dead ground. Our patrols reconnoitred the ground on the night of the 31/1 and found this line extended along the front of the battalion on our right | |
| DO | 1/2 Apl | | Relieved and proceeded by march route to BIENVILLIERS where the battalion embussed for HALLOY, and rested for the night. | |
| HALLOY | 3 Apl | 6/30am | Proceeded by march route to MONDICOURT PAS and embussed for BONNIÉRES. | |
| BONNIERES | 4 Apl | 9/30am | Entrained at FREVENT and detrained at HOPOUTRE where busses conveyed the Battalion to Rest Billets at WINNIZEELE. | |
| WINNIZEELE | 5/6 Apl | | The Battalion rested, and commenced reorganising & refitting. 420 Reinforcements were received. | |
| DO | 7 Apl | 9/30am | The Battalion proceeded by march route to the forward Area and spent the night at ST LAWRENCE CAMP, G10.a central (Sheet 28) | |

1875 Wt. W593/826 1,000,000 4/15 J.B.C. & A. A.D.S.S./Forms/C. 2118.

24 K. (4 sheets)

Instructions regarding War Diaries and Intelligence Summaries are contained in F. S. Regs., Part II. and the Staff Manual respectively. Title Pages will be prepared in manuscript.

# WAR DIARY
*or*
~~INTELLIGENCE SUMMARY~~
*(Erase heading not required.)*

Army Form C. 2118

| Place | Date | Hour | Summary of Events and Information | Remarks and references to Appendices |
|---|---|---|---|---|
| St. LAWRENCE CAMP. BRANDHOEK | 8th April | | The Battalion rested this day. Orders were received to entrain at BRANDHOEK at 1620 pm to proceed up the line to relieve the 2nd K.O.S.B. in the PASSCHENDAELE sector. Detrained at BRIDGE HOUSE (Bel. 28NW) at 8pm & met guides for the line. The Battalion held the sector from the left of PASSCHENDAELE D6b8.4 to V30b1.4 (map C2 1-10,000), 2 Company in the front line, 1 in support & 1 in reserve. | [initials] |
| CARTE KEEP & MILLS KEEP | 12th April | | There was little activity on either side & the line was held until dusk on the 12th April when owing to enemy pressure south of YPRES it was decided to compress the SALIENT & the Battalion was ordered to fall back to 2 strong points along the OXFORD & CAMBRIDGE ROADS (BEL. 28NW) viz CARTE KEEP & MILLS KEEP. This manoeuvre was accomplished successfully without loss, the 10th QUEENS R.W.S. REGt. who held the sector on our right taking over our sector as well as their own & forming an outpost line on the old front line. | [initials] |
| LOW FARM | 13th | 7pm | The Battalion was ordered to move forward & relieve the 12th East Surreys in a line from POTSDAM D26c6.8 to BECK HOUSE, D19d1.2 with Bn. H.Q. at LOW FARM D25a7.5 (map 28N.E.) This was accomplished by 8.30 pm. | [initials] |
| YPRES MENIN Rd | 15th | 8pm | The 14th & 15th were spent by improving the line held. A further compression of the SALIENT having been decided upon the Battalion was ordered to fall back & dig a line of resistance from WHITE CHATEAU, I10c5.5 (Exclusive) to | [initials] |

1875 Wt. W593/826 1,000,000 4/15 J.B.C. & A. A.D.S.S./Forms/C. 2118.

Army Form C. 2118

# WAR DIARY
*or*
# INTELLIGENCE SUMMARY
*(Erase heading not required.)*

Instructions regarding War Diaries and Intelligence Summaries are contained in F. S. Regs., Part II. and the Staff Manual respectively. Title Pages will be prepared in manuscript.

| Place | Date | Hour | Summary of Events and Information | Remarks and references to Appendices |
|---|---|---|---|---|
| YPRES MENIN R^D | 16^th to 25^th Apl. | | I 4 d 3 5 (Ap 28 NW) having the 20^th DLI on their left & the 2^nd Y&L 6^th DIV. on their right. One Company (B) was left in the forward area (POTSDAM to BECK HOUSE) as an outpost. The next 10 days were spent in building the line, 2 Coys in the front line & 1 Coy on a reserve line 3 to 400 yards behind. On Saturday 20^th Apl 'B' Coy was relieved by 'C' in the forward outpost line. The latter Coy in the early morning of the 25^th carried out a very successful raid on the enemy lines. Two parties under 2/Lt J J Mackintosh & 2/Lt J T Smellie respectively went over at 4 am after a barrage by Trench Mortars & attacked 2 enemy strong points, each party succeeding in bringing back a prisoner. | [initials] |
| YPRES RAMPARTS | 25^th to 27^th Apl. | 7 pm | The Battalion was relieved by the 10^th QUEENS R.W.S. REG^T & went into Brigade support in Trenches in & around YPRES. with B^TN H.Q. on the RAMPARTS. | [initials] |
| YPRES OUTPOST LINE | 28^th | 1 am. | The Battalion was ordered to go up to the old line which they had been building & to hold same as an outpost line, the POTSDAM – BECK HOUSE outposts having been withdrawn. The Battalion now held from | [initials] |

1875 Wt. W593/826 1,000,000 4/15 J.B.C. & A. A.D.S.S./Forms/C. 2118.

Army Form C. 2118

Instructions regarding War Diaries and Intelligence Summaries are contained in F. S. Regs., Part II. and the Staff Manual respectively. Title Pages will be prepared in manuscript.

# WAR DIARY
*or*
# INTELLIGENCE SUMMARY
*(Erase heading not required.)*

| Place | Date | Hour | Summary of Events and Information | Remarks and references to Appendices |
|---|---|---|---|---|
| YPRES OUTPOST LINE | 28th to 30th Apl. | | WHITE CHAU I10c 5.5 (Exclusive) to the POTIJZE ROAD I4b 1.4 (Exclusive) having on its left the 11th QUEENS R.W.S. REGT (123 BRIGADE) forming with this battalion the outpost line for the 41st DIVISION. During this period there was considerable movement on the part of the enemy who had followed up the withdrawal from the forward zone & were taking up positions opposite our line. Of this movement our Lewis gunners & snipers took full advantage. The Battalion was disposed in depth with 2 Coys in the line & 2 in support, each of the latter having 2 platoons in close support of the front line & 2 in reserve some 400-500 yards behind. | [initials] |

H A Robinson Lt. Col

1875 Wt. W593/826 1,000,000 4/15 J.B.C. & A. A.D.S.S./Forms/C. 2118.

Instructions regarding War Diaries and Intelligence Summaries are contained in F. S. Regs., Part II. and the Staff Manual respectively. Title Pages will be prepared in manuscript.

# WAR DIARY
or
# ~~INTELLIGENCE SUMMARY~~
*(Erase heading not required.)*

Army Form C. 2118



| Place | Date | Hour | Summary of Events and Information | Remarks and references to Appendices |
|---|---|---|---|---|
| YPRES OUTPOSTS PILKEM LINE | 1st/2nd May | | The Battalion remained in the outpost line harassing the enemy as much as possible. Having completed 5 days on outpost duty the Battalion was relieved by the 12th EAST SURREYS at 9 pm on the 2nd. Relief completed by midnight. | |
| DAMBRE CAMP | 3rd May | 4am | By march route by platoons independently to DAMBRE CAMP B27c.9.9. Battalion being reported all present in camp at 4 am | |
| " | 3rd to 9th May | | Spent in work on the Corps "Green Line" from B26d 6.8 to H3a 3.1 and in training, musketry & Lewis Gun | |
| SIEGE CAMP | 9th to 11th | 3am | DAMBRE CAMP being badly shelled, battalion moved to SIEGE CAMP – B20d 9.2. Work & training carried on. All Coys fired on Range & Lewis gun teams did likewise. | |
| PILKEM LINE YPRES RESERVE | 11th to 19th | 5pm | Battalion moved up the line, being in the sector EAST & SOUTH of YPRES, and relieved the 1st BUFFS in BRIGADE RESERVE. BTN H.Q. at H18a 1.6. B Coy in the DOLLS HOUSE LINE (I14c); C Coy in CANAL SWITCH (I13a&c) & A & D Coys in V2 & V3 (H11d & 12a&c) | |

1875 Wt. W593/826 1,000,000 4/15 J.B.C. & A. A.D.S.S./Forms/C. 2118.

25.K

Army Form C. 2118

# WAR DIARY
*or*
# ~~INTELLIGENCE~~ SUMMARY
*(Erase heading not required.)*

Instructions regarding War Diaries and Intelligence Summaries are contained in F. S. Regs., Part II. and the Staff Manual respectively. Title Pages will be prepared in manuscript.

| Place | Date | Hour | Summary of Events and Information | Remarks and references to Appendices |
|---|---|---|---|---|
| RAMPARTS YPRES SUPPORT. | 19th May to 23rd | 9pm. | Battalion moved up into Support relieving the 10th Bat QUEENS R.W.S. Rgt. Bn Hdqs in the RAMPARTS (I 14 b 2.8) with A Coy in the ZILLEBEKE SUPPORT LINE (I 15 b & d & 9 d); D Coy in strongpoint around the ECOLE (I 9 c); C Coy in part of RAMPARTS in HORNEWORKS LINE (I 14 b & d) and B Coy in the RAMPARTS (I 14 b). | [initials] |
| ECOLE YPRES. | 23rd to 25th May | 10pm | Took over part of the front line on the left of the 10th QUEENS R.W.S. Regt. from I 16 a 6.8 to I 10 c 5.7 with one Coy ("B") & Headquarters moved to ECOLE. I 9 c. | [initials] |
| | | 11pm | Relieved by 12th EAST SURREY REGT. Relief complete by 12.45 am. | |
| SIEGE CAMP. | 26th May | 4am | By march route to SIEGE CAMP (B 27 a 3.8) going into Divisional Reserve. The whole battalion bathed & complete change of clothing provided. | [initials] |
| | 27th | 10am | Battalion stood-to on receipt of orders from Brigade that enemy had taken SCOTTISH WOOD. & moved forward & occupied a line N of the YPRES-VLAMERTINGHE ROAD in H 10 b. Orders were then received to withdraw to the Battalions position in the GREEN LINE from H 3 a 3.4 to B 26 d 7.8 with Hdqrs at VLAMERTINGHE CHau. | [initials] |
| | | 6pm | The situation on the battlefront having been restored the battalion moved back to SIEGE CAMP. | |

1875 Wt. W593/826 1,000,000 4/15 J.B.C. & A. A.D.S.S./Forms/C. 2118.

Instructions regarding War Diaries and Intelligence Summaries are contained in F. S. Regs., Part II. and the Staff Manual respectively. Title Pages will be prepared in manuscript.

# WAR DIARY
*or*
# ~~INTELLIGENCE SUMMARY~~

(1)

*(Erase heading not required.)*

Army Form C. 2118.

#26 RF

V/I 26

| Place | Date | Hour | Summary of Events and Information | Remarks and references to Appendices |
|---|---|---|---|---|
| SIEGE CAMP. 28NW. B20d. | June 1st 2nd 1918. | | The Battalion continued its work on the GREEN LINE & also carried on General training. | [initials] |
| | 3rd | 8.30 am. | Relieved by the 1/5th WEST YORKSHIRE REGT. Proceeded by light | [initials] |
| | | 12 Noon | railway from MISSION JUNCTION (B27c.) to PUGWASH near PROVEN. (Sheet 27 F 7.) | |
| | | 4pm | Entrained at PROVEN & proceed to WATTEN (HAZEBROUCK 5A. 3C.); detrained at 8pm. | |
| | | 8pm | By march Route to training area WULVERDINGHE (HAZ. 5A. 2D) arriving 9.30pm. | |
| WULVERDINGHE. (HAZEBROUCK 5A) | June 4th 8th | | Battalion cleaned up & commenced General training which continued for the next ~~four~~ days | [initials] |
| AUDENFORT (CALAIS 13) | 8th | 4pm. | By march route to new training area with headquarters at AUDENFORT (CALAIS 13). arriving at 1pm. | [initials] |
| " | 9th to 24th | | General training continued, practice being carried out in open warfare fighting, attack, defence, wood fighting etc. All Companies fired on the range a number of days & Lewis gunners had a great deal of firing practice also. | [initials] |

26.R (2 sheets)

2449 Wt. W14957/M90 750,000 1/16 J.B.C. & A. Forms/C.2118/12.

Instructions regarding War Diaries and Intelligence Summaries are contained in F. S. Regs., Part II. and the Staff Manual respectively. Title Pages will be prepared in manuscript.

# WAR DIARY
*or*
~~INTELLIGENCE~~ SUMMARY

*(Erase heading not required.)*

(2)

Army Form C. 2118.

| Place | Date | Hour | Summary of Events and Information | Remarks and references to Appendices |
|---|---|---|---|---|
| WULVERDINGHE (HAZEBROUCK 5A) | June 25th | 8.30 am<br>4 pm | Battalion returned by march route to WOLVERDINGHE re-occupying the same billets as from June 4 to 8th, arriving at 4 pm. | [initials] |
| OUDERZEELE AREA (HAZEBROUCK 5A) | 26th | 8.50 am<br>5 pm | Proceeded by march route to the OUDERZEELE AREA arriving at 5 pm with Battn. H.Q. at LOOGE HOEK (HAZEBROUCK 5A) | [initials] |
| " | 27th to 29th | | Cleaned up & carried on training for the next 3 days. | |
| ABEELE AREA (SHEET 27) | 30th | 6 pm | By march route to Bivouacs at Sheet 27 L 33. C and D. arriving at 9/30 P.M. | [initials] |

H. A. Robinson
Lieut. Col. Commanding
26th (S) Bn Royal Fusiliers

2449 Wt. W14957/M90 750,000 1/16 J.B.C. & A. Forms/C.2118/12.

4

Instructions regarding War Diaries and Intelligence Summaries are contained in F. S. Regs., Part II. and the Staff Manual respectively. Title Pages will be prepared in manuscript.

# WAR DIARY
*or*
~~INTELLIGENCE SUMMARY~~
*(Erase heading not required.)*

Army Form C. 2118.

26th. Bn. Roy. Fus. (1)

VR 27

| Place | Date | Hour | Summary of Events and Information | Remarks and references to Appendices |
|---|---|---|---|---|
| SCHERPENBERG Sht 28 S.W. | July 1st 1918 | 8 pm | The Battalion moved up the line going into support to the 20th Battalion D.L.I. on the SCHERPENBERG with Battalion Hdqtrs at M 17 b 9.7. & remained there for 5 days. Working parties were provided for front & support lines every night. | |
| WESTOUTRE AREA Sht 27 NE & 28 SW | July 5th | 12 mnt. | Relieved by 20th Battn D.L.I. & moved back to Reserve in the WESTOUTRE - GOOD MILL line with Battalion Hdqrs at L 30 c 8.5. Sht 27 NE & arrived in | |
| | 6th | 5 am | billets in the area at 5 am. Remained in Reserve & carried out work on the Reserve line & New Brigade Hdqtrs. | |
| SCHERPENBERG | July 10th | 9 pm | Battalion went up the front line relieving the 10th Battalion (Queens) R.W.S. Regt. | |
| | 11th | 1 am | & relief was completed by 1 am. The line was held in the normal way | |
| | 13th | 1 am | An attempt was made to raid an enemy post. The men in it were bombed but no prisoners could be captured. | |
| " | 15th | 10 pm | Relieved by 20th Batt D.L.I. & moved back into support to position occupied previously from 1st to 5th inst. Work carried on as usual for next 5 days. | |
| Westoutre area | 20th | 10 pm | Relieved by 20th Batt D.L.I. & moved back into Reserve positions occupied previously | |
| | 21st | 5 am | from 6th to 10 inst. Arrived at billets by 5 am | |

27 K (3 sheets)

2449 Wt. W14957/M90 750,000 1/16 J.B.C. & A. Forms/C.2118/12.

Army Form C. 2118.

(2)

Instructions regarding War Diaries and Intelligence Summaries are contained in F. S. Regs., Part II. and the Staff Manual respectively. Title Pages will be prepared in manuscript.

# WAR DIARY
*or*
# INTELLIGENCE SUMMARY
*(Erase heading not required.)*

| Place | Date | Hour | Summary of Events and Information | Remarks and references to Appendices |
|---|---|---|---|---|
| Reninghelst Sht 28 N.W. | July 22nd to 25th | 9.30 pm | Battalion moved into new Reserve position holding position on the Westoutre – Goedmoet line from M10a 9.8 to M4d 7.8 (28SW) with Batt. H.Qrs at RENINGHELST BRASSERIE G34d 30.70 (28 N.W.). Work on the line & on new forward fire positions carried on. | [illegible] |
| | " | 10 pm | The Battalion proceeded up the line & relieved the 10th Batt QUEENS RWS Regt in the front line of the Brigade Sector with Headquarters on the | [illegible] |
| SCHERPENBERG Sht 28 SW | 25th/26th | | SCHERPENBERG at M17b 85.60. The Battalion took with them for instructional purposes the Headquarters of the 1st Batt 106th Inf. Regt 27th Division American Expeditionary Force together with one Company (D). This company was split up amongst the Battalion, one platoon (40 OR) going with each Coy & being again split up down to 2 americans to each section. | |
| | 26th/27th | | The americans were reformed into platoons relieving one platoon of each Company who were withdrawn into trenches & Bivouacs around HEKSKEN CABt M9a (Sht 28SW). | [illegible] |
| | 27th/28th | | The American Coy was reformed & relieved B Coy 26th Royal Fusiliers in support line about WEDGEWOOD M18c & d, this Coy being withdrawn to HEKSKEN as above, the platoons of A C & D rejoining their Companies. | [illegible] |

2449 Wt. W14957/M90 750,000 1/16 J.B.C. & A. Forms/C.2118/12.

Instructions regarding War Diaries and Intelligence Summaries are contained in F. S. Regs., Part II. and the Staff Manual respectively. Title Pages will be prepared in manuscript.

# WAR DIARY
*or*
# INTELLIGENCE SUMMARY
*(Erase heading not required.)*

(3) Army Form C. 2118.

| Place | Date | Hour | Summary of Events and Information | Remarks and references to Appendices |
|---|---|---|---|---|
| SCHERPENBERG Sht. 28 S.W. | 28th / 29th July 18 | night | D Coy American was relieved by C Coy American & the latter Company went thro' the same process of training for the next 3 days as had D Coy | [initials] |
| | to 31st | 10pm | The Battalion was relieved by the 1st Battalion 106th Infantry Regt American & on relief moved into support with H.Qrs at M17 b 9.7 relieving 10th R.M.S Regt | [initials] |
| | 28th | 12.30 am | A successful raid was carried out on an enemy post. A raiding party from B Coy consisting of 3 Officers & 45 O.R. went over at 12.30am with Artillery, & M.G. & L.T.M. Co-operation. Two prisoners belonging to the 9th Coy 107 Regt 55 Div were captured & the whole party returned without any loss. | [initials] |

[signature] Major
Comm. D. 28th Bn Royal Fusiliers

2449 Wt. W14957/M90 750,000 1/16 J.B.C. & A. Forms/C.2118/12.

Army Form C. 2118.

# WAR DIARY
or
# INTELLIGENCE SUMMARY
(Erase heading not required.)

26th Bn. Royal Fusiliers (1)

WO 28

Instructions regarding War Diaries and Intelligence Summaries are contained in F. S. Regs., Part II. and the Staff Manual respectively. Title Pages will be prepared in manuscript.

| Place | Date | Hour | Summary of Events and Information | Remarks and references to Appendices |
|---|---|---|---|---|
| SCHERPENBERG Sh 28 SW | Aug 1st 2nd 1918 | | The Battalion remained in Support for the next 2 days carrying on the normal routine, working Parties etc | [initials] |
| | 2nd | 11.30 pm | Relieved by the 20th Battalion Durham Light Infantry & on relief proceeded by march route to Reserve positions in the WESTOUTRE - GOED MOET MILL line | [initials] |
| | 3rd to 10th | 3am | with Headqtrs at G 34 d 3 8. Battalion carried on with training for the next 8 days, one company in turn being on Work at New Brigade Hdqtrs. All Coys also worked on improving their own sector in the Reserve line | [initials] |
| LAPPE AREA (Sh 27) | 10th | 11 pm | Relieved by the 20th Batt. DURHAM LIGHT INFANTRY & on relief proceeded by march route to rest area with Headquarters at R.3.d 95-95. | [initials] |
| | 11th to | | The next 8 days were spent in training + 2 days work was done on the WESTOUTRE-GOED MOET MILL LINE. (Sh 28) | |
| SCHERPENBERG | 18th | 9pm | By march route up the line, taking over the same front sector as before & relieving the 3rd Battalion 108th Regiment 27th American Division. Headquarters on the Scherpenberg as before. Relief completed by 11-40 pm | |
| | 19th to 23rd | | The next five days were spent in the line carrying on the normal routine. | |
| | | 11 pm | Relieved by 20th Batt. Durham Light Infantry + on relief moved into Support | |

28 K (2 sheets)

2449 Wt. W14957/M90 750,000 1/16 J.B.C. & A. Forms/C.2118/12.

'711

Instructions regarding War Diaries and Intelligence Summaries are contained in F. S. Regs., Part II. and the Staff Manual respectively. Title Pages will be prepared in manuscript.

# WAR DIARY
*or*
# INTELLIGENCE SUMMARY
*(Erase heading not required.)*

(2)

Army Form C. 2118.

| Place | Date | Hour | Summary of Events and Information | Remarks and references to Appendices |
|---|---|---|---|---|
| SCHERPENBERG (SH 28 SW.) | 24th to 26th | | Next 3 days spent in support carrying on with work as usual. | HA |
| | | 10pm | The 124th Brigade extending its front, the Battalion moved up into the front line taking over the left sub-sector of Brigade front & relieving the 23rd Battalion MIDDLESEX REGT with Headquarters at M 12 c 90-30, one Company being in the front line one in close support at FERMOY FARM & 2 in the SCHERPENBERG- | |
| " | 27th to 30th | | DICKEBUSCH LAKE LINE. The next 4 days were spent in normal trench warfare & day patrols. | HA |
| | 31st | 3am | It being suspected that the enemy had retreated before us in the KEMMEL AREA patrols were ordered to push forward & reached the top of MONT KEMMEL at 6.40am, the hill being finally occupied at 8.20am. The battalion pushed forward & contact was finally gained with the enemy on a line running through N° 27 d & 33 b from | HA |
| SHT 28 SW | | | N to S. This line was held for the remainder of the day & the battalion was relieved at 5am on the 1st Sept. by the 8th Batt Kings own SCOTTISH RIFLES. | |

H. A. Robinson
Lt. Col

2449 Wt. W14957/M90 750,000 1/16 J.B.C. & A. Forms/C.2118/12.

Instructions regarding War Diaries and Intelligence Summaries are contained in F. S. Regs., Part II. and the Staff Manual respectively. Title Pages will be prepared in manuscript.

# WAR DIARY
*or*
# INTELLIGENCE SUMMARY
*(Erase heading not required.)*

Army Form C. 2118.

26 RF

VOL 29



| Place | Date | Hour | Summary of Events and Information | Remarks and references to Appendices |
|---|---|---|---|---|
| Sht-28SW | Sept 1st | 8am | The battalion being relieved by the Battalion SCOTTISH RIFLES returned to its old positions in front of the SCHERPENBERG – LA CLYTTE ROAD | |
| | | 10pm | Relieved by the 1/1st BATN HEREFORD REGt & on relief proceeded by march route to rest area in neighbourhood of HOOGRAAF CABt. with H'qtrs at G20b5.3 (Sht28NW) | |
| Sht28NW | 2nd | 6am | arriving at 6am & rested in billets until the evening. | |
| DICKEBUSCH | | 8pm | Proceeded up the line into DICKEBUSCH SECTOR going into reserve & relieving the 2nd BATN 105th REGT 27th AMERICAN DIV. with H'dqtrs at H26d3.3 (Sht28NW) | |
| " | 3rd & 4th | 11pm | Remained in Reserve for the next 2 days under Brigade orders to move at a moments notice until the evening of the 4th when the Battalion went into the line relieving the 20th BATN DURHAM L.T INFT in the Rt SUB SECTOR of the Brigade FRONT east of VIERSTRAAT with H'dqtrs at N4 Cent. (Sht28SW). | |
| Sht28SW. | 5th to 8th | | The position in the front line being somewhat obscure the Battalion was ordered to restore the situation & push the line forward. This operation was carried out during the next 4 days & nights – (see attached REPORT of OPERATIONS 4th to 8th) on the night of the 5th the Battalion relieved the 10th Batt QUEENS RWS Regt & took over the whole of the BRIGADE FRONT being attached to the 123rd BRIGADE. | |

2449 Wt. W14957/M90 750,000 1/16 J.B.C. & A. Forms/C.2118/12.

Instructions regarding War Diaries and Intelligence Summaries are contained in F. S. Regs., Part II. and the Staff Manual respectively. Title Pages will be prepared in manuscript.

# WAR DIARY
*or*
# INTELLIGENCE SUMMARY
*(Erase heading not required.)*

(2)

Army Form C. 2118.

| Place | Date | Hour | Summary of Events and Information | Remarks and references to Appendices |
|---|---|---|---|---|
| SHT 28 NW. DICKEBUSCH | 9th Sept. | 2 am | Relieved by the 10th BATTN R.W. KENT REGT. & moved into Brigade Support round DICKEBUSCH LAKE with Hdqtrs in the BUND at H28d90.05 (Sh28NW) | [initials] |
| | to 11th. | 11pm | Remained in support for the next 3 days until relieved by the 10th BATTN R.W.S. REGT. (QUEENS) & returned to the 124th BRIGADE in RESERVE at DOMINION CAMP G23b (Sh28NW) | [initials] |
| DOMINION CAMP (Sh28NW.) | 13th to 15th | 1.30am | Relieved by the 11th Battn QUEENS R.W.S. Regt. & proceeded by march route to WIPPENHOEK 'B' siding (Sheet 27.) Entrained for Training Area at 6am changing to metre guage at LUMBRES at 10am & arriving at BONNINGUES (HAZEBROUCK 5A) & detraining at 12 noon. Thence by march route to RECQUES training area (CALAIS 13) arriving in billets at 1pm. Bttn Hdqrs at AUDENFORT & 1 Coy. 2 Coys at AUDREHEM & remaining Coy at LE POIRIER. | [initials] |
| [illegible] (CALAIS 13) | 15th to 27th. | 1pm | Following days were spent in strict training. Battalion & Brigade field days were held & all Coys fired on ranges — rifle & Lewis gun. Two night operations were held. Sunday 22nd was devoted to Battalion Sports. | [initials] |

2449 Wt. W14957/M90 750,000 1/16 J.B.C. & A. Forms/C.2118/12.

Army Form C. 2118.

(3)

# WAR DIARY
*or*
# INTELLIGENCE SUMMARY
*(Erase heading not required.)*

Instructions regarding War Diaries and Intelligence Summaries are contained in F. S. Regs., Part II. and the Staff Manual respectively. Title Pages will be prepared in manuscript.

| Place | Date | Hour | Summary of Events and Information | Remarks and references to Appendices |
|---|---|---|---|---|
| TORONTO CAMP (Sht 28) | Sept. 27th 12 noon | 12 noon | Battalion proceed by march route from AUDENFORT to BONNINGUES (HAZEBROUCK 5A) & entrained for RENINGHELST (Sht 28) detraining at 8 pm and thence by march route to TORONTO CAMP (Sht 28 G18a) arriving at 9 pm. | [initials] |
| Sht 28 | 28th | 6am | Commencement of active operations. | |
| | | | The Battalion proceed by march route to Brigade assembly area at SWAN CHATEAU (Sht 28 I.19c) to await orders. These were received at 10.15 am & the march commenced to the forming-up line behind MT SORREL (Sht 28 I 30a) where the battalion formed up at 1 pm on a bearing of 58° T. At 3 pm orders where received for the advance to commence on a bearing of 146° T the final objective being a distance of 4000 yards with the Right of the Brigade on KORTEWILDE (Sht 28 J13b), the 26th Battalion ROYAL FUSILIERS being on the left of the Brigade frontage & covering 750 yards having the 10th BAT. QUEENS R.W.S. Regt on its right. The Battalion advanced steadily having 2 Coys in front & 2 in support, each Coy having 2 platoons in front each with 2 sections leading & covered by ground scouts. Considerable opposition was met both from Enemy M.G. posts & snipers but these were gradually outflanked & surrounded. The advance proceeded in bounds of 500 yards and | [initials] |

Army Form C. 2118.

# WAR DIARY
*or*
# INTELLIGENCE SUMMARY

*(Erase heading not required.)*

Instructions regarding War Diaries and Intelligence Summaries are contained in F. S. Regs., Part II. and the Staff Manual respectively. Title Pages will be prepared in manuscript.

| Place | Date | Hour | Summary of Events and Information | Remarks and references to Appendices |
|---|---|---|---|---|
| Sht 28. | 28th Sept 1918 | 6.30 pm | The final objective was reached at 6.30pm. The enemy counter attacked on the left Coy front, but this was completely repulsed after a sharp fight + prisoners taken. The line being finally established & consolidated at 7pm running from P11a 3.7 to P8d 6.5 being in touch both the 10th Batt. Queens on the Right + 35th DIV. on the left. | [illegible] |
| | 28/9/18 – 29/9/18 | | The Battalion was engaged in Active Operations as per attached copy of report. | [illegible] |

[illegible signature]
Major
for O/C 26th (S) Battn. Royal Fusiliers

2449 Wt. W14957/M90 750,000 1/16 J.B.C. & A. Forms/C.2118/12.

REPORT OF OPERATIONS.

4/9/18 to 8/9/18.

1. On the night Sept. 4/5th, the 26th Battn. Royal Fusiliers relieved the 20th Bn. D.L.I. in the Rt. sub sector of Lt. Bde. taking up positions as follows:-

Rt. Coy. New Reserve Trench from N.12.a.05.20 to junction of railway N.12.b.15.45.

Lt. Coy. 1 Platoon in trench from N.12.b.15.45 to N.12.b.65.75.
1 Platoon do. do. N.6.d.20.10 to N.12.b.80.75
2 Platoons do. do. N.12.b.80.75 to O.7a.25.90.

2 Coys. in Support in the VIERSTRAAT SWITCH from N.11 Cent. to N.5.b.5.1.

2. During the early morning of the 5th, the Rt. Coy. pushed forward and occupied a line along the RAILWAY from N.12.d.05.90 to N.12.b.10.50 with 3 platoons and 1 platoon in Support in NEW RESERVE TRENCH.

3. Between 4 and 5 p.m. on the 5th, the Rt. Coy. pushed forward and occupied CHINESE TRENCH from N.12.d.05.80 to CHICORY LANE O.7.a.12.42 with 3 platoons and 1 platoon in Support on the Railway and the Lt. Coy. occupied CHICORY LANE up to the junction with CHINESE TRENCH.

4. During the night of the 5/6th, the 26th Royal Fusiliers took over the whole of the Brigade Front relieving the 10th Battn. Queens R.W.S. Regt. in the Lt. sub sector, the line being then held as follows:-

Rt. Coy. 3 Platoons in CHINESE TRENCH from N.12.d.05.80 to O.7.a.12.42 with forward post at O.7.a.35.25 and 1 platoon in support on railway.

Centre Coy. From O.7.a.12.42 along CHICORY LANE N.W. to N.12.b.85.73 thence N.E. to Road O.1.c.25.05 with forward post at O.7.a.40.80 and platoon in support along trench from N.12.b.30.77 to N.12.b.80.71.

Lt. Coy. From O.1.c.25.05 to junction of trench and railway at O.1.a.45.15 with forward post at O.1.c.82.54 and platoon in support at N.6.d.98.00.

Support Coy. 2 platoons in New Reserve Trench and 2 platoons in BOIS CARRE TRENCH.

5. During the night of 6/7th the Lt. Coy pushed forward and occupied OLD FRENCH TRENCH from O.1.c.25.05 to junction with VOORMEZEELE SWITCH at which point a liason post was established with the Division on the left. The Centre Coy. pushed forward posts from junction of CHINESE TRENCH and CHICORY LANE to junction of OLD FRENCH TRENCH and ROAD at O.1.c.25.05.

6. On the night of the 7/8th posts were pushed forward and established all along the Battalion Front as follows:-

Rt. Coy. L.G. Post at N.12.d.10.70 - forward platoon at junction of light railways at N.12.d.92.85 leaving 2 platoons in CHINESE TRENCH and one in Support on Railway.

Centre Coy. Posts at O.7.a.35.25 and O.7.a.40.70 leaving remainder of 3 platoons in posts from O.7.a.15.45 to O.1.c.25.05 and one in support from N.12.b.30. /

Army Form C. 2118

Instructions regarding War Diaries and Intelligence Summaries are contained in F. S. Regs., Part II. and the Staff Manual respectively. Title Pages will be prepared in manuscript.

# WAR DIARY

*or*

~~INTELLIGENCE SUMMARY~~

*(Erase heading not required.)*

| Place | Date | Hour | Summary of Events and Information | Remarks and references to Appendices |
|---|---|---|---|---|
| SIEGE CAMP | 28th May to 31st | | The next 4 days were spent in work upon the Battalion sector of the GREEN LINE & in general training, musketry, Lewis Gun etc. | [illegible] |

H. A. Robinson Lt. Col.

1875 Wt. W593/826 1,000,000 4/15 J.B.C. & A. A.D.S.S./Forms/C. 2118.

# R E P O R T   O N   O P E R A T I O N S.

28-9-18 to ~~[illegible]~~ 30/10/18

SHEET 28

At 6 a.m. September 28th, the Battalion proceeded by march route to Brigade Assembly Area at SWAN CHATEAU (I.19.c.) to await orders. These were received at ~~xxxx~~10.15 a.m. and the march commenced to the forming-up line behind MT. SORREL (I.30.a.) where the Battalion formed up at 1 p.m. on a bearing of 56 deg. T. At 3 p.m. orders were received for the advance to commence on a bearing of 146 deg. T. the final objective being a distance of 4000 yards with the right of the Brigade on KORTEWILDE (J.13.b.), the 26th Bn. ROYAL FUSILIERS being on the left of the Brigade frontage and covering 750 yards having the 10th Bn. "Queens" R.W.S. Regt. on its right. The Battalion advanced steadily having two Coys. in front and two in Support. Considerable opposition was met with from enemy M.G. posts and snipers but these were gradually outflanked and surrounded. The advance proceeded in bounds of 800 yards and the final objective was reached at 6.30 p.m., when a Company of the enemy were seen to mass with the intention of counter-attacking and restoring the WARNETON LINE on the Left. Coy. front. The Left.Coy. reinforced by two platoons from Support immediately attacked with the bayonet dispersing the enemy with heavy casualties before the counter-attack developed. About 30 prisoners were taken. The line was finally established and consolidated at 7 p.m. running from P.14.a.3.7 to P.8.d.6.5. being in touch with 10th Bn. "Queens" on the Right and 35th Division on the Left.

Casualties 28-9-18:-

| | |
|---|---|
| Killed ... ... | 3 |
| Wounded .... ...) | 19 |
| Missing (Blvd Wnd.) | 3 |
| Sick.. ... ... | 1 |

On September 29th, the advance was continued at 7 a.m. the Battalion objective being from DELEBEQUE FARM (P.21.a.7.6) inclusive to P.15.b.7.3. a distance of 1500 yards. More resistance was met with than on the previous day from isolated M.G. posts and snipers, but these were dealt with with slight loss by mutual co-operation between the Front Coys. and the objective gained by 8.30 a.m. The Left Coy who had advanced the whole distance with an open flank came under heavy M.G. fire during the later stages of the advance and during consolidation from the neighbourhood of TICUROUX FARM. These M.G's. were dealt with by L.T.M. and L.G. fire and by patrols and were forced to withdraw, but continued to harass the line from a distance all day. During the morning the 10th Royal West Kent Regt. passed through the Front Line, but on reaching the LYS were forced to withdraw and fell back by dusk on to our line.

Casualties 29-9-18:-

| | |
|---|---|
| Killed | 6 |
| Wounded .... ...) | 17 |
| Missing (Blvd Wnd.) | 3 |
| Sick... ... ... | 1 |

On September 30th, the Battalion resumed the advance at 5.30 a.m. the objective being the KORENTJE - LES CASERNES Road, a distance of 3000 yards. The line advanced rapidly in spite of open flanks. M.G. teams holding out in isolated posts were forced to withdrawn leaving their guns and one gun with a team of twelve was surrounded and captured in SCHOONVELD FARM. By 8.30 a.m. the objective was gained and posts had pushed forward to the Railway. Patrols during the morning cleared GODSHUIS taking prisoners and reported the ground clear of enemy as far as the LYS. The enemy were seen rapidly withdrawing from the other side of the river and were engaged with L.G. fire. COMINES appeared to have been evacuated and WERVICQ not strongly held. This was reported.

Casualties 30-9-18:-

| | | |
|---|---|---|
| Killed. | ... ... | 3 |
| Wounded | (... ...) | 7 |
| Missing | (Blvd Wnd.) | 1 |
| Sick.. | ... ... | 3 |

Fifteen Field Guns, and at least 100 prisoners including Six Officers were taken between the second pause and final objective. Our total casualties were:-

| | | | |
|---|---|---|---|
| OFFICERS. | Wounded | 2 | |
| OTHER RANKS. | Killed. | 3 | |
| | Wd. bvd. Killed | 1 | |
| | Died of Wounds | 2 | |
| | Wounded. | 69 | |
| | Missing | 9 | believed Wounded. |

On the morning of the 15th orders were received to push out patrols if possible as far as the LYS. Three patrols of one Officer and 8 other ranks each supported by 1 Officer and 25 other ranks, were accordingly sent out at 0930. These patrols pushed on against considerable machine gun fire, and sniping, but by 1155 were all in touch on the WEVELGHEM - GULLEGHEM ROAD between M.2.c.3.7, and M.32.c.8.2. and with the 35th Division on their left, but were held up by heavy Machine Gun fire from the WEVELGHEM - COURTRAI Railway in front and from WEVELGHEM on the right. The right patrol cleared all opposition, from the Northern outskirts of WEVELGHEM with the loss of one officer wounded, but were not strong enough to detail a party from their own front to deal with the town. At 1400 the enemy was reported by our own patrol, and by the 35th Division to be massing in strength on the railway in M.2.b. and G.33.c. The Artillery were informed and engaged the enemy, no counter-attack developing. Our patrols were ordered to establish themselves on the line of the WEVELGHEM - GULLEGHEM ROAD between the Battalion Boundaries M.2.c.3.2. and G.32.central, and this line was handed over the same night to 2/4th R. Sussex Regiment.

[signature]

Captain & A/Adjutant,

19/10 /18. 26th (S) Bn. Royal Fusiliers.

REPORT ON OPERATIONS.
October 14th and 15th, 1918.

The Battalion was in position on the tapes by 0400, and dug in to obtain temporary cover till Zero Hour. The enemy was very alert and his guns active. As the forming up line, especially on the left, was in his barrage line, and there was a considerable amount of wire to clear on the left between ourselves and the 122nd Infantry Brigade, the order was given to advance at 0525. This brought the Battalion on to the heels of the 122nd Infantry Brigade at 0532, and undoubtedly saved many casualties as the enemy replied very quickly and heavily to our barrage. The whole Battalion, however, was clear with the exception of the left Support Company which suffered heavily, losing 2 Officers and 25 other Ranks.

During the advance to the first and second pause, a thick fog rendered all supervision of units larger than a section or half Platoon impossible. Officers and senior N.C.Os, however, took command of the nearest body of men to them, and, collecting stragglers of all units on the way, marched by compass bearing on to the second pause, this being reached by all Officers with a large proportion of their men by 0700. Up to this point very little opposition had been met with, but several small parties under Officers had worked right forward and covered by the fog had entered pillboxes and farms immediately on top of the barrage and taken prisoners and machine guns.

At 0700 Battalion Headquarters moved forward to JOHNSON FARM in order to get into touch with the situation, and was established there at 0815.

Meanwhile Companies had re-organised to a large extent during the second pause andhad begun to push on . Immediately strong resistance was met with from ANCONA FARM, ADELAIDE HOUSE, MUTUAL FARM and other strong points; the advance was also checked by enemy batteries firing at point blank range through the fog. Patrols were sent forward to locate these, but progress was slow until after 0800 when the fog began to lift. The enemy at this stage attempted to limber up his guns and get away, but was forced by xxxxx close pressure and strong Lewis Gun and Rifle fire to abandon several guns the Right Company capturing one Battery intact with the gunners who had been left to remove the breach blocks. The advance was very rapid on the left where Captain SPOTTISWOODE with a few of his own Company and some men of the 35th Division established a post at WIJNBERG CROSS ROADS as early as 1000. The Right Company which came under very heavy Artillery fire at close range from the direction on MENIN was unable to advance so quickly, but had succeeded by 1100 in establishing a post at RADISH FARM where touch was gained later in the day with 20th Bn. Durham Light Infantry, enabling them to move to the left on to their own front. The centre Company encountered some opposition from scattered farms and pillboxes, but working steadily forward began to establish themselves on the final objective by noon. The Power Station at BUFF MILL was strongly held, but was taken in the flanks and captured with its garrison of 2 Officers and 12 men.

At 1300 the post at WIJNBERG which had not at that time gained touch with its right, was heavily counter-attacked from the direction of READER FARM, and, after suffering casualties, forced back on BACHELOR CROSS ROADS. Here it held until more men arrived, when Captain SPOTTISWOODE initiated a counter-attack which drove the enemy back to his original position, the post at WIJNBERG being re-established.

By 1400 touch was gained along the whole line, and Companies were able to re-organise and consolidate on their own fronts, consolidation on the final objective between PARAGON FARM and BAILIFF CROSS ROADS with touch on both flanks being completed by 1600 with Battalion Headquarters established at ADELAIDE HOUSE.

to N.12.b.80.71.

| | |
|---|---|
| Left, Coy. | Posts at O.1.c.90.25 and O.1.c.97.60 leaving remainder of 3 platoons in OLD FRENCH TRENCH with Liason post at O.1.d.35.95 and one platoon in Support at N.6.d.98.99. |

7. In these positions the line was handed over to the 10th Battn. R.W. Kents on the night 8/9th September.

At dusk on the 1st October, the Battalion was relieved in the line by two Coys. 23rd London Regt. and at 4 a.m. on the 2nd marched via TENBRIELEN to AMERICA Cross-Roads (P.12.b.8.0.) taking up position at dawn along the AMERICA - KRUISEECKE Road with the 20th D.L.I. on the Left, the Brigade being in Divisional Reserve. A hostile counter-attack developed at dusk from the direction of GHELUWE and the Battalion was ordered forward and took up position on the forward slopes. The Battalion was later withdrawn and remained in position behind the AMERICA - KRUISEECKE Road during the night.

At 5 a.m. on the 3rd position was again taken up and retained all day on the forward slopes facing GHELUWE in view of a probable enemy counter-attack. This did not materialise and at dusk the Battalion moved up to the line and relieved the left sub-sector of the 87th Brigade, 2nd Bn. South Wales Borderers (K.29 central to 34 central). With the exception of a small minor operation on the left, this line was held without event until the night 7th/8th when the Battalion was relieved in the line by the 10th Royal West Kent Regt. and proceeded by road and train to the ABEELE area. One prisoner (unter offizier) was taken on the night of the 5th and two prisoners including an officer on the 6th.

<u>Casualties 1-10-18 to 7-10-18:-</u>

| | | |
|---|---|---|
| Killed | ... ... | 7 |
| Wounded | ... ... | 42 |
| Missing | (Blvd Wnd.) | 1 |
| Sick.. | ... ... | 8 |

75

Instructions regarding War Diaries and Intelligence Summaries are contained in F. S. Regs., Part II. and the Staff Manual respectively. Title Pages will be prepared in manuscript.

# WAR DIARY
*or*
# INTELLIGENCE SUMMARY
*(Erase heading not required.)*

Army Form C. 2118.

26th Bn. Royal Fusiliers

WO 31

31.K. (3 sheets)

| Place | Date | Hour | Summary of Events and Information | Remarks and references to Appendices |
|---|---|---|---|---|
| COURTRAI AREA | 1/11/18 | | The Battalion left Rest Billets at 1100 and proceeded to the KROTE AREA where dinners were served prior to moving into the line as Battalion in Brigade Reserve. | RB |
| O.18. b. 4.3. Sheet 29 | 2/11/18 to 4/11/18 | | Battalion in Brigade Reserve holding the line. Lewis Gun training & firing were carried out. | RB |
| VICHTE | 4/11/18 | | The Brigade was relieved in the line by the 123rd Infantry Brigade, 11th Bn "Queens" relieving the Battalion, which proceeded by march route to VICHTE arriving about 1400 hours. | RB |
| DO | 5/11/18 to 6/11/18 | | Training was carried out daily between the hours of 0900 to 1200 and 1400 to 1630. | RB |
| DO | 7/11/18 | 1100 | The Battalion proceeded by march route to DEERLYCK, arriving in billets about 1300. | RB |
| DEERLYCK | 8.11.18 | | Special training for crossing the SCHELDT and Lewis Gun training were carried out daily. | RB |
| do | 9.11.18 | 0915 | The Battalion proceeded by march route to TIESHEM, arriving at 1600 & billetted for the night, the battn being in Bde Reserve. The enemy withdrew from the SCHELDT on the night of the 8th/9th | RB |
| TIESHEM | 10.11.18 | 0720 | The Brigade moved to the MARQUETTE area, the Battalion marching in Brigade Reserve and billetting for the night in M 21 d (Sheet 30) at about 1800. | RB |
| M.21 a (Sheet 30) | 11.11.18 | 0900 | News of the Armistice was received at 0900. The Battalion immediately moved off | RB |

2449 Wt. W14957/M90 750,000 1/16 J.B.C. & A. Forms/C.2118/12.

Army Form C. 2118.

# WAR DIARY
*or*
# INTELLIGENCE SUMMARY
*(Erase heading not required.)*

Instructions regarding War Diaries and Intelligence Summaries are contained in F. S. Regs., Part II. and the Staff Manual respectively. Title Pages will be prepared in manuscript.

| Place | Date | Hour | Summary of Events and Information | Remarks and references to Appendices |
|---|---|---|---|---|
| | 11.11.18 | Continued | passing through the 123rd Infantry Brigade and joining the remainder of the Brigade in NEDERBRAKEL at 1300 remaining in Brigade Reserve. | Reference Maps TOURNAI 5, BRUSSELS 6. ABB |
| NEDERBRAKEL | 12.11.18 | 0415 | C Coy moved forward and took up an outpost position on the GRAMMONT-VRIJHEID road within the divisional boundaries, posts being all in position by 0715. | ABB |
| | | 0845 | The remainder of the Battalion moved off, joining the rear of the Brigade Column and reaching billets at HEMELVERDEGHEM by 1200. | ABB |
| | | 0500 | C Coy moved forward to IDEGEM and established posts on the road and bridge at LUST and on the bridge at IDEGEM | ABB |
| HEMELVERDEGEM | 13.11.18 | 0630 | A Coy moved forward to MOENEBROEK (P10 a) establishing posts on all roads leading from west. C Coy withdrew forward posts and picqueted roads and bridge west and south of IDEGEM. Reorganisation complete by 0930. | ABB |
| | | 0930 | Remainder of Battalion moved to IDEGEM, H.Qrs being established there by 1130. | |
| IDEGEM | 14-11-18 to 17/11/18 | | The Battalion was reorganised and refitted. Training was carried out by the companies not engaged on Outpost. | ABB |
| Do | 18/11/18 | | The Battalion proceeded by March Route to DENDERWINDEKE, "B" Company taking up the Outpost Line on the NINOVE [illegible] — ENGHIEN ROAD from Kilo 9 on the Right to DENDERWINDEKE (inclusive) on the left, establishing a liaison post with 123rd Infantry Brigade on the right. | ABB |

Instructions regarding War Diaries and Intelligence Summaries are contained in F. S. Regs., Part II. and the Staff Manual respectively. Title Pages will be prepared in manuscript.

# WAR DIARY
*or*
# INTELLIGENCE SUMMARY
*(Erase heading not required.)*

Army Form C. 2118.

| Place | Date | Hour | Summary of Events and Information | Remarks and references to Appendices |
|---|---|---|---|---|
| DENDERHINDEKE | 19/11/18 | | The day was spent in cleaning up & drill under Company arrangements. | TOURNAI 5. BRUSSELS 6. [initials] |
| DO | 20/11/18 | 0745 | The Battalion proceeded by March Route to the VIANE – BIEVENE Area and arrived in billets at BIEVENE about 1330 hours. | [initials] |
| BIEVENE | 21/11/18 to 30/11/18 | | This period was spent in cleaning up, training from 0900 to 1230 hours (including route marches) and Recreational Training from 1400 to 1600 hours. On the 26th the Divisional Commander presented Medal Ribbons to those who had been awarded Decorations since 29/9/18. | [initials] |

[signature]
Lieut-Col Commanding
26th (S) Battn Royal Fusiliers

ORDERLY ROOM
2 DEC. 1918
No. [illegible]
ROYAL FUSILIERS

2449 Wt. W14957/M90 750,000 1/16 J.B.C. & A. Forms/C.2118/12.

REPORT ON OPERATIONS, 21st October to 28th October, 1918.

REFERENCE MAP:- SHEET 29.

On the 21st during the advance on the River L'ESCAUT, the Battalion was in Brigade Reserve, two Companies following the 10th Bn "Queens" R. W. S. Regt. in close support.

The advance progressed rapidly without incident until the 10th Bn. "Queens" R.W.S. Regt. withdrew to cross the COURTRAI - BOSSUYT CANAL, when the Companies in Close Support advanced over the LAATSTE-OORTNE - HOOGSTRAATJE ridge to fill the gap. The advance on the forward slope, however, was checked by the very heavy and accurate Machine Gun fire from HOOGMOLEN and the East side of the Canal. The 10th "Queens" R.W.S. Regt. were prevented by the same fire from crossing the Canal, and orders were therefore issued for the Battalion to consolidate on the line approximately along the road from O.28.d.9.0. to U.5.d.2.3., touch being established with the 20th Bn. Durham Light Infantry on the right.

| | | | |
|---|---|---|---|
| Casualties:- | Killed. | ~~XXXXX~~ | 1 Other Rank. |
| | Wounded | | 6 Other Ranks. |

During the 22nd and 23rd October, the line was held without change while the attempt was made to clear the HOOGMOLEN Ridge by attacks on the East side of the Canal.

| | | | |
|---|---|---|---|
| Casualties:- | Killed. | | 8 Other Ranks. |
| | Wounded. | 1 Officer | 16 do. |
| | Missing | | 3 do. |

On the night 23/24th the Battalion took over part of the line held by the South Wales Borderers in O.6.d. and O.12.a., and orders were received on the night of the 24th for the advance on the L'ESCAUT to be resumed in the morning, the Battalion being the left front Battalion.

| | | |
|---|---|---|
| Casualties:- | Wounded. | 5 Other Ranks. |

At 01.15 the Battalion concentrated in assembly positions along the road running through, O.6.b., O.6.a - O.12.a.3.9, and proceeded to dig in until Zero hour. The enemy kept up moderate dispersed ~~fire~~ shell fire during the night, only slackening down after dawn. At 09.00, on the commencement of our barrage, the whole line closed under the barrage and moved forward at 09.04.

The enemy appeared to have withdrawn his front posts to a depth of about 400 yards on our immediate front, and relied upon a barrage to break up our advance. Heavy casualties were suffered in passing through the barrage, four Officers being wounded within the first five minutes. There was also fairly heavy machine gun fire from both flanks, which increased as the advance continued, Machine Guns coming into action from the Farms and High Ground around P.7.c. and P.7.d. The windmill at P.7.d.2.4 especially causing casualties as the Battalion entered the village round P.7.c.6.4. To silence these enemy Machine Guns the ~~Battalion~~ RIGHT FRONT COY. worked round the Right Flank into dead ground along the road from P.7.c.6.4 to P.13.a.7.9, passing into 20th Bn. D. L. I. front ~~xxx~~ for this purpose, and two ~~xxx~~ Vickers Guns attached to the Battalion brought fire to bear from the Right Flank, while the left flank pushed steadily ahead over the KASSELRYBEEK up the higher ground in P.7.d. There were three more casualties to Officers and several to men, but by 10.30 the village and windmill had been taken; from the windmill itself one enemy machine gun and sixteen men were captured.

From 10.30 to 12.30 re-organisation wherever possible took place in dead ground, and the line held by the Battalion was as follows:-

"A" Company around Farm at P.13.a.7.8, and along road running North of it.

"C" Company in dead ground in P.7.d.2.4.

"B" and "D" Companies along crest in P.7.b. and P.7.d.

This was a line approximately 1000 yards short of the first pause line, but enemy Machine Gun fire was very accurate and casualties had been severe. It was necessary, therefore, to reorganise before pushing forward.

forward.

At 12.30 the advance was recommenced. On the right a Composite Company was made out of "A" and "C" Companies owing to casualties to Officers and men, and a determined attempt to penetrate the enemy positions by means of infiltration on both sides of the windmill took place. At the same time "B" and "D" Companies attempted to work forward into P.8.a. and c. This attack on the left flank penetrated as far as OOTEGHEM, but the casualties were too heavy to admit further progress. At the same time the Camerons on the left were ordered to retire, and, in conformity with them, the left Companies of the Battalion swung back and eventually took up their position along the road at the forward crest at P.7.d.9,3 to P.8.c.7.7

On the Right Flank the Composite "A" and "C" Company were also met by extremely accurate Machine Gun fire in their attempt to move forward. The sections sent round the left of the windmill were unable to move forward and were withdrawn and sent round the right flank to rejoin their platoon, and together these sections penetrated as far as P.13.a.5.5, beyond which point further progress was impossible. As the point reached by the Battalion was on the 20th Bn. D. L. I. front and Machine Gun fire from P.14.a. and b began to die down, O/C "A" and "C" Company ordered his Company to side-step a distance of 300 yards, and at 15.30 this was carried out by sections and a position at P.13.b.8.8 was occupied. In doing this Machine Gun fire was drawn from the left, i.e. the Eastern slopes of OOTEGHEM, and the men commenced to dig in.

At this point the Commanding Officer was wounded while re-organising the line of the left flank, and Captain A. SPOTTISWOODE took over command of the Battalion. This was at about 16.00, and at dusk the 10th Bn. "Queens" R.W.S. Regt. passed through the 20th Bn. D. L. I. and by dark had reached P.13.b.6.6 with their left resting on P.7.d.6.0. "A" and "C" Company were then ordered to withdraw and move forward fill the gap between P.7.d.9.3, and the "Queens" left flank at P.7.d.6.0 a continuous line being established.

| | | | | |
|---|---|---|---|---|
| Casualties. | Killed | 1 Officer | 14 | Other Ranks. |
| | Wounded | 7 " | 72 | do. |

At 12.00 on the 26th the Battalion was ordered to carry forward its line along the original line of advance in a South East direction towards the LESCAUT. Two parties, of three platoons each, with Officers, pushed forward through KLOOSTERHOEK to near LANGESTRAAT where the line was taken over by 10th Bn. "Queens" R.W.S. Regt, touch being established by the Battalion with D. L. I. on the right and the Camerons on the left.

At dusk the Battalion moved back into rest billets in the COURTRAI Area.

[signature]
Captain & A/Adjutant,
26th (S) Bn. Royal Fusiliers.

3/11/18.

COPY No. 1. Commanding Officer.
2. The Adjutant.
3. File.
4. DRONE.
5. War Diary.
6. O/C. "ALE".
7. " "BEER".
8. " "CIDER".
9. " "DOPE".
10. Headquarters.
11. Quartermaster.
12. Medical Officer.
13. DROSS.
14. Spare.

----------------------

Army Form C. 2118.

Instructions regarding War Diaries and Intelligence Summaries are contained in F. S. Regs., Part II. and the Staff Manual respectively. Title Pages will be prepared in manuscript.

# WAR DIARY
*or*
~~INTELLIGENCE SUMMARY~~
*(Erase heading not required.)*

26th Royal Fusiliers.

VR 32

| Place | Date | Hour | Summary of Events and Information | Remarks and references to Appendices |
|---|---|---|---|---|
| BIEVENE | 1/12/18 to 11/12/18 | | This period was devoted to Training and Route Marches between 0900 hours and 1230 hours, and Recreational Training from 1400 to 1600 hours. On the 11th the Divisional Commander presented French Medals to Officers and Other Ranks at GRAMMONT. | TOURNAI BRUSSELS 5/6 RNB. |
| BIEVENE | 12/12/18 | 0735 | The Battalion commenced the march to the HUY AREA and arrived in billets at ENGHIEN about 11.30 hours. | RNB. |
| ENGIEN | 13/12/18 | 0820 | The march was continued to HAL where the Battalion arrived about 12/30 hours. | RNB. |
| HAL | 14/12/18 | 0750 | The march was continued to WATERLOO, arriving in billets about 1245 hours. | RNB. |
| WATERLOO | 15/12/18 | | The Battalion rested for the day. | RNB. |
| DO | 16/12/18 | 0730 | The march was continued to WAYS DE GENAPPE, reaching billets about 1400 hours | RNB. |
| WAYS DE GENAPPE | 17/12/18 | 0840 | The march was continued to NAGWALEE, arriving about 1300 hours. | RNB. |
| NAGWALEE | 18/12/18 | 0710 | The march was continued to TEMPLOUX arriving billets about 12/30 hours. | RNB. |
| TEMPLOUX | 19/12/18 | 1015 | The march was continued to BONNINE and GELBRASSE AREA reaching billets about 14.30 hours. | RNB |

82.K (2 sheets)

2449 Wt. W14957/M90 750,000 1/16 J.B.C. & A. Forms/C.2118/12.

Instructions regarding War Diaries and Intelligence Summaries are contained in F. S. Regs., Part II. and the Staff Manual respectively. Title Pages will be prepared in manuscript.

# WAR DIARY

*or*

~~INTELLIGENCE SUMMARY~~

*(Erase heading not required.)*

Army Form C. 2118.

| Place | Date | Hour | Summary of Events and Information | Remarks and references to Appendices |
|---|---|---|---|---|
| BONNINE | 20/12/18 | 0910 | The march was continued to HUY reaching billets about 1400 hours. The Battalion being billetted in the Barracks HUY. | PNB |
| HUY | 21/12/18 to 31/12/18 | | This period was spent in training from 0900 to 1230 hours and Recreation 1400 to 1630 hours. Educational Classes were held daily from 30/12/18. | PNB |

H.K. Robinson Lt. Col. COMMANDING, 26th (S) BN. ROYAL FUSILIERS.

LONDON DIVISION

(LATE 41ST DIVISION)

124TH INFY BDE

# 26TH BN ROY. FUSILIERS

JAN - SEP 1919

Instructions regarding War Diaries and Intelligence Summaries are contained in F. S. Regs., Part II. and the Staff Manual respectively. Title Pages will be prepared in manuscript.

# WAR DIARY
*or*
# INTELLIGENCE SUMMARY
*(Erase heading not required.)*

Army Form C. 2118.

26th Battalion Royal Fusiliers

Vol 33

| Place | Date | Hour | Summary of Events and Information | Remarks and references to Appendices |
|---|---|---|---|---|
| HUY | 1/1/19 | | This day was a whole holiday for the Battalion. Football matches were played in the afternoon. | ABD |
| HUY | 2/1/19 to 4/1/19 | | Training from 0900 to 1230 hours. Recreational Training 1410 to 1630 hours. Educational Classes daily. | ABD |
| HUY | 5/1/19 | | Church parade in the KURSAAL, HUY. | ABD |
| HUY | 6/1/19 7/1/19 | 0830 | The Battalion proceeded by march route to ANDENNE and entrained for Germany. Detrainment took place at BENSBERG and the Battalion marched to STEINENBRUCH and rested for the night. | ABD |
| STEINENBRUCK | 8/1/19 | | Proceeded by march route to EHRESHOVEN. | ABD |
| EHRESHOVEN | 9/1/19 to 31/1/19 | | Training during the mornings — including Educational Training. Recreation in the afternoons. Concerts were given weekly by the Battalion Concert Party. | ABD |

Jan - Sep '19

G. A. Robinson Lt Col COMMANDING.
26th (S) BN. ROYAL FUSILIERS.



33 K

Instructions regarding War Diaries and Intelligence Summaries are contained in F. S. Regs., Part II. and the Staff Manual respectively. Title pages will be prepared in manuscript.

# WAR DIARY
*or*
# INTELLIGENCE SUMMARY.
*(Erase heading not required.)*

I 6 R 7 Army Form C. 2118.

| Place | Date | Hour | Summary of Events and Information | Remarks and references to Appendices |
|---|---|---|---|---|
| COLN KALK | 1/4/19 to 30/4/19 | | This period was spent chiefly in re-organising the Battalion. The 53rd Royal Fusiliers joined on 2/4/19 and were absorbed into the Battalion. Guards on Dumps and Stores were found by the Battalion Alternate weeks. | |
| " " | 1/4/19 to 8/4/19 | | Lieut. Col. H.A. ROBINSON D.S.O. Commanded the Battalion. | |
| " " | 9/4/19 | | Lieut. Col. W.W. CHARD M.C. Assumed Command. vice Lieut Col. H.A. Robinson D.S.O. to England for demobilization | |
| " " | 14/4/19 | | Br. Lieut. Col. C.J. HICKIE Assumed Command. vice Lieut Col. W. W. Chard. M.C. | |
| " " | 27/4/19 | | Major W.W. CHARD M.C. Again assumed Command. vice Lieut Col. C. J. HICKIE to United Kingdom on leave. | |

ORDERLY ROOM -2 AUG. 1919 No. 19.34 26th (S) BN. ROYAL FUSILIERS

C. J. Hickie
Lieut. Colonel.
Commanding. 26th (S) Battn. Royal Fusiliers

34 K
1 sheet

D. D. & L., London, E.C.
(A8004) Wt. W1771/M231 750,000 5/17 Sch. 52 Forms/C2118/14

Instructions regarding War Diaries and Intelligence Summaries are contained in F. S. Regs., Part II. and the Staff Manual respectively. Title pages will be prepared in manuscript.

# WAR DIARY
*or*
# INTELLIGENCE SUMMARY.
*(Erase heading not required.)*

26 K7

Army Form C. 2118.

35 K (1 sheet)

| Place | Date | Hour | Summary of Events and Information | Remarks and references to Appendices |
|---|---|---|---|---|
| " COLN KALK | 1/5/19 to 5/5/19 | | Training was carried out in the morning. Sports and recreation in the afternoon. | |
| " " | 6/5/19 | | The Commander in Chief, Army of the Rhine, inspected the Battalion on the EXERTZIER PLATZ. | |
| " " | 7/5/19 to 13/5/19 | | This period was spent in Training, Education and Sports. | |
| VOLBERG | 14/5/19 | | The Battalion entrained at CÖLN KALK Station and proceeded to VOLBERG AREA relieving 9th Bn. East Surrey Regt. | |
| " | 15/5/19 to 31/5/19 | | Training Education and Sports were carried out during this period. | |
| | 1/5/19 to 15/5/19 | | Major W.W. CHARD, M.C. Commanded the Battalion. during absence of Lieut Col. C.J. HICKIE on leave. | |
| | 16/5/19 to 20/5/19 | | Major S.A. DALE Commanded the Battalion. vice Major W. W. CHARD. M.C. to United Kingdom on leave. | |
| | 21/5/19 to 31/5/19 | | Lieut. Col. C.J. HICKIE Commanded the Battalion. on rejoining from leave. | |

ORDERLY ROOM -2 AUG. 1919 No. A 34 26th (S) BN. ROYAL FUSILIERS

C J Hickie Lieut. Colonel
Commanding 26th (S) Battn. Royal Fusiliers

D. D. & L., London, E.C. (A8004) Wt. W1771/M2 31 750,000 5/17 Sch. 52 Forms/C2118/14

Army Form C. 2118

26 R7

Instructions regarding War Diaries and Intelligence Summaries are contained in F. S. Regs., Part II. and the Staff Manual respectively. Title Pages will be prepared in manuscript.

# WAR DIARY
*or*
# INTELLIGENCE SUMMARY
*(Erase heading not required.)*

| Place | Date | Hour | Summary of Events and Information | Remarks and references to Appendices |
|---|---|---|---|---|
| HOFFNUNGSTAHL and VOLBERG. | 1/6/19 to 2/6/19 | | Training and Education were carried out during the morning. Sports and recreation in the afternoon. | |
| — | 3/6/19 | | The King's Birthday. The Commanding Officer addressed the Battalion on parade in the morning. The remainder of the day was observed as a holiday. | |
| — | 4/6/19 | | The Corps Commander, Sixth Corps, inspected the Battalion. | |
| — | 5/6/19 to 17/6/19 | | The following wire was received from 3rd London Infantry Brigade:- "J day is June 20th. J - 3 day is today". | |
| UNTER VILKERATH | 18/6/19 | | J - 2 Day. The Battalion proceeded by march route to UNTER VILKERATH via OVERATH and bivouaced, thus allowing a clear day's rest before a long march. | |
| — | 19/6/19 | | Battalion rested. During the day intimation was received that no further advance was likely until the following Tuesday June 24th. This intimation was confirmed on June 20th. | |
| — | 20/6/19 to 30/6/19 | | J day postponed. Training proceeded with. Telegram about 20.00 hours "Germany has decided to sign" On 28th June news was received that the Peace Treaty had been signed today about 8pm. | |
| | 1/6/19 to 30/6/19 | | Lieut.Colonel C.J. HICKIE, C.M.G. commanded the Battalion during this period. | |



C J Hickie
LIEUT.COLONEL.
Commanding 26th (S) Bn. The Royal Fusiliers.

1875 Wt. W593/826 1,000,000 4/15 J.B.C. & A. A.D.S.S./Forms/C. 2118.

36 K
1 sheet

26 R7 Army Form C. 2118.

Instructions regarding War Diaries and Intelligence Summaries are contained in F. S. Regs., Part II. and the Staff Manual respectively. Title pages will be prepared in manuscript.

# WAR DIARY
*or*
# INTELLIGENCE SUMMARY.
*(Erase heading not required.)*

UNTER VILKERATH

| Place | Date | Hour | Summary of Events and Information | Remarks and references to Appendices |
|---|---|---|---|---|
| UNTER VILKERATH | 1/7/19 | | "D" Company proceeded by march route to OVERATH. | |
| OVERATH | 2/7/19 | | The remainder of the Battalion proceeded by march route to OVERATH relieving the 17th Bn. Royal Fusiliers. | |
| -- | 3/7/19 | | This day was observed as a general holiday to celebrate the signing of Peace. | |
| -- | 4/7/19 to 23/7/19 | | The Battalion commenced firing General Musketry Course - two Companies firing and two carrying out general training and education. | |
| -- | 24/7/19 | | The Divisional Commander inspected the Battalion. | |
| -- | 25/7/19 to 31/7/19 | | Two Companies General Musketry Course and two Companies training and education. | |
| -- | 29/7/19 | | 3rd London Infantry Brigade Sports were held at CLEF. | |
| -- | 30/7/19 | | 3rd London Infantry Brigade Horse Show was held at OVERATH. The chief event, i.e. Turn-out of 5 vehicles was won by this Battalion. | |
| | | | Lieut.Colonel C.J. HICKIE, C.M.G. commanded the Battalion during the whole of the above period. | |

ORDERLY ROOM 2 AUG 1919 1939 26th ROYAL FUSILIERS

C J Hickie
LIEUT.COLONEL.
Commanding 26th (S) Bn. The Royal Fusiliers.



37 K (1 sheet)

Instructions regarding War Diaries and Intelligence Summaries are contained in F. S. Regs., Part II. and the Staff Manual respectively. Title pages will be prepared in manuscript.

# WAR DIARY
*or*
# INTELLIGENCE SUMMARY.
*(Erase heading not required.)*

Army Form C. 2118.



| Place | Date | Hour | Summary of Events and Information | Remarks and references to Appendices |
|---|---|---|---|---|
| OVERATH | 1/8/19 to 11/8/19 | | The Battalion continued firing the General Musketry Course. | |
| -- | 12/8/19 | | "D" Company proceeded by train to ANTWERP relieving guards found by NORTHERN Division. | |
| -- | 13/8/19 to 19/8/19 | | The Battalion finished firing General Musketry Course and commenced practicing for Brigade Rifle Meeting. General Training and Education carried out daily by men not firing on range. | |
| -- | 20-21-22/8/19 | | 3rd London Infantry Brigade Rifle Meeting. | |
| -- | 25/8/19 | | "A" and "B" Companies relieved two Companies of 23rd Bn. Royal Fusiliers in the Outpost Line. Company Headquarters - "A" Company, DRABENDERHOHE. "B" Company, GRUTZENBACH. | |
| MARIALINDEN | 26/8/19 | | Remainder of Battalion proceeded by march route and completed the relief of the 23rd Bn. Royal Fusiliers at MARIALINDEN. | |
| -- | 26-27-28/8/19 | | Divisional Rifle Meeting was held at EHRESHOVEN. The Battalion scored 73 points, being 4th highest in the Division and 1st in 3rd London Infantry Brigade. | |
| | | | Lieut.Colonel C.J. HICKIE, C.M.G. commanded the Battalion during this month. | |
| | | | C.J. Hickie<br>LIEUT.COLONEL.<br>Commanding 26th (S) Bn. The Royal Fusiliers. | |

T2134. Wt. W708—776. 500000. 4/15. Sir J. C. & S.

38 K

Instructions regarding War Diaries and Intelligence Summaries are contained in F. S. Regs., Part II, and the Staff Manual respectively. Title pages will be prepared in manuscript.

# WAR DIARY
*or*
# INTELLIGENCE SUMMARY.
*(Erase heading not required.)*

26 R7

Army Form C. 2118.

| Hour, Date, Place | Summary of Events and Information | Remarks and References to Appendices |
|---|---|---|
| MARIALINDEN 1.9.19 to 6.9.19 | Lieut.Col.C.J.HICKIE. C.M.G. Commanded the Battalion. | |
| do. 7.9.19 to date. | Major E. A.S. GELL, D.S.O., M.C. Commanded the Battalion. | |
| OVERATH. 16.9.19 | London Division Horse Show was held at OVERATH. The Chief event i.e. Officers' Jumping was won by the Transport Officer of this Battalion, also Turn-out of Field Kitchen was won by this Battalion. | |
| MARIALINDEN. 30.9.19. | Lewis Gunners of this Battalion Commenced firing Lewis Gun Course. General Training and Education carried out daily. Two Companies were in the Outpost Line during the whole of this period. Battalion Headquarters and one Company were at MARIALINDEN. "D" Company still detached at ANTWERP during this period. | |

E. A. S. Gell
Major,
Commanding 26th (S) Bn. The Royal Fusiliers.

www.ingramcontent.com/pod-product-compliance
Lightning Source LLC
Chambersburg PA
CBHW080847230426
43662CB00013B/2040